A Theology *for* Family Ministries

A Theology *for* Family Ministries

Michael & Michelle Anthony

B&H ACADEMIC
Nashville, Tennessee

A Theology for Family Ministries

ISBN: 978-0-8054-6421-4

Published by B&H Publishing Group
Nashville, Tennessee

Dewey Decimal Classification: 306.85
Subject Heading: CHURCH WORK WITH FAMILIES \
FAMILY \ FAMILY LIFE

Printed in the United States of America

2 3 4 5 6 7 8 9 10 11 12 • 17 16 15 14 13 12 11
SB

The family was God's idea. It was the first institution He ever created and it is a gift with which we have been blessed.

To our families—the Anthony's, the Van Groningen's, and those yet to come from our children. Thank you for the way you have shaped our lives and let us see Christ in you!

—Michael & Michelle Anthony

Contents

Contributors

Dr. Karen Jones is professor of Ministry and Missions at Huntington University. Dr. Jones earned B.S. and M.S. degrees from Southwest Missouri State University. She served as a public school teacher and a youth minister before earning a Ph.D. and an M.A. from Southwestern Baptist Theological Seminary. She has more than 15 years of experience working with youth in the local church and continues to minister to them by directing student mission projects each year, both in the United States and internationally.

Dr. Frederick Cardoza is chair of the Department of Christian Education at the Talbot School of Theology. He is also the director of Distributed Learning and Instructional Technology at Biola University. Dr. Cardoza earned a Ph.D. in leadership from The Southern Baptist Theological Seminary and a M.A. from Southeastern Baptist Theological Seminary.

Dr. Michael S. Lawson is senior professor of Christian Education at Dallas Theological Seminary. He earned a Ph.D. from The University of Oklahoma and a Th.M. from Dallas Theological Seminary. He has devoted more than 30 years to pastoral work and Christian education in many countries.

Dr. Richard R. Melick Jr. is director of the Academic Graduate Studies Program and professor of New Testament at Golden Gate Baptist Theological Seminary. He earned his Ph.D. from Southwestern Baptist Theological Seminary and his M.Div. from Trinity Evangelical Divinity School. A former pastor of two churches and numerous interim pastorates, he is a frequent speaker for Bible conferences.

Dr. Timothy P. Jones is associate professor of Leadership and Church Ministry at The Southern Baptist Theological Seminary where he earned his Ph.D. He earned his M.Div. from Midwestern Baptist Theological Seminary. He is also the editor of *The Journal of Family Ministry*. Dr. Jones has more than 15 years of vocational ministry experience as a children's minister, student minister, administrative pastor, and senior pastor.

Dr. Randy Stinson is the dean of the School of Church Ministries at The Southern Baptist Theological Seminary where he also earned a Ph.D. and a Th.M. He earned a M.Div. from Southeastern Baptist Theological Seminary.

Dr. Stinson also serves as the president of The Council on Biblical Manhood and Womanhood. He has served as a senior pastor as well as other church staff positions.

Curt Hamner is the director of Between Two Trees Ministries and a professional marriage and family education consultant. Curt earned his M.A.B.S. from Dallas Theological Seminary and a B.A. from Biola University. He and his wife are also Certified Marriage and Family Relationship Coaches, and he has 30 years' experience as a pastoral counselor. Curt has served as a senior pastor and associate pastor of several churches including Fullerton Evangelical Free Church.

Dr. Leon M. Blanchette Jr. is an associate professor of Christian Education in the School of Theology and Christian Ministry at Olivet Nazarene School of Theology and Christian Ministry. Dr. Blanchette earned an Ed.D. from The Southern Baptist Theological Seminary and a M.A. from Trevecca Nazarene University. He has served as a children's pastor for 18 years in the Church of the Nazarene and serves as the director of the children's ministry undergraduate degree and the family ministry graduate degree programs.

Dr. Gordon R. Coulter is associate professor of Ministry for the C. P. Haggard Graduate School of Theology at Azusa Pacific University. He earned an Ed.D. from Biola University, Talbot School of Theology and a M.A. from Azusa Pacific University. He serves as a pastor of a multiethnic church.

Dr. James W. Thompson is the associate dean of the Graduate School of Theology and professor of New Testament at Abilene Christian University. He earned a Ph.D. from Vanderbilt University and a M.Div. from Abilene Christian University. Prior to his coming to Abilene Christian University, he served as professor and president of the Austin Graduate School of Theology in Austin, Texas.

Kit Rae is the families pastor at **ROCK**HARBOR Church in Costa Mesa, California. He has more than 13 years of ministry experience and is increasingly passionate about what the future of children's ministries holds with the integration of spiritual formation and the family. He earned his B.A. from Biola University in Christian Education, and his M.A. in Spiritual Formation and Soul Care from the Talbot School of Theology.

David Keehn is associate professor of Christian Education at the Talbot School of Theology where he earned a M.A. degree. Professor Keehn has served for more than 20 years in youth ministry in both large and small churches. His expertise is developing ministry programs to reach and disciple the Millennial generation and their families. He has spoken at numerous conferences and continues to be involved on a church pastoral staff in Dana Point, California.

Unit 1

The Changing Face of the North American Family

1 The Morphing of the Family

Michael J. Anthony
Biola University

I grew up watching the popular sitcom television shows of the 1950s and 1960s. Episodes of *Ozzie and Harriet, Father Knows Best, Leave It to Beaver, The Donna Reed Show,* and *The Dick Van Dyke Show* were weekly staples in our home. We would gather around the TV as a family and watch together while they generated laughter, finger pointing, and the occasional postepisode family discussion. We looked forward to the evening when our favorite show was on, and we would organize our time accordingly.

The writers and producers could capture the essence of our family even though they had never come to interview or visit us in our home. It was as if they had little spy cameras in our house so the things we were dealing with as a family became the theme of next week's episode. Obviously, our family wasn't alone in this observation. These popular portrayals of the "all-American family" were a snapshot of what was happening across the country. And where reality did not match the television show, the actors provided role models for how most Americans wanted to emulate their households.

As the popular Bob Dylan songs goes, "The Times They Are a Changin'." The family of the twenty-first century has morphed into so many different configurations since those popular shows first aired that even sociologists are hard pressed to define them all. What was once simply referred to as a "nuclear family" has now morphed into labels such as "nontraditional families," "fragmented families," "single-parent families," "gay-partner families," "blended families," and a host of other descriptions.

The purpose of this chapter is to explore and present some of the variations of families common in our culture today. If we are going to establish a theology of family ministries, we will need to take a hard look at what the Scriptures teach about the composition of the home (chapters 4–8) and then present strategies and models for helping these families live out their God-given mandates (chapters 9–12). However, before that can begin, we need to acknowledge that we do not live in a vacuum and families, as we once knew them, have changed dramatically over the past few decades. This first unit is designed to present the reader with a snapshot of current social and cultural existence as it pertains to the North American family. It may not always be pretty, but it is reality, and that is the intersection between biblical ideal and ministry practice.

Still the Gold Standard

The traditional nuclear family (e.g., dad, mom, and two kids) was the ideal model during the aftermath of the Second World War. The postwar baby boom explosion launched America into an unprecedented season of family growth. The percentage of married adults hovered close to 95 percent of the population.[1] However, this model was short lived as the 1960s brought about a turbulent era of transition. Young adults deferred marriage, opting for a carefree existence of experimentation with drugs, rock music, and sexual freedoms.

> The growing demand for gender equality encouraged women to stand on their own, get in touch with their own strengths, and not rely on marriage and family as their sole source of security and identity. Marriage was still seen as a desirable objective by most men and women, but self-fulfillment and gratification were increasingly important motivators.[2]

Marriages that began after the war faced difficult times, and soon many were ending in divorce. As one author put it, "[T]he Cleavers are only available on reruns now, and the prominence of the breadwinner-homemaker family rapidly declined in the last third of the twentieth century. Married women moved into the work force, divorce rates rose, and more children were born out of wedlock."[3] The percentage of single-parent homes was on the rise in ways America had never known before. Sociologists were in a quandary to predict what the future held. This was new territory for the American family to be sure.

Throughout the next decades and into the twenty-first century, America has come to see new variations in what was once viewed as the gold standard of the American dream. The traditional family model is on the

---

[1] C. Koons and M. J. Anthony, *Single Adult Passages: Uncharted Territories* (Grand Rapids, MI: Baker Books, 1991), 49.

[2] Ibid.

[3] A. J. Cherlin, "Public Display: The Picture-Perfect American Family? These Days, It Doesn't Exist," *The Washington Post*, September 7, 2008, Sec. "Outlook," B01.

ne, but it has not been abandoned. A 2008 *Washington Times* article orted on a recent Census Bureau study that revealed "the most popular nily type remained the nuclear family: Nearly 43 million children, or 58 percent, lived with their married biological parents. The number of parents in two-parent homes swelled even larger, to 51 million, when adoptive parents, remarried parents and unmarried-but-cohabitating parents were added in. Another 19 million children lived in single-parent homes, nearly 17 million with their mothers."[4]

Although the variations have expanded and become far more creative in nature than our grandparents ever dreamed possible, the traditional nuclear family of two parents with children remains the foundation of American society.

Changing Paradigms of the Family

What are these new paradigms of family that we see throughout our society today? Definitions have had to expand and reconfigure what was once a fairly stable construct to examine. But when it comes to describing the all-American family today, it is time to take out a fresh piece of paper to describe what you see. Take a glance, for example, at some of these recent statistics that represent some of these familial changes:

- About one out of six 15-year-old girls will give birth before reaching the age of 20, according to the National Center of Health Statistics.
- In 1950 women made up 28 percent of the workforce. Today that figure is 48 percent.
- Multigenerational families have increased by 60 percent since 1990, according to www.togetheragain.com.
- A new Census Bureau American Community Survey shows that the number of parents younger than age 65 in households was up 75 percent between 2000 and 2007. It would appear families are not putting their aging parents in nursing homes as frequently as before.
- In the early 1960s, almost 60 percent of families had children younger than 18 living at home; that percentage in 2009 had dropped to just 46 percent.
- Married couples are older now. In 1968 less than 30 percent of married men were 55 and older. Today, nearly 40 percent are

---

[4] C. Wetzstein, "U.S. Families Data Remains Steady: Nuclear Model Most Popular," *The Washington Times*, February 21, 2008, Sec. "Nation," A04.

that age; the percentage of married women 55 and older has increased from 22 percent to 33 percent.

- Twenty percent of women ages 40 to 44 have no children, double the level of 30 years ago; women who do have children in that age category have fewer of them—an average of 1.09 children today compared to 3.1 children in 1976.
- Of women who gave birth in 2006, 36 percent were separated, widowed, divorced, or never married. Five percent were living with a partner.
- Research indicates that a 10 percent increase in welfare benefits increases by 12 percent the chances that a poor young woman will have a baby out of wedlock before she reaches the age of 22. This is true for both black and white girls.

In summary, the American family today is a household with fewer children and both parents working outside the home, with mothers giving birth to children at an ever older age, having far fewer children, and spacing them out farther than in years past. Never-married young teen mothers no longer disappear to have their baby with a relative out of state but remain home without raising an eyebrow. Aging parents live with their children longer before going into a retirement home.[5] This captures a brief look at our current condition, but looking below the surface one finds deeper issues that affect the future and have profound implications for how the church will minister to this new landscape of the American home. We'll take a look at five trends that are affecting the new face of the American family.

The Changing Face of the American Family

1. A Significant Increase In Premarital Cohabitation. Back in 1984 a team of researchers examined the relationship between living together before marriage and the couple's level of satisfaction after they got married. Compared with those who had never lived together before marriage, those who had lived together scored significantly lower in both perceived quality of marital communication and in marital satisfaction overall. This was particularly true for the women in the study.[6] In other words, those who had lived together prior to getting married discovered that they were not as happy as those who had chosen not to live together.

Today the number of couples living together prior to getting married, if they get married at all, has skyrocketed. What was once a social

---

[5] M. Zuckerman, "Rebuild the American Family, Starting with Mom and Dad," *Daily News*, October 7, 2007, Sec. "Editorial," 41.

[6] A. Demaris and G. R. Leslie, "Cohabitation with the Future Spouse: Its Influences upon Marital Satisfaction and Communication," *Journal of Marriage and the Family* (1984): 46, 77–84.

taboo has become common among young adults. For example, in 1997 the total number of unmarried couples in America topped four million, up from less than half a million in 1960.[7]

> It is estimated that about a quarter of unmarried women between the ages of 25 and 39 are currently living with a partner and about half have lived at some time with an unmarried partner (the data are typically reported for women but not for men). Over half of all first marriages are now preceded by cohabitation, compared to virtually none earlier in the century.[8]

This trend among America's younger generation shows no signs of letting up, and for them it makes a lot of sense.

> For today's young adults, the first generation to come of age during the divorce revolution, living together seems like a good way to achieve some of the benefits of marriage and avoid the risk of divorce. Couples who live together can share expenses and learn more about each other. They can find out if their partner has what it takes to be married. If things don't work out, breaking up is easy to do. Cohabiting couples do not have to seek legal or religious permission to dissolve their union. Not surprisingly, young adults favor cohabitation. According to surveys, most young people say it is a good idea to live with a person before marrying.[9]

The appeal for these young couples in love is motivated by a variety of factors, but regardless of which factor tops a couple's particular list, inherent dangers also are associated with living together prior to marriage. Some of these dangers include the loss of self-esteem when one partner chooses to leave; the insecurity that follows into a marriage relationship (because couples who cohabitate tend to be less dedicated to long-term commitments); the fact that couples who lived together tend to drop out of marriage quicker than those who did not live together; the fact that those who live together before getting married have higher rates of

---

[7] U.S. Bureau of the Census, Marital Status and Living Arrangements: March, 1997. As quoted in "Should We Live Together? What Young Adults Need to Know About Cohabitation Before Marriage: A Comprehensive Review of Recent Research." The National Marriage Project Rutgers, January 1999. *Smart Marriages,* January 1999, ¶ 1, http://www.smartmarriage.com/cohabit.html.

[8] L. Bumpass and H. Lu, "Trends in Cohabitation and Implications for Children's Family Contexts," unpublished manuscript, Madison, WI: Center for Demography, University of Wisconsin, 1998. Quoted in "Should We Live Together?" Ibid.

[9] D. Popenoe and B. D. Whitehead, "Should We Live Together? What Young Adults Need to Know About Cohabitation Before Marriage: Executive Summary," *Smart Marriages.* Ibid.

depression than their married peers; and, perhaps most importantly, the women are more likely to suffer physical and sexual abuse.[10]

Those who have children and choose to live together before getting married perhaps face the greatest danger. One might think that because of the "trial nature" of such a relationship, couples would wait to have children until they knew for sure that they would stay together (and therefore get married), but the demographic data indicate that such is not the case. In 1987 only 21 percent of couples that lived together also had a child in their home. Today that number has jumped to 36 percent.[11] It is estimated that nearly 50 percent of all children born in America today are born into a family where the parents are not married. Couple this trend with the knowledge that couples living together are far more likely to end their relationship than those who are married, and it does not take much to realize that children of cohabitating couples are at far greater risk of feeling isolation, anxiety, and abandonment compared to intact (married) couples.

In a national study of couples entitled "The State of Our Unions: The Social Health of Marriage in America," couples who choose to live together without getting married do so for at least one of four reasons. First, they are looking to get to know their partner better than they could if they lived in separate apartments. In essence, you can think you know someone until you move in and see him or her for who they *really* are. That is when you really know them. Second, it is viewed as a test of compatibility in several critical factors: emotional, relational, financial, and perhaps even spiritual. This around-the-clock test is essential before making the plunge into a legally binding relationship. Third, it gives each of them an opportunity to avoid the hazards they saw played out in their parents' marriage relationships. The chances of being trapped in an unhappy marriage (like their parents) are diminished through this trial period. Last, couples choose to live together for a variety of financial reasons. They simply need time to build that nest egg, to finish paying off their student loans, or to save up for the down payment on a house.[12]

This increase in couples living without the "notarized seal" is forcing churches to rethink their approach to family ministry in ways most ministry leaders would not have considered a decade or two ago. For example,

---

[10] J. E. Stets, "Cohabiting and Marital Aggression: The Role of Social Isolation," *Journal of Marriage and the Family* (1991), 53:669–80. One study found that, of the violence toward women committed by intimates and relatives, 42 percent involves a close friend or partner, whereas only 29 percent involves a current spouse. Ronet Bachman, "Violence Against Women" (Washington, DC: Bureau of Justice Statistics, 1994), 6. As quoted in "Should We Live Together?" Ibid.

[11] Ibid.

[12] D. Popenoe and B. D. Whitehead, "The State of Our Unions 2000: The Social Health of Marriage in America," The National Marriage Project, The State University of New Jersey-Rutgers, June 2000, 12.

when a young couple living together chooses to attend church (although fewer cohabitating couples attend church compared to their married peers), which Sunday school class do they attend? Do they go to the single adult class because they are not officially married? Do they go to the young marrieds class even though they are not married? If they want to hold a home Bible study in their home, does the church support it? What if they want to volunteer to serve in the children's or youth ministry areas? These and a host of other questions pose challenging dilemmas for ministry leaders today, and I do not see the challenges getting any easier any time soon.

2. The Increase in Gay/Lesbian Unions. Although by most accounts the conservative evangelical approach is to condemn all gay and lesbian unions, there is no arguing that they are on the rise and that their impact is being felt across all corners of society. It is not unusual for children to have their same-gender parents attend a parent night in an elementary classroom. The governmental workforce employs gays and lesbians as does the military, and it is a commonly accepted practice in most business enterprises. Gone are the days when deciding whether to accept them into our culture is an option. They are here in force and show no signs of diminishing. So let's deal with the current reality and figure out a way to reach a growing segment of our population with a gospel message they need to hear.

According to the most recent U.S. Census data, there are at least 707,000 same-sex couples.[13] Some believe this number is grossly underreported because many in this form of union feel too intimidated to indicate their relationship on a government form,[14] in part because doing so would prevent them from receiving any of the 1,138 federal benefits that are made available to married couples.[15] However, there is no denying the pressure our society is facing by this well-funded and popular movement. Ever since the New York police tried to arrest people for attending a gay bar in Greenwich Village back in 1969, the gay rights movement has been relentless in its efforts to legitimize their view of marriage.

It may surprise you to know the degree to which gays and lesbians are represented in our society today. For example:

- At the time of this writing, though, the military's "don't ask, don't tell" policy does not permit lesbians and gay men to serve openly, census data make clear that they are actively serving in the armed forces, in guard and reserve units, and have served in the military throughout the later part of the twentieth century. Estimates suggest that gay men and lesbians represent

[13] 2004 American Community Survey data from the United States Census Bureau, www.gaydemographics.org/USA/USA.htm.

[14] n.a. "Marriage Equality: Why Marriage?" 2009, ¶ 6. www.fairwisconsin.com/issues/marriageequality/whymarriage.html.

[15] n.a. "The Issues," *National Gay and Lesbian Task Force Newsletter*, 2009, ¶ 1. thetaskforce.org/issues/marriage_and_partnership_recognition.

2.5 percent of active-duty personnel. When the guard and reserve are included, nearly 65,000 men and women in uniform are likely gay or lesbian, accounting for 2.8 percent of military personnel.[16]

- More than 7,400 companies now offer equal benefits to the same-sex partners of their employees. Divergent national, state, and local laws affecting same-sex couples and their families, however, are sending businesses into unclear territory.[17]
- Gay and lesbian couples appear to be "urban pioneers," willing to live in and possibly transform distressed urban areas. They are more likely than their heterosexual counterparts to live in racially and ethnically diverse neighborhoods that have more college-educated residents, older housing stock, and both higher crime rates and higher property values.[18]
- Same-sex couples with children often live in states and large metropolitan areas not known for large gay and lesbian communities. Mississippi, South Dakota, Alaska, South Carolina, and Louisiana are where same-sex couples are most likely raising children.[19]

Highest Concentration of Same-Sex Couple Households[20]

By State	By Large Metro Area
1. Vermont	1. San Francisco, CA
2. California	2. Oakland, CA
3. Washington	3. Seattle-Bellevue-Everett, WA
4. Massachusetts	4. Fort Lauderdale, FL
5. Oregon	5. Austin-San Marcos, TX
6. New Mexico	6. New York, NY
7. Nevada	7. Los Angeles-Long Beach, CA
8. New York	8. Albuquerque, NM
9. Maine	9. Atlanta, GA
10. Arizona	10. Jersey City, NJ

16 n.a. "Gay and Lesbian Demographics: A Research Focus of the Urban Institute," Washington, DC, The Urban Institute. ¶ 2. www.urban.org/toolkit/issues/gayresearchfocus.cfm#RecentFindings. For additional statistics of gays and lesbians in the military, see also Gary J. Gates, "Gay Men and Lesbians in the U.S. Military: Estimates from Census 2000" (Washington, DC: The Urban Institute, 2004).

17 B. Witeck and G. Gates, "Same Sex Marriages: What's at Stake for Business?" (Washington, DC: The Urban Institute, July 21, 2004), ¶ 4.

18 K. McKenzie and L. Good, "The Gay and Lesbian Atlas Displays First Detailed Portrait of Same-Sex Households across the United States" (Washington, DC: The Urban Institute, March 30, 2004), ¶ 4.

19 Ibid.

20 G. Gates and J. Ost, "Facts and Findings from The Gay Lesbian Atlas" (Washington, DC: The Urban Institute, March 30, 2004), ¶ 4, www.urban.org/publications/900695.html.

Not long ago I had a counseling appointment with a young woman who wanted to talk about her impending separation. She had been living with her female partner for several years. Each of them had chosen to have two children via artificial insemination by the same male donor. In essence, each of the four children had two mothers and the same father (although they had never met him). They had recently decided to end their union and were facing the challenge of trying to figure out how to navigate what was a painful passage for all concerned. I asked a few probing questions about her spiritual journey, and I was a little surprised to discover that she had grown up in a conservative evangelical home and had once attended a well-known evangelical college. She dropped out of school when she was "discovered and rejected" and never felt accepted by the church again. I asked if she had ever taken her children to Sunday school, and she laughed. "What would I put down on the parent information card? There are no categories for the type of union I'm in. I obviously don't belong, and 'my kind' aren't wanted in most churches today."

Let's postpone my response for the time being and focus on the bigger issue. Is there a place for gays and lesbians in the church today? Are they welcome, or, like the lepers in Jesus' day, are they kept at arms' distance and told to stay away until they repent and "clean up their act"? What would your church do if this young woman walked in the door on Sunday morning looking for help? Knowing that she was in deep emotional pain, would you tell her to leave and take her children with her? Would you welcome her children and try to find a way to minister in the name of Jesus? These hard questions foster deep theological (and emotional) debate. These kinds of scenarios will only come more frequently as the decades of the twenty-first century roll along. The increase in gay and lesbian unions and the common place we now associate with these new family paradigms is going to have an impact on the way we do ministry in the years ahead.

3. The Continuing Increase in Single-Parent Families. Back in the early days of Colonial America, the single-adult population hovered around 3 percent. There were a number of reasons for this. Society as a whole did not value breaking what they perceived to be the foundation of society. In addition, the church did not condone divorce or support those who broke their marriage vows of "'till death do us part." But perhaps the strongest reason for the low rate of divorce was economic. America was primarily an agrarian culture, and life on the farm required large families. Everyone helped, whether out in the fields or in the home. Those who chose to leave their families on the farm for an independent lifestyle were frowned upon and ostracized.[21] It was not until the 1960s that America experienced a significant increase in the number of single-parent households. "The number of households headed by single or divorced women has increased by 46 percent since 1980. In 1977 almost 18 million children were living in single-parent homes in the United States. Today that number has experienced a 100 percent increase."[22]

You may be interested to know some demographic data about the average American single-parent household that lives in your community today.

The Average Single-Parent Home[23]

- There are approximately 13.6 million single parents in the United States today, and those parents are responsible for raising 21.2 million children.
- Approximately 84 percent are led by mothers; 16 percent are led by fathers.
- Of single custodial mothers, 44 percent are currently divorced or separated, 33 percent never married, and only 1 percent are widowed.
- Of single custodial fathers, 57 percent are divorced or separated, 18 percent never married, and only 1 percent are widowed.
- Of custodial single-parent mothers, 79 percent are employed, 50 percent work full-time, and 29 percent work part-time.
- Almost 28 percent of custodial mothers live in poverty, compared to 11 percent of custodial fathers. Only 31 percent of all single parents receive some form of public assistance.
- Almost 38 percent of custodial mothers are 40 years old or older.
- Of custodial mothers, 56 percent are raising one child from the absent parent, and 44 percent have two or more children living with them.

Churches continue to face challenges in terms of family ministry programming as it relates to single-parent families, but significant progress has been made in recent decades. For decades the single-parent family was an enigma to the church as the stigma over divorce influenced the distribution of limited resources. For example, why would a church budget for

---

21 Koons and Anthony, *Single Adult Passages*, 48.

22 Amy B., "The Changing American Family—Are Family Values Declining?" *Associated Content*, November 21, 2009, 1. www.associatedcontent.com/article/2404864/the_changing_american_family_are_family.

23 Timothy S. Grall, "Custodial Mothers and Fathers and Their Child Support: 2005," United States Census Department. Issued August 2007. As quoted in J. Wolf "Single Parent Statistics." ¶ 4, www.singleparents.about.com/od/legalissues/p/portrait.htm.

divorce recovery workshops when they did not believe in divorce in the first place? Why invite single parents and their children to your church when you wanted to promote the traditional nuclear family as your only acceptable role model for the family? These and a host of other questions had to be faced and answered by churches across America in the 1980s and 1990s. Now in most churches the stigma of being divorced has lessened, and churches greet single-parent households with open arms—albeit somewhat reluctantly. Nevertheless, this trend will not decline in the generations to come. If anything, it will continue its rise and probably become more commonplace in the next decade.

4. Blended Families Will Continue Their Meteoric Rise. One of the reasons this trend will continue to rise in the generations to come is coupled with the divorce rate that continues to hover around the 45 to 50 percent rate. Even among evangelical Christians, the divorce rate is close to that of society as a whole. In essence divorce affects families in the church just as much as those who are on the outside looking in. Pastors have been forced to rethink their attitude toward remarriage in recent years, and most churches no longer view the remarried adult as living in adultery. Broader definitions are used that now allow divorced adults to remarry and bring their newly reconfigured families back into the church with them. This has resulted in a proliferation of blended families in the local church where once they were rarely seen. According to Jill Curtis, "65% of remarriages include children from previous relationships, so the number of families 'blending' to create stepfamilies is ever-increasing."[24]

The new husband and wife may enter into the relationship flush with newfound love and affection, but it is rare for the children to go into the new family configuration with the same feelings. Many of the children enter the blended family with feelings of anxiety, fear, and uncertainty. This stress often compounds after the wedding ceremony, and it doesn't take long before what seemed like such a blessed arrangement has become a source of discord, sometimes leading to another marital breakup. This is even more accentuated if the cause of the marriage ending was the death of the spouse. Feelings of allegiance are often associated with the children, and they are too young to understand that finding a new love does not mean the living spouse does not still love and respect the one who passed away. A good snapshot of what children in blended families need is described in the box on the following page.[25]

---

[24] J. Curtis, "Blended Families: Preparing to Form Healthy Step Families Before the Wedding," *I Do, Take Two. Guide to Second Weddings, Second Marriages and Vow Renewals,* 2009, ¶1, www.idotaketwo.com/second_marriage_children.html.

[25] G. Kemp and J. Segal, "Stepparenting and Blended Family Advice," *Helpguide.org,* March 9, 2009, www.helpguide.org/mental/blended_families_stepfamilies.htm.

What Do Kids in Blended Families Need?

- Safe and secure—Children want to be able to count on their parents. Children of divorce have already felt the upset of having people let them down and may not be eager to give second chances to their parents or stepparents.
- **Loved**—Kids like to see and feel your affection, although it should be a gradual process.
- **Seen and valued**—Kids often feel unimportant or invisible when it comes to decision making in the new blended family. Recognize their integral role in the family when you are making decisions.
- **Heard and emotionally connected to**—Kids are eager for real connection and understanding. Creating an honest and open environment free of judgment will help them feel heard. Show them that you can view the situation from their perspective.
- **Appreciated and encouraged**—Children of all ages respond to praise and encouragement and like to feel appreciated for their contribution.
- **Limits and boundaries**—Children may not think they need limits, but a lack of boundaries sends a signal that the child is unworthy of the parents' time, care, and attention. As a new stepparent, you should not step in as the enforcer at first; work with your spouse to set limits.

The church can do a lot to help stepfamilies during this transitional time. Start with identifying the real needs in the stepfamily. For example, what was the issue that precipitated the new family model? Dealing with the death of a parent, especially for young children, is different from the issues associated with a divorce. If there was abuse in the home prior to the marriage ending, do not overlook the trauma the children are experiencing. Abandonment also brings a host of emotional issues that need to be unpacked. Specific situations require more specific intervention programs. The church can help the stepfamily transition by providing counseling for children, spouses, and other related family members.

As difficult as it may be for some churches, they are going to have to come to grips with the fact that blended families are not going away. Take the time to examine the teachings of Scripture in light of our call to be redemptive and merciful. The pastor would do well to lead his leadership team through a formulated theology related to blended families and preach a series on this position. The church will be looking for cues from the pastoral leadership to know how they should respond. Churches that are viewed as welcoming and accepting will find their services well attended by blended families of all sorts.

Another issue the pastoral staff will need to work through is the degree of leadership men and women from blended families will be allowed to assume. For example, will those who are divorced be allowed to serve in leadership roles such as deacon or elder? Will they be allowed to host a home Bible study? What about other leadership roles in various age-level departments? On what basis will such decisions be made? I bring this up because it is better to form a position before the need arises and emotions get attached to decisions. When you do this, however, keep in mind that no family is perfect, and the church is called to model redemption, grace, and kindness.

The following tips may help your church as they determine how best to advise and minister to stepparents and their children.[26]

Tips for Establishing Healthy, Happy Stepfamilies

- **Go slowly.** Do not expect to fall in love with your partner's children overnight. Take it slowly, and get to know them. Love and respect have to be learned, and a stepparent has to earn them.
- **All brothers and sisters have "falling out" periods,** so don't assume all family arguments are the result of living in a blended family.
- **Beware of favoritism.** Be fair. Do not overcompensate by favoring your stepchildren. This is a common mistake, made with the best of intentions, in an attempt to avoid indulging your biological children.
- **Communicate.** Be sure to discuss everything. Never keep emotions bottled up or hold grudges.
- **Make special arrangements.** If some of the kids "just visit," make sure they have a locked cupboard for their personal things. Bringing toothbrushes and other standard fare each time they come to your home makes them feel like visitors, not members of the blended family.
- **Find support.** Locate a stepparenting support organization in your community. You can learn how other blended families address some of the challenges of blended families.
- **Spend time every day with your child.** Try to spend at least one "quiet time" period with your child (or children) daily. Even in the best of blended families, children still need to enjoy some "alone time" with each parent.
- **Patience is a virtue.** Don't just cross your fingers and hope the kids will like each other. They need time to get to know their stepbrothers or stepsisters. It should not be hurried.

[26] Curtis, "Blended Families," ¶ 8.

5. Teen Attitudes about Marriage. The final trend we will explore relates to the changing perspective teenagers have regarding marriage. Where once their views were shaped by their own experience (and to a large degree they still are housed here), today there is growing evidence to support the view that the media is the largest influence in shaping their worldview.

This plugged-in and turned-on generation that lives connected to electronic devices. It is a rare child that is not in some way connected to a larger social network found through sites such as MySpace, Facebook, Twitter, Habbo, Hi5, Ning, and so on. These sites provide a sense of connection that the teen generation values today. They want community and find it through a terminal and keyboard. It may seem strange to their parents, but it is their reality, and we would do well to learn about it.

Beyond these cyber communities, values are also being shaped through television shows depicting dysfunctional families. You may have grown up watching television shows such as *The Wonder Years, Saved by the Bell,* and *Beverly Hills 90210.* Although they may have seemed "edgy" to you at the time, they pale in comparison to the shows affecting teen values today. Shows such as *The Simpsons, South Park, The Robot Chicken, Family Guy,* and a multitude of teen soaps are forming values beyond what you think possible. The writers and producers of these shows seem to think just because they cloak their characters in cartoon animation they are less accountable for their raunchy content and baseless values.

A common theme in many of these shows is that the father is either absent or, at best, acts like an imbecile. The mother is usually domineering, cynical, and contemptuous. The children are sarcastic and cutting of their parents and other siblings in their home. Is it any wonder teens bring the values (and vocabularies) of these shows into their own homes?

When such media-generated values are allowed to affect their view of marriage and the family, there is little cause for hope. Many worry what will happen when these teens become the parents of the next generation—and for good reason. Data show that many of these young teens will indeed conceive a child before they reach their twenties.

In case you feel confident that churched kids have radically different values concerning premarital sex, marriage, and the family, consider the following reality check. Statistics show that even Christian teens are succumbing to the same lifestyle choices of their non-Christian peers.

> A recent study of teenagers who pledged in the 90s to remain virgins until marriage found that 88 percent of them had since violated their pledge. The study also found that their behavior, both before and after losing their virginity, was more risky than that of teens who had not committed to such an absolute value. While they were still virgins,

> pledgers were six times more likely than non-pledgers to engage in oral and anal sex, probably out of concern for preserving their "technical virginity." Teens who took the pledge did start having sexual intercourse a little later, on average, than teens who didn't, and they had fewer sexual partners. But they were much less likely than the other teens to use contraception and ended up with the same rates of sexually transmitted diseases.[27]

Teen values, both those in the church and those outside looking in, are being radically shaped by our culture. Through every portal—television, Internet, movies, and music—teen values are being pulled farther and farther away from what we once knew as traditional family values.

There's No Place Like Home

The prominent trends of increasing premarital cohabitation, the increase in gay and lesbian unions, the continuing increase in single-parent families, the rise in blended families, and the attitude among many teens regarding their view of marriage and the family combine to make for a significantly different familial landscape in the years ahead.

The postmodern world in which we live works overtime trying to force us into accepting its relativistic values. The world says, "Just because you have different standards of behavior from someone else doesn't give you the right to impose your views on them." "Celebrate diversity" is the battle cry of a world that wants to be left alone to explore and experiment with lifestyle choices that run contrary to the teachings of Scripture. This argument is not new. John Stuart Mill called for "experiments in living" back in 1859. In his book *On Liberty* he argues for the celebration of personal freedoms, and he goes so far as to advocate public benefits of lifestyle experimentation. He believed we would learn from this clash of values and that the end result would be a more harmonious existence. History has proved him wrong.[28] Said one family researcher as she looked back over the past few decades:

> For the best part of thirty years we have been conducting a vast experiment with the family, and now the results are in: the decline of the two-parent, married-couple family has resulted in poverty, ill-health, educational failure, unhappiness, anti-social behavior, isolation and social exclusion for thousands of women, men and children.[29]

---

[27] S. Coontz, "Family Values: Actions Speak Louder Than Words," *Seattle Pi*, May 13, 2005, ¶ 7, www.seattlepi.com/opinion/224048_values13.html.

[28] R. O'Neill, "Experiments with Living: The Fatherless Family," *The Institute for the Study of Civil Society*, September 2002, 2, www.civitas.org.uk/pubs/experiments.php?PHPSESSID=04a5571963443f82281d8c0bd4332322.

[29] Ibid.

It is as though people believe their choices do not have consequences, but clearly they do. What is worse is that these lifestyle choices also have implications and consequences for the generation to come.

Divorce, for example, has far-reaching implications for the children in a household. Homes without fathers are riddled with long-term consequences for both the custodial mother and her children. Consider for a moment the following statistics about children who grow up in a family without a father:

- They are more likely to engage in premarital sexual activity.
- They are more likely to abuse alcohol and marijuana.
- They are more likely to become the victim of child abuse.
- They are more likely to experience depression and other forms of mental illness.
- They are more likely to underperform at school and eventually drop out.
- They are more likely to commit suicide.
- They are more likely to experience sexual identity problems.

The results of countless investigations have come to the same general conclusion: When the father is absent from the home, the effects are significantly more detrimental to the children than for those children whose father is present.

Dorothy concluded at the end of *The Wizard of Oz,* "There's no place like home." However, research shows that not all homes are of equal value to the well-being of the child. Children raised in homes where there is constant abuse (e.g., emotional, physical, sexual) may be better off living with only one parent than in an unsafe environment. It is unfair for people (including ministry leaders) to judge prematurely whether the departing parent is automatically at fault. Is it better to stay and subject yourself and your children to physical or sexual abuse than to leave and create an environment that is more conducive to safety and nurture? These are tough issues but issues the contemporary ministry leader faces on a regular basis. Gone are the days of simple answers for simple dilemmas. The greater question is, What is the church doing to help, encourage, and support these families who find themselves at life's edges?

It is not the home that automatically makes the environment safe and nurturing. It is a safe and nurturing home that is most conducive to a healthy family. Quality also has to be factored into the equation. Once we start doing this higher level of critical thinking, however, we open ourselves up as ministry leaders to misunderstanding and ridicule. Quoting a verse and sending a battered wife home to her abusive spouse to prove her submission does little to solve the long-term problem; in many cases, it does far more harm.

The Scriptures are given to guide us in important decisions that affect our lives, but the complexity of some societal situations could not have been foreseen so many years ago. Wisdom has to be applied to contextualize the application of biblical principles. God knew that. That is why we read, "But if any of you lacks wisdom, let him ask of God, who gives to all men generously and without reproach, and it will be given to him" (James 1:5 NASB). Not all passages are applied in a literal fashion—otherwise heaven would be filled with blind and lame believers because they took literally the words of Jesus when He declared:

> And if your hand or your foot causes you to stumble, cut it off and throw it from you; It is better for you to enter life crippled or lame than having two hands or two feet, to be cast into the eternal fire. And if your eye causes you to stumble, pluck it out, and throw it far from you. It is better for you to enter life with one eye, than having two eyes, to be cast into the fiery hell. (Matt 18:8–9 NASB)

We are calling for ministry leaders who, while having one foot firmly planted in the pages of Scripture, have the other foot planted in a broken and fallen world filled with people who need direction to the foot of the cross. The condition of the postmodern family is nothing like Dorothy's home in the final scenes of *The Wizard of Oz,* but that does not mean it cannot still be a place of safety, comfort, and warmth.

Conclusion

It has been my intention at the outset of this book to lay a foundation for family ministry models that are firmly based on a sound theology. Too many ministry programs exist today because they are expedient and trendy. They may draw a crowd, but all too often they lack biblical veracity. Ministry leaders who have a passion for God's Word have written each of the chapters of this book. They believe it is given for the purpose of teaching, correction, and training in right living (2 Tim 3:16). The challenge is in interpreting and applying these passages in light of our ever-changing society. Not all Scripture speaks to each contemporary need. For example, little is said about youth ministry in Scripture, but that does not mean it has no value and is not a necessary component of our churches today. The same argument could be made for camping ministry, child evangelism, recovery ministries, and a host of other contemporary programs.

The family has changed a great deal since the days of the Old and New Testament. Family and gender roles have gone through radical transitions. Many of the changes in society have been for the good. Women have the opportunity to receive an education and work outside the home if they choose. Governments are far more democratic than in the days of Scripture. Minorities have received far more rights, and slavery, at least for the majority of the world, has come to an end. Change has led to progress in so many areas. Some would argue that change in the family is also an improvement. Some would argue to the contrary, and perhaps some would prefer to go back to "the good old days." For the latter audience the family is viewed through a lens of cynicism.

> The current wave of pessimism about the family's future can be attributed to an outmoded set of views about how families work. A major cause of this pessimism involves out-dated myths, and specifically, the idea of a perfect, self-sufficient nucleus family and the parent's exclusive responsibility for what and who the child becomes. Families have never been, nor will they ever be, the perfect, independently-operating building blocks of our American society. Rather, they are deeply influenced by broad social and economic forces over which they have no control.[30]

Lest you be tempted to conclude that the changes are over and we have arrived at the final frontier, let me warn you that society is far from done tinkering with the concept of family.

Dr. Katherine Rake, a prominent family researcher and executive director of the Family and Parenting Institute, predicted:

> [T]here will be no such thing as a "typical family" in the next 10 to 20 years. People are constantly redefining what it means to be a family. What we are seeing is that family shape is changing all the time, the notion of a traditional nuclear family . . . certainly isn't the norm now. Because people are having children later and because there is more divorce and separation, what is happening is that people draw on resources from right across the family and their families can be more involved.[31]

---

[30] Amy B., "The Changing American Family," 1.

[31] J. Bingham, "Nuclear Family Is Broken Warns Parents' Group," *Telegraph,* November 29, 2009, ¶ 9, www.telegraph.co.uk/family/6686407/Nuclear-family-is-broken-warns-parents-group.html. For additional articles regarding future family trends see also www.familyandministryinstitute.org.

Although the family may continue to change and morph into models and paradigms that bring discomfort and angst to some of us, we rest in the assurance that God has a plan for those who live in any of these new configurations of what we now call *family.* Each of the following chapters will examine some of the issues introduced in this first chapter with the hope that the ministry leader might be more informed both biblically and philosophically to make wise and discerning choices as to how best he can reach those who reside in this broken world. No one model will work for everyone. Not all will agree on what is essential or even biblical for that matter. But we need to be careful not to get discouraged and lose heart. We need to heed the admonition of the apostle Paul where he says, ". . . the one who sows to the Spirit will from the Spirit reap eternal life. Let us not lose heart in doing good, for in due time we will reap if we do not grow weary. So then, while we have opportunity, let us do good to all people, and especially to those who are of the household of the faith" (Gal 6:8b–10 NASB).

2 The Family in Formational Years

Karen E. Jones
Huntington University

Parents begin preparing for the healthy development of their children from the time they learn they are expecting. Mothers avoid taking anything into their bodies that might threaten the health of the unborn child, and they schedule regular visits with their physicians, who monitor the growth of the baby. After the child is born, parents purchase car seats, cribs, high chairs, and toys that meet high safety standards. As the child grows, they choose fast-food restaurants that provide healthy children's meals and purchase bicycle helmets and protective sports and recreational equipment in an attempt to keep them safe. Age restrictions on driving and restrictions on the purchase of alcohol and tobacco products are designed to protect children as they grow from adolescence into adulthood. Parents not only want to keep their children safe, but they also want to know that their children are developing normally. They consult experts and read magazines, books, and Web sites to find out whether their children are reaching developmental milestones on time. Parents also are concerned about their children's cognitive development, and they invest in educational DVDs, books, preschools, tutoring, and educational camps and programs to help them reach their full potential. Healthy social and emotional development is also a concern, as evidenced by organized playdates and trophies awarded to all children who participate in a sport.

It is appropriate for parents to be concerned about their children's needs and always want the best for them because children are a gift and a blessing from God (Ps 127:3–5; Gen 30:20; 1 Sam 1:11). The Bible provides numerous examples of children bringing pleasure to their parents, such as when Sarah rejoiced at Isaac's birth (Gen 21:6–7). Jesus said, "A woman giving birth to a child has pain because her time has come; but when her baby is born she forgets the anguish because of her joy that a child is born into the world" (John 16:21).[1] When teaching about the importance of persistent prayer, Jesus made reference to parents' natural desire to provide for their children. "Which of you, if his son asks for bread, will give him a stone? Or if he asks for a fish, will give him a snake?" (Matt 7:9–10). When Jairus, a synagogue ruler, lost his young daughter, Jesus brought her back to life and asked her parents to provide her with food (Luke 8:49–55). In a time when children were often devalued, Jesus found time to welcome them and publicly affirm their innocence and openness (Matt 19:13–15). In his letters to the churches at Ephesus and Colossae, Paul instructed parents to avoid the kind of discipline that would lead to anger or distress in their children, showing a concern for their emotional health (Eph 6:4; Col 3:21). He spoke about his ministry among the Thessalonians as being gentle, just "like a mother caring for her little children," and dealing with them as a father would his children, with encouragement and comfort (1 Thess 2:7–11).

The only reference to Jesus' childhood is found in the second chapter of Luke. At the age of 12, instead of being where he was supposed to be, Jesus caused his parents a great deal of stress when they had to return to Jerusalem to find him after the Passover celebration. Right after this incident is recorded in Luke 2:41–51, the Bible includes one short verse that provides a unique perspective on Jesus' continued development into adulthood. "Jesus grew in wisdom and stature, and in favor with God and men" (Luke 2:52). Not only does this passage refer to physical and intellectual growth, but it also makes note of Jesus' social development, in terms of positive interpersonal relationships, and his inner spiritual growth. God was pleased with the person Jesus was becoming. We will unpack this passage in greater detail in chapter 12.

Much attention is given to helping children develop physically, intellectually, and even socially and emotionally, but parents are not given a lot of help in knowing how to aid in the moral or spiritual development of their children. Although societies depend on the continued transmission of morals and values from one generation to the next, little is done to ensure success. Entertainment rating systems and family settings and protections can be applied to computers and gaming systems, but even these actions seem directed more at keeping children physically safe and protecting them from cognitive content than they are aimed at character development. This does not mean, however, that parents are unconcerned about the moral and spiritual development of their children.

Parental Goals for Child Development

In the Building Strong Families study, Search Institute asked parents how they defined success in their parental role. The top definition was "having children who are respectful, exhibit good behavior,

[1] Unless otherwise noted, all citations from Scripture in this chapter are taken from the NIV.

and have positive values."[2] For the majority of parents, this probably involves religious training or spiritual development. Studies have consistently found that most people in the United States believe in God and even identify with a religious denomination. The developmental sciences have tended to marginalize spiritual development, however, although evidence suggests that it is a powerful force and important dimension of human growth. Existing research is focused mainly on adults, "despite mounting evidence that the first two decades of life are particularly vital in how spirituality is developed, thwarted or misdirected. Issues of beliefs, meaning, purpose, identity and relationships are particularly salient during adolescence."[3] All aspects of a person's life and development are interrelated, but the spiritual dimension has the power to integrate them into a whole self. Out of one's moral and spiritual self the best and worst of humanity is evident; consider the source for generosity and genocide, sacrifice and slavery, altruism and terrorism. Research suggests that desired life outcomes are positively associated with spirituality and that an inverse relationship exists between negative life outcomes and spirituality.[4]

In addition to raising children who display positive values, such as honesty, self-confidence, and loyalty, some child development experts place the greatest significance on helping children find a balance between a strong sense of self and a healthy respect for others, to love themselves and to practice self-control in such a way that they can develop healthy relationships with other people.[5] This view is a basic tenet of transactional analysis, popularized by Dr. Thomas Harris in his 1967 best seller, *I'm OK—You're OK*.[6] Although this book/philosophy was instrumental in ushering in the self-esteem movement in child development, it is not entirely inconsistent with Christian theology. Leviticus 19:18 instructs God's children to "love your neighbor as yourself." Jesus made reference to this Old Testament teaching several times, including during his Sermon on the Mount: "So in everything, do to others what you would have them do to you, for this sums up the Law and the Prophets" (Matt 7:12). In Mark 12:30–31a, when asked which of the commandments was the greatest, Jesus responded, "Love the Lord your God with all your heart and with all your soul and with all your mind and with all your strength. The second is this: 'Love your neighbor as yourself.'" Parents, then, should

---

[2] J. Roehlkepartain and E. Roehlkepartain, *Embracing Parents* (Nashville: Abingdon Press, 2004), 47.

[3] J. O. Balswick, Pamela Ebstyne King, and Kevin S. Reimer, *The Reciprocating Self* (Downers Grove, IL: InterVarsity, 2005), 263.

[4] E. C. Roehlkepartain et al., "Spiritual Development in Childhood and Adolescence: Moving to the Scientific Mainstream," in *The Handbook of Spiritual Development in Childhood and Adolescence*, ed. Eugene C. Roehlkepartain et al. (Thousand Oaks, CA: Sage Publications, Inc., 2006), 9–11.

[5] W. Wayne Grant, *Growing Parents Growing Children* (Nashville: Convention Press, 1977), 56.

[6] T. A. Harris, *I'm OK—You're OK* (New York: HarperCollins, 1967).

strive to help their children develop a positive sense of self, which enables them to enjoy healthy relationships with others. Notice, however, that Jesus identified this as the second most important commandment, not the first. The primary goal of parents should be to nurture within their children a love of God, which is holistic. This foundation of faith will enable them to understand their worth as unique creations of a loving Father, giving them the freedom to love genuinely and accept others.

In their book *The Reciprocating Self: Human Development in Theological Perspective,* Balswick, King, and Reimer propose a comprehensive understanding of the goal of human development that closely aligns with Jesus' teaching, including each of the key components: love of God, self, and others. They articulate a developmental teleology, which suggests that because persons are created in the image of God, the goal of human development is to become a fully reciprocating self. This self is one that recognizes God's intention for individuals first to understand their own uniqueness and then enter into relationships with the divine and other persons. Only through these mutual relationships, where both distinctness and unity are experienced, can human beings fully develop. The persons of the Trinity model this idea of distinct yet unified. "Both the self and other are recognized and appreciated as unique, differentiated selves. Such a relationship enables the self and other to become more fully what God created them to be."[7] For children to live and mature into persons who have a healthy view of self and enjoy fully reciprocating relationships with God and others they must be loved and nurtured in ways that allow them to experience positive moral and spiritual growth. How can this be accomplished? What can parents do to help their children acquire morality and faith and grow spiritually?

The Role of Parents in the Spiritual Development of Children

In the *Republic,* Plato argued that the children of the guardian class should be a common possession of the city, that a child should not even know his own parents. By raising children this way, the rulers could gain control over the entire reproductive process and make sure that only the best men and women would procreate to produce the ideal children for the society.[8] A subtle shift toward this position has been occurring in recent decades, although most would not agree with Plato's rationale. For instance, it has become more common to hear phrases such as, "It takes a village to raise a child," and to sell public policies on the basis of what they will do for children. Government and societal institutions, including churches and schools, have begun to redefine the family structure.

[7] Balswick, King, and Reimer, *The Reciprocating Self,* 43.
[8] Plato, *Republic,* trans. G .M. A. Grube, rev. C. D. C. Reeve (Indianapolis: Hackett, 1992), 457d.

Although it is true that the entire faith community, as the family of God, has a responsibility to help nurture the growth and development of all children, the Bible places the primary responsibility for this critical task on the parents. The home was the center of religious training and education in Israelite families, and it was the father's responsibility to make sure this happened. Education had a dual purpose. First, it was focused on transmitting God's covenant and the history of how God continued to honor that covenant. Second, it was aimed at instructing children in how to live an ethical life.[9] The father served as the family priest in early Israel, offering sacrifices and performing circumcision, a spiritual act of obedience (Gen 8:20; 12:7–8; 21:4).

Deuteronomy 6:7 records Moses' belief in the centrality of this educational role when he instructed parents not only to obey the laws God gave him but also to impress them upon their children, to "talk about them when you sit at home and even when you walk along the road, when you lie down and when you get up." In the future, when their children questioned the laws and stipulations God placed on them, parents were to be prepared to teach them accurately about God's provision and faithful love and the blessings that would result from their obedience (Deut 6:20–25). The Passover observance was also centered in the home and was another opportunity for parents to teach children about God's faithfulness. "And when your children ask you, 'What does this ceremony mean to you?' Then tell them" (Exod 12:26–27a).

Throughout the Bible, parents are admonished to teach their children. Proverbs 22:6 is one of the most referenced passages on the role of parents. "Train a child in the way he should go, and when he is old he will not turn from it." Training involves more than telling but carries with it the idea that a skill or ability has been achieved. When parents successfully teach their children how to make moral decisions on their own, they can be confident that the training also will guide their future life choices.

Luther emphasized the importance of parenting, saying, "Most certainly father and mother are apostles, bishops, and priests to their children, for it is they who make them acquainted with the gospel. In short, there is no greater or nobler authority on earth than that of parents over their children, for this authority is both spiritual and temporal."[10] Churches are beginning to refocus their attention on the importance of spiritual formation in the home, recognizing that faith is fostered and modeled; it is more caught than taught. Researchers have consistently found that a person's sense of being cared about and supported is

---

[9] R. L. Honeycutt Jr., "The Child Within the Old Testament Community," in *Children and Conversion*, ed. Clifford Ingle (Nashville: Broadman, 1970), 31.

[10] M. J. Bunge, "Biblical and Theological Perspectives on Children, Parents, and 'Best Practices' for Faith Formation: Resources for Child, Youth, and Family Ministry Today," *Dialog: A Journal of Theology* 47:4 (Winter 2008): 352.

strongly related to a variety of desirable life outcomes, and the support of parents is most influential.[11] Parental support is associated with positive outcomes in children, such as lower levels of delinquency, substance abuse, and early sexual intercourse and higher levels of academic performance and better mental health.[12]

Parents often take measures to provide religious instruction for their children. In a study by Search Institute, 76 percent of the respondents reported that they made sure their children participated in some type of religious organization at least weekly.[13] However, religion is not faith, nor does religious training necessarily result in moral living or spiritual faith. Religion is a more cognitive concept that can be taught, but religion does not automatically translate into faith and spiritual development. Jesus often called out the Pharisees and other religious leaders of his day for their lack of true righteousness, pointing out that it is possible to be outwardly religious yet far from God (Matt 5:20). Even a religiously devout and wealthy young man who kept all the commandments was found to be unworthy of the kingdom of God because his faith in money was greater than his trust in God (Mark 10:17–23). In Col 2:16–23, Paul makes clear that religion that is not based on faith in Christ is meaningless. In verse 8 of that same chapter, Paul warns: "See to it that no one takes you captive through hollow and deceptive philosophy, which depends on human tradition and the basic principles of this world rather than on Christ." Providing only for religious instruction, apart from a concern for moral and faith development, is an inadequate foundation for the spiritual growth of children.

Moral Development

Concepts of character and acceptable standards of right and wrong are both questions of morality. Moral development theorists attempt to explain how persons acquire these basic values, which guide their thoughts, feelings, and behavior. Moral development has two dimensions: the intrapersonal, which involves a sense of self and regulates a person's activities when no one else is involved, and the interpersonal, which is evident in a person's social interactions, especially in conflict situations.[14]

James Rest identified four components of morality: interpreting a situation that will call for a response, considering the needs of everyone who will be affected by the response, making a decision about what specific

---

[11] P. C. Scales and Nancy Leffert, *Developmental Assets,* 2nd ed. (Minneapolis: Search Institute, 2004), 23.

[12] Ibid., 24.

[13] Roehlkepartain, *Embracing Parents,* 57.

[14] L. J. Walker and R. C. Pitts, "Naturalistic Conceptions of Moral Maturity," *Developmental Psychology* 34 (1998): 403–19, quoted in John W. Santrock, *A Topical Approach to Life-Span Development* (New York: McGraw-Hill Higher Education, 2002), 419.

response to make, then implementing that commitment by taking action and responding. Moral failures take place when an individual fails at any one of these four components.[15] The account of the Good Samaritan is an example of how these four components work together to result in an act of morality. Seeing the victim of robbers lying beside the road, the Samaritan realized the man's need for help. Then, unlike the priest and Levite who came before him and refused to become involved, the Samaritan man felt pity on the stranger and decided to care for him. After doing what he could to treat the man's wounds on the side of the road, he took him to an inn to provide further care and even made provisions for the victim's continued well-being when he had to leave him (Luke 10:30–37).

How does a person develop this type of moral behavior? Various theorists have focused on different aspects of development to answer this question. Sigmund Freud's psychoanalytic approach suggests that children identify with their parents and internalize their own standards of right and wrong to avoid punishment and gain their parents' affection. This leads to the formation of the superego, the moral component of the personality. His views draw upon his concept of the oedipal conflict, in which a young child has a strong desire to replace the same-sex parent and win the affection of the other parent. The child fears punishment if his feelings are discovered, so the hostility is turned inward, resulting in feelings of guilt. This guilt, according to Freud, is responsible for keeping children from immoral behavior. This view is narrow, however, and does not take into account more positive feelings and emotions that can contribute to morality.[16]

Jean Piaget formulated his theory, based on moral reasoning, by observing children playing marbles. He paid particular attention to their thoughts about and adherence to the rules. He discovered that younger children did not even seem aware that there were rules to the game. Those between the ages of two and six years recognized that rules existed and attempted to adhere to them, although they did not seem to understand their purpose or why they should be followed. Children in the concrete operations stage of cognitive development viewed the rules as important and unchangeable, and those who had moved into formal operational thinking approached them as simply agreements reached by mutual consent that could be changed.[17]

Piaget used these observations and further discussions with children to formulate his theory of how they think about morality. He considered children younger than age 4 to be premoral because they are still

---

[15] D. H. Dirks, "Moral and Faith Development in Christian Education," in *Foundations of Ministry*, ed. M. J. Anthony (Grand Rapids: Baker Books, 1992), 116–17.
[16] J. W. Santrock, *Life-Span Development*, 11th ed. (New York: McGraw-Hill Higher Education, 2008), 280.
[17] W. R. Yount, *Created to Learn* (Nashville: B&H, 1996), 104.

egocentric and unable to consider the perspective of others. From ages four to seven, children display heteronomous morality, in which they think of rules and justice as unchangeable. The determination of whether something is good or bad is determined by the consequences and not the intentions of an action.

For children at this level of moral development, a child who accidentally hits another child while playing is just as immoral as one who deliberately hauls off and punches a playmate, and both should be punished for breaking a rule. At this stage children believe in imminent justice—the idea that punishment will immediately follow whenever rules are broken regardless of whether the act is witnessed by anyone else. This is why young children often begin to worry or even cry when they do something wrong, even if they are not punished. Children between the ages of seven and ten are in a transitional phase of development, according to Piaget, in which they may show signs of either heteronomous morality or autonomous morality, the next stage of development.[18]

In this final stage children begin to realize that rules and laws can be changed or even broken. They are able to consider persons' intentions apart from their actions. They realize that punishment is not inevitable and not always automatic.[19] These changes occur as children become more sophisticated in their thinking and begin to negotiate with their peers. Parents are not as effective as peers at advancing moral reasoning, in Piaget's view, because they hold all of the power in the parent–child relationship and tend to hand down rules that are nonnegotiable.[20]

Kohlberg's model of moral development is based on Piaget's cognitive stage theory. He used 20 years of interviews with children, posing hypothetical moral dilemmas, as the basis for his view that there are six universal, sequential stages of moral development. People move from one stage to the next as they gain life experience through their interactions with people, ideas, and situations.[21] Kohlberg described three levels of moral thinking—preconventional, conventional, and postconventional—and each level is characterized by two stages.

Preconventional reasoning: Good and bad are determined by external rewards and punishment.

- The first stage is heteronomous morality, or obedience and punishment, and is most closely associated with early childhood. Judgments are based on rules, especially when there is evidence of immediate consequences for breaking them. Children obey because they are told to and to avoid being punished for their disobedience.

---

[18] Santrock, *Life-Span Development,* 280.
[19] Dirks, "Moral and Faith Development in Christian Education," 121.
[20] Santrock, *Life-Span Development,* 281.
[21] Dirks, "Moral and Faith Development in Christian Education," 121.

- In stage two—individualism and exchange—older children are able to recognize that people have different viewpoints. They make decisions based on their own needs and, to a lesser extent, the interest of others. For instance, they may treat others fairly if they think the other person will reciprocate.

Conventional reasoning: Individuals apply standards of right and wrong set by others in authority.

- Stage three is interpersonal relationships, generally demonstrated by early adolescents but often found in adults also. Judgments are made on the basis of trust, loyalty, and caring for others. Children and adolescents who want to be thought of in positive terms by parents or teachers will often adopt their standards of right and wrong.
- In stage four—maintaining the social order—judgments are made in terms of what will be best for society as a whole. This is typically characteristic of older adolescents and adults who are able to understand the concepts of justice and duty and the reason for laws.

Postconventional reasoning: Moral judgments are tied to abstract principles that benefit humanity as a whole.

- Stage five is social contract and individual rights. Judgments are based on what makes for societal goodness, recognizing that maintaining the social order does not necessarily mean that the society is a good or fair place to live. Standing up against communistic or totalitarian governments is an example of this type of moral judgment. A consideration of the rights of individuals often may transcend the law.
- Universal principles constitute the sixth stage. Moral judgments recognize that all people have value and should be treated accordingly. Human rights and what is just for all persons is a consideration. People should act in accordance with their conscience, regardless of the consequences.[22]

Kohlberg recognized that his theory did not account for God and faith in the moral equation, so he eventually added a seventh stage that focused

---

[22] Balswick, King, and Reimer, *The Reciprocating Self*, 248–51.

on ultimate questions about the meaning of life.[23] It is irrational to believe that elements of faith and spirituality do not influence moral development until a seventh stage is reached. Kohlberg's theory has also been criticized for placing too much importance on sequential stages, focusing more on moral thinking than actions, confusing moral issues with social conventions, and being biased toward Western males.[24] Others have found that preschool children, contradictory to Kohlberg's findings, are capable of acting and reasoning beyond the stage one obedience and punishment orientation and often demonstrate acts of sharing, helping, and comforting with the intention of meeting other's needs.[25]

The ability to relate to others in healthy ways and appreciate and understand their uniqueness is at the heart of moral growth. Robert Selman studied this aspect of development, specifically focusing on how taking the perspective of others contributes to moral and ethical decisions. He found that higher levels of perspective taking allow persons to accept others' differences and make it easier to offer forgiveness without holding a grudge.[26] Kohlberg also believed that the give and take of peer relationships offers children an opportunity to take the perspective of another person, which tends to advance moral reasoning. However, like Piaget, he did not see family relationships as important to the development of morality because they do not often provide opportunities for the give and take that is found among peers.[27] More recent studies dispute this notion, finding that family boundaries—the rules, standards, and norms that pertain to behavior—are often directly or indirectly associated with higher self-esteem; greater psychosocial competence and peer likability; higher school achievement; and decreased problem behaviors, such as reduced alcohol and substance use.[28] A well-known study by Colby and Damon also found that influential relationships, such as the parent–child bond, can evoke emotions that bring about transformation, leading to the formation of a strong moral identity.[29] Additional studies on adolescents have concluded "that relationships are a significant means by which moral identity is transformed."[30]

In addition to the importance of human relationships, Colby and Damon were surprised to discover from their research participants many specific "accounts of how God's influence was the basis for their moral identity."[31] Philippians 2:13 teaches us that God is working within the life of the believer to bring about transformation, so these find-

---

[23] C. P. Massey, "Preschooler Moral Development," in *Handbook of Preschool Religious Education*, ed. D. Ratcliff (Birmingham: Religious Education Press, 1988), 90.
[24] Yount, *Created to Learn*, 117–18.
[25] Massey, "Preschool Moral Development," 86–87.
[26] Dirks, "Moral and Faith Development in Christian Education," 124–25.
[27] Santrock, *Life-Span Development*, 360–61.
[28] Scales and Leffert, 77.
[29] Balswick, King, and Reimer, *The Reciprocating Self*, 253–54.
[30] Ibid., 257.
[31] Ibid.

ings are not surprising for the Christian. God's desire for his followers is to be continually conformed to the image of Christ, a process of development that will only be completed when Christians are ultimately united with Him (Rom 8:29; 1 John 3:2). Conformity to Christ's image includes the process of developing a moral lifestyle and incorporates the hallmarks of the various theories of moral development advanced by Piaget, Kohlberg, and others.

Christians are to conduct themselves as worthy of the gospel by serving others in humility and looking after the interests of others (Phil 1:27; 2:3–4). They are to be generous and share with those in need; speak truthfully; avoid dishonesty; show kindness; and be encouraging, compassionate, and forgiving (1 Tim 6:18; Eph 4:25–32). Titus 3:1–2 and 1 Peter 2 offer instruction on living in society and submitting to rulers and authorities. Other passages address the proper attitude the believer should hold toward government (Acts 5:29; Rom 13:1).

Micah 6:6–8 is a reminder that God is more concerned with the moral lifestyle of his followers than their religious acts:

> With what shall I come before the Lord and bow down before the exalted God? Shall I come before him with burnt offerings, with calves a year old? Will the Lord be pleased with thousands of rams, with ten thousand rivers of oil? Shall I offer my firstborn for my transgression, the fruit of my body for the sin of my soul? He has showed you, O man, what is good. And what does the Lord require of you? To act justly and to love mercy and to walk humbly with your God.

Although the Pharisees had an abundance of outwardly focused religious behavior, they demonstrated a low level of internal moral development, focusing on obedience to religious rules at all cost. For this reason, among others, Jesus called them out for their hypocrisy (Matt 15:1–9; Luke 11:37–53). He also challenged the social conventions of the day, choosing to place people's needs above the law and treating all people with respect, even an adulterous Samaritan woman (Mark 3:1–6; John 4:4–26). He stood up against injustice and taught the importance of loving everyone, even one's enemies, and showing kindness to those who have nothing to offer in return (Mark 11:15–18; Luke 6:27–36).

The Bible teaches that there is a need for moral growth in all persons. The first nine chapters of Proverbs provide wisdom for young people to guide them into moral living. This is not something that comes naturally because all humans have inherited a sin nature and all will sin (Rom 5:12; 3:23). The law was given to help people realize their own sinfulness. It is not possible to do good entirely out of sheer will or intent, as emphasized by Paul in Rom 7:15–20. However, resisting the temptation of immorality is not impossible (1 Cor 10:13). Donald Joy suggests that Christians consider the following when dealing with issues of moral development:

1. God's unconditional love and prevenient grace provide the basis for our inclination toward justice and righteousness.
2. Immature understandings of God's role in life and the meaning of life are to be expected as a part of the developmental process.
3. God may be expected to represent himself faithfully to any person at an appropriate structural level.
4. A faith response that presupposes that life is larger than disease and death must be more appropriately analyzed.[32]

Parental Contributions to the Moral Development of Their Children

Parents must be present in the lives of their children if they are to foster moral growth. As early as infancy, children attach to significant caregivers who will have the greatest influence on all aspects of their lives, for better or for worse. When parents relinquish this role by giving over significant periods of their children's lives to the care and influence of others, they are also diminishing their potential to help shape the moral development of their children. Modeling the values they esteem, such as empathy, honesty, self-control, generosity, and fairness, will have a more powerful impact on their children than verbal instruction. Children learn through the imitation of significant others. When children attempt to dress, act, or speak like their parents, they are also beginning to internalize the parents' values and morals.

Parents who offer their children unconditional love and acceptance and foster intimacy by genuinely listening to their children are laying the foundation for their children to develop healthy relationships and are more likely to have a positive impact on their moral development.[33] It is important for parents to communicate with their children and to share their own thoughts and feelings at age-appropriate levels of disclosure, but it is even more important that they allow children to express honestly their own viewpoints without fear of being ridiculed or dismissed.

Children also develop their moral values from reward and punishment. Establishing rules and standards of acceptable behavior are important, but rules should also be accompanied by rationale. Children need to know why certain rules exist. At an early age children

[32] Massey, "Preschool Moral Development," 91.
[33] Balswick, King, and Reimer, *The Reciprocating Self*, 56.

choose their actions—whether they will adhere to certain rules—on the basis of the consequences they can expect. When good behaviors are rewarded and inappropriate actions are punished, they are shaped into acting morally. One problem with this approach to instilling moral values is the child's fear of getting in trouble for breaking rules, which can lead to lying and deceit. This is actually counterproductive to the development of genuine spiritual formation.

Parents who reward children for honesty, even when they are admitting wrongful acts, and who help them make amends for their behavior, can help children internalize a desire to act morally. The conscience develops in early childhood as children internalize their parents' standards of right and wrong. It is important to respond to their misbehavior with grace and not shame so they are able to make the distinction between their behavior and their identity. It is healthy for a child to develop a sense of guilt when their actions warrant it, but guilt can become destructive when parents discipline their children in such a way that they begin to see themselves as unforgivable or worthless.

Parents can also encourage moral development in their children by giving them opportunities to act on their values. This means they must be empowered and allowed to make age-appropriate choices. Although reasoning abilities are limited by children's levels of cognitive development, they can be led to think through possible outcomes of various decisions they might face. Parents can remind them of Christian principles and encourage them to evaluate their choices in light of Scripture. Children develop empathy when they are encouraged to consider how their own actions might affect others. This becomes more relevant as children grow in their cognitive ability to consider others' points of view, but there are those who believe that empathy can even be nurtured in children younger than the age of three. This process of putting oneself in another's shoes, also known as role taking, is considered by some to be the most important experience for helping children in their moral development.[34] The power of role taking is especially strong when children are closely attached. They want to please their parents or other significant persons, so they make a concerted effort to understand what they would want and then attempt to imitate that response.[35]

Adolescents are especially influenced by social learning, adopting the beliefs, values, and behaviors of those they respect and admire. Unlike younger children, their ability to engage in abstract thinking and higher-order reasoning enables them more easily to detect hypocrisy in the lives of their parents and other authority figures. If there is discontinuity between

---

[34] L. Kohlberg, *The Psychology of Moral Development: Essays on Moral Development*, vol. 1 (San Francisco: Harper & Row, 1981), 74.

[35] C. Stonehouse, *Joining Children on the Spiritual Journey* (Grand Rapids: BridgePoint Books, 1998), 113.

the actions and teachings of these significant others, then the adolescent loses respect for them and is less likely to internalize their moral teachings. However, when adolescents and their parents enjoy a relationship of mutual love and care, youth are more likely to adopt their parents' moral standards and behaviors. If parents are absent from their lives, adolescents will seek significant relationships elsewhere, taking on the morals of those from whom they seek approval and acceptance.

In *The Religious Potential of the Child,* Sofia Cavalletti suggests that the *foundation* for moral growth must begin in early childhood. For her, morality is:

> a certain orientation of the whole person in life, the leaning forward of the being toward a point; we could compare this to heliotropism, that movement whereby plants turn toward the sun. . . . The relation between orientation and actions is like a plant and its fruits; there are living fruits only if the plant is healthy and rooted deeply in the earth. Actions are the manifold expressions of the global orientation of the person. This fundamental orientation should already be established by the time the older child begins to ask his first questions in regard to the value of individual actions. . . . Before the older child comes to consider the details of reality, he should first be helped to find a universal key that allows him to approach these details in the right way. Before the older child begins to question himself whether this or that action is good or bad, we should have provided him with a "yardstick" with which he can give his own response when the time comes; we should give the older child a reference point to orient himself in the new horizon that is opening before him. The yardstick must already be prepared by the time he needs it. The adult's hurried intervention in the moment when the moral crisis is already in action is undoubtedly detrimental. The older child will either rebel against an inopportune intrusion, or he will become accustomed to using someone else's yardstick; then morality will not be the child's own listening to the voice of the Spirit, but rather obedience to an external law. Thus the older child—and often the adult as well—will stay on a level of moral immaturity.[36]

This description of moral growth presupposes a foundation of faith, a relationship with God, which can serve as the reference point for life decisions.

---

[36] S. Cavalletti, *The Religious Potential of the Child,* trans. P. M. Coulter and J. M. Coulter (Ramsey, NJ: Paulist Press, 1983), 151–52.

Faith Development

Faith is what gives purpose to morality, "without faith it is impossible to please God" (Heb 11:6). When morality is based on cultural or societal standards alone, there is no true north with which to align one's moral compass, no "why" behind moral codes or laws other than to help people live in harmony and uphold social structures, and these codes can change from generation to generation. Christian parents know that faith is more than moral living, and it is more than what persons do to try and earn salvation. James 2:14–26 teaches the reality that saving faith is evidenced through one's actions, but as Paul writes in Gal 2:16, human deeds do not have the power to save. Ephesians 2:8–9 states that "it is by grace you have been saved, through faith—and this not from yourselves, it is the gift of God—not by works, so that no one can boast." Not only is one saved through faith, but the Bible also teaches that the just person continues to live by faith (Hab 2:4; Rom 1:17; Heb 10:38).

Although faith is a gift from God, Scripture speaks of faith as being developed. In 2 Thess 1:3, Paul expresses his thankfulness that the believers' "faith is growing more and more" and that their love for one another is also growing. Just as children develop cognitively, physically, and emotionally, their spiritual selves are also growing and dynamic. In 1 Pet 2:2–3, Peter encourages this growth. "Like newborn babies, crave pure spiritual milk, so that by it you may grow up in your salvation, now that you have tasted that the Lord is good." As theorists have attempted to understand this concept of growing in spiritual faith, they have created their own developmental models, which can be useful in understanding how children conceptualize faith and respond to religious and moral instruction.

David Elkind used Piaget's understanding of child development to study the religious thinking of children. From ages five to seven, children described people of different religions according to external characteristics, with no attention to beliefs or motivations. From about ages seven to nine, children thought of religious identity with respect to birth or observable behaviors, such as religious participation. Beginning around age ten, children began to understand religious identity as something internal.[37]

James Fowler's theory of faith development was influenced by the research of Lawrence Kohlberg, Jean Piaget, and Erik Erikson in their studies of moral, cognitive, and psychosocial development, respectively. Fowler defined faith in three parts: as "a dynamic pattern of personal trust in and loyalty to a center or centers of value, trust in and loyalty to images and realities of power, and trust in and loyalty to a shared master

---

[37] D. Elkind, *The Child and Society: Essays in Applied Child Development* (New York: Oxford University Press, 1979).

story."[38] Catherine Stonehouse relates Fowler's three-part definition specifically to Christian faith by equating the center of value to something bigger than we are—God, the Creator and Redeemer. The image of power is the Lord of the universe, the ultimate power on whom we depend, and the shared master story is found in the Bible, God's revelation of love and redemption.[39]

According to Fowler, faith development is best described in sequential stages, which are invariant and qualitatively different. The first prestage, undifferentiated faith, corresponds to the first two years of life. In these early years infants learn to trust in and experience love from their caregivers, a necessary foundation for mature faith.[40]

- The first identifiable stage begins when thought and language come together. From about ages three to seven children experience intuitive-projective faith, in which they are powerfully and often permanently influenced by the examples, images, and stories of adults, usually their parents. The imagination of children plays a major role in their intuitive understandings and feelings about life.[41]
- Stage two is ushered in by the child's ability to think concretely. This stage, mythic-literal, typically begins around age seven or eight when the child is able to begin considering the perspective of others. The literal stories, beliefs, and traditions that characterize the child's faith community become personal, and symbols of the faith take on a literal meaning. Children transition to the next stage as they begin to reflect on apparent contradictions in stories, which lead them to reflect on their meaning. This transition is possible when a child is able to engage in formal operational thought and mutual perspective taking.[42]
- Stage three, synthetic-conventional faith, is most characteristic of adolescents, but it is also the stage where many adults remain. The outside world gains more influence in the life of adolescents, and their faith must provide them with a coherent way of making sense of the values and information they are encountering as they try to develop a sense of personal identity. In many ways this is a conformist stage, in that teenagers are still attuned to the expectations and judgments

---

[38] J. W. Fowler, *Weaving the New Creation: Stages of Faith and the Public Church* (New York: HarperCollins, 1991), 100–101.
[39] Stonehouse, *Joining Children on the Spiritual Journey*, 147–49.
[40] J. W. Fowler, *Stages of Faith: The Psychology of Human Development and the Quest for Meaning* (San Francisco: HarperCollins, 1995), 121.
[41] Ibid., 133–34.
[42] Ibid., 149–50.

of significant others, such as their parents. They begin to synthesize their values and beliefs into a coherent faith that makes sense. Their beliefs and values are deeply felt, but they have not yet examined them systematically.[43] When young people leave home for the first time, they often engage in a more critical evaluation of their beliefs and values that can usher in the next stage of development.

- Stage four is individuative-reflective faith, in which late adolescents or young adults begin to take more responsibility for their own beliefs and attitudes. Individuals often face the tension between identifying with a group and the power of their own strongly felt but yet unexamined, individual beliefs. Faith symbols take on conceptual meanings as young adults clarify their own worldview.[44]

- The final two stages, conjunctive and universalizing faith, are typically evident only in middle and late adulthood. In the conjunctive stage, middle adults tend to reevaluate their lives and beliefs and become more open to others. They have a stronger desire to invest in the faith development of others.[45] Some people in late adulthood may realize a universalizing faith, which is characterized by a recognition of the supremacy of God's kingdom that calls them to a radical commitment to justice and love. They exhibit a selfless passion for a world transformed according to God's intentions.[46]

For V. Bailey Gillespie, the faith experience is best understood in terms of seven major generic faith situations, similar to Fowler's stages, that correspond with the key developmental periods of the life cycle.

- **Situation 1:** Borrowed Faith—early childhood. Trustworthiness is established, and young children are able externally to experience their parents' faith.

- **Situation 2:** Reflected Faith—middle childhood. Children realize they are members of faith communities, and they experience God's love and care reflected back to them from these groups. The actual experience of faith feelings begins. Stories and images are important, and heroes of the faith, such as Noah or Jesus, can become important role models.

---

[43] Ibid., 172–73.
[44] Ibid., 182–83.
[45] Ibid., 197–98.
[46] Ibid., 201, 210.

- **Situation 3:** Personalized Faith—early adolescence. Questioning, searching, committing, and life examination characterize this stage. Faith becomes a verb as it is owned by the youth. Reflection and reason become major factors in faith development, which is often misinterpreted by adults as rebellion or rejection.
- **Situation 4:** Interior or Established Faith—later youth. Beliefs are solidified, at least for the time being, and adolescents have a desire to testify to what they believe.
- **Situation 5:** Reordered Faith—young adult. Personal faith is reinterpreted as the cognitive process of theological reflection is revisited. As lifestyles change, faith is often placed on hold until parenthood or a crisis or challenge confronts them.
- **Situation 6:** Reflective Faith—middle adult. The experience of faith reduces life to the basics, such as God and the future, and life is viewed in a broad perspective.
- **Situation 7:** Resolute Faith—older adult. Faith reaches beyond the here and now into the future. God's comfort is felt and His actions begin to make sense and offer hope.[47]

Regardless of the faith model, there is agreement that the power and influence of parents on the life of the child are significant. Until children are old enough to begin thinking logically, their faith is largely borrowed from their parents. This places the primary responsibility for spiritual development within the home. As with moral development, some of the most effective ways parents can nurture the development of their children's faith is by spending time with them, living out their faith through their words and actions, and providing for their secure attachment by meeting their physical and emotional needs (see chapter 10 for more material related to this topic).

For children to own their own faith, they must first witness the faith in their parents' lives and hear stories of how God has blessed and protected them. Visual symbols and markers can remind children of God's presence and importance in the lives of their families and provide opportunities for parents to retell their faith stories. Joshua 4:6–7 offers an example of just such a faith symbol. On entering the promised land, Joshua led the Israelites to set up a marker that would remind them and future generations of God's trustworthiness. He explained the significance of the task by telling the people: "In the future, when your children ask you,

---

[47] V. B. Gillespie, *The Experience of Faith* (Birmingham: Religious Education Press, 1988), 79–82.

'What do these stones mean?' tell them that the flow of the Jordan was cut off before the ark of the covenant of the Lord. When it crossed the Jordan, the waters of the Jordan were cut off. These stones are to be a memorial to the people of Israel forever."

Parents can help faith develop by teaching the Bible to their children and introducing them to biblical characters whose actions or commitments display faith in action. Romans 10:13–17 also emphasizes the importance of directly proclaiming the good news because faith comes by hearing. In essence, Jesus' Great Commission, found in Matt 28:18–20, is a command to continue to pass along the faith from one generation to the next. It is a message for all believers, not just pastors and evangelists. Unfortunately, parents often rely on religious institutions to talk with their children and adolescents about matters of faith, when they are the ones in the position of greatest influence. A study of 8,000 adolescents whose parents were members of 11 different Protestant and Catholic denominations found "that only 10% of these families discussed faith with any degree of regularity, and in 43% of the families, faith was never discussed."[48]

Many Christian parents become fearful when their teenagers begin to express doubts about their faith and what they have been taught since childhood. However, it is important to allow adolescents to wrestle with questions of the faith so they can claim it for their own rather than relying on the borrowed faith of their parents. It is not necessary for parents to have all the answers to their questions, but they should respond to them honestly out of their own experiences of God working in their lives. They can offer to help the searching teen find answers to any questions, but parents should never pretend to know what they cannot know or offer childish Sunday school responses that do not recognize the adolescent's ability to think abstractly. Parents often mistake their teenager's spiritual growing pains as a rejection of the faith. However, the National Study of Youth and Religion, a significant analysis of the religious and spiritual lives of teenagers in the United States, found that the majority of teenagers are similar to their parents when it comes to religion. They share their beliefs, continue in the same religious traditions, and usually attend religious services with one or both of them.[49]

One approach to spiritual growth places too much reliance on the power of the self instead of on the power of the Holy Spirit. When parents rely too heavily on child discipline practices that focus on doing the right thing, they can help their children in their moral development but may stunt or distort their spiritual formation. It can lead to the practice of "activities such as the spiritual disciplines, obedience to Scripture, or

---

[48] M. P. Strommen and R. A. Hardel, *Passing on the Faith* (Winona, MN: Saint Mary's Press, 2000), 14.
[49] C. Smith with M. L. Denton, *Soul Searching* (New York: Oxford University Press, 2005), 68.

ministry to others as a way of dealing with the guilt and shame that are produced by our failures in the spiritual life."[50] These activities are not bad things per se, but they are not the result of the Spirit's transformative power in our lives when they are done as a way to atone for sin, and they are not necessarily contributing to spiritual growth. It can develop adolescents who routinely vow to do better next time, making amends out of guilt but never confessing to God or allowing him to change them. The law, which helps people understand what they have done wrong, was given to lead persons to Christ (Gal 3:23–25). The belief that it is possible to do God's will by sheer willpower is often acquired and reinforced in childhood. Parenting should help counteract the effects of original sin, not project blame and instill guilt and shame that lead to a sense of personal inadequacy for which the child tries to atone. Not only can this damage the parents' relationship with their children, but it can also do harm to the child's relationship with God. Children need to know that their parents love them no matter what and that God loves them not just when they are good. Otherwise, the child will grow up trying to please God through spiritual disciplines and by trying to be good instead of developing an open and honest relationship with him.[51]

Conclusion

Even when parents do everything they know to do, the ultimate decision for how children will live their lives is a matter of free will and personal choice. It is not always an easy task, watching them grow and beginning to make their own decisions on issues of morality and faith. Paul described this process so poignantly in Gal 4:19: "My dear children, for whom I am again in the pains of childbirth until Christ is formed in you." The caring parent can, and should, provide for the positive moral and spiritual development of their children by giving them a firm foundation that will nurture their faith. The most important and powerful thing they can do, however, is continually to pray for their children. Parents can count themselves successful if, when they come to the end of their lives, they can pray Jesus' prayer for His own children, when His earthly ministry was coming to a close.

> I have revealed you to those whom you gave me out of the world. They were yours; you gave them to me and they have obeyed your word. Now they know that everything you have given me comes from you. For I gave them the words you gave me and they accepted them. . . . I pray for them. I am not praying for the world, but for those you have given

---

[50] M. W. Austin, *Wise Stewards: Philosophical Foundations of Christian Parenting* (Grand Rapids: Kregel, 2009), 94.
[51] Ibid., 93–95.

me, for they are yours. All I have is yours, and all you have is mine. And glory has come to me through them. I will remain in the world no longer, but they are still in the world, and I am coming to you. Holy Father, protect them by the power of your name . . . so that they may be one as we are one. While I was with them, I protected them and kept them safe . . . My prayer is not that you take them out of the world but that you protect them from the evil one. . . . Sanctify them by the truth; your word is truth. (John 17:6–17)

3 Crisis on the Doorstep

Freddy Cardoza
Talbot School of Theology

The Crisis on "My" Doorstep

My ancestry is a genealogist's nightmare. My father never knew his biological father. Once he was born, his single, immigrant mother quickly married another man to establish respectability. My grandmother's husband was an alcoholic who became increasingly physically violent toward her and abusive to the family. Then, when my father was only four, she developed cancer and died. The day after she was buried, Dad's stepfather deserted him and his newborn sister on the doorstep of a New England orphanage—never to have contact again. That was 1950. My father was abruptly forced to enter the world of foster care and continued to move from house to house until a Portuguese–Italian couple unable to have children adopted him. For that reason I now bear the name Cardoza. *Just writing those words is surreal.*

My mother also had a challenged past. She grew up poor in the Deep South. She was raised in an old farmhouse without plumbing or running water and, for a time, no electricity. Her father was a serious "rubbing alcohol–drinking alcoholic" who was finally kicked out and divorced by my grandmother, who then raised my mother and her six older siblings. After graduation my mother entered the air force. That is where she met and married my father. Whether they were in love, infatuated, or something like it, their relationship began to deteriorate during her pregnancy. The short-lived marriage had dissolved by the time my twin brother and I were a year old.

My family was broken before I even knew what a family was. My mother, brother, and I returned to her home state of Tennessee, where we moved in with her extended family in the same home in which she was raised. By working two to three jobs, Mom was finally able to buy a used car and move us to a one-bedroom apartment in the housing projects. Despite having government assistance through food stamps, times were tough, and we soon moved in again with our extended family—my grandmother, uncle, Mom, and us boys—once they had enough money for a down payment on a single-wide trailer.

Elements of my story are unique, but many of these themes are shared by generations of others who were also raised in dysfunctional homes. The pages that follow take a decidedly different tone from this personal introduction. In them we explore some of the major challenges faced by American children, parents, and families in the sociological context of the early twenty-first century. Hard statistical data and anecdotal evidence are analyzed to understand better the familial crisis that looms pervasively around society at large and within the broad diversity of our nation's families. These findings are intertwined with a degree of cultural exegesis where the traumatic effects of family strain and fragmentation are unpacked in greater detail. Throughout these discussions we will address what the church can do within its family ministries to better assist dysfunctional homes in their quest for stability and health.

A Sociological Overview of American Families

Chapter 1 explored how the ideal of a nuclear family has been assaulted and, as a result, suffered increasing deterioration within American society. This has resulted from a myriad of ideological and lifestyle choices being made by large percentages of people in the general public. This phenomenon has caused the proliferation of alternative views about the nature of the family, including a stalwart challenge to redefine *family* in the courts.[1] At issue is not only the more obvious issue of same-sex marriages but also the elimination of language that prohibits "nonfamily households" of all types to obtain the same legal status of the traditional family.[2] In other words, the goal of some proponents in this movement is the elimination of any fundamental definition of *family*.

In conjunction with the family and ministry challenges that have been outlined, a number of uniquely sociological factors are affecting today's households. In some cases the morphing of the family he has described has produced these crises. In other cases the current familial crisis has been the result of broad, destructive dynamics occurring within culture and society at large.

Although there is no single and authoritative list of the great challenges of our time, research and ministry experience provides us with insights to many of the major crises affecting today's families. In a recent study,

---

[1] B. Egelko, "High Court Says No to Same-Sex Marriage Review," *San Francisco Chronicle*, August 11, 2005, B-4.

[2] T. Coleman, "Mini-Battle over Definition of 'Family' Has National Significance" (February 26, 2006), http://www.unmarriedamerica.org/column-one/2-27-06-definition-of-family.htm.

respondents were asked to identify the most significant or challenging issues facing their young children (younger than age 13); issues such as school performance, peer pressure, media use, and family struggles were among the top responses.[3] When asked about their teenage children, parents in that study mentioned some of these same issues in addition to substance abuse and several issues related to personal and family finances. Other sources identified similar issues and related causes.

These factors led to the identification of several causes and effects jeopardizing today's families. Through a process of elimination and consolidation designed to accommodate the limitations of this chapter, six themes have been selected to better illustrate the common dysfunctions affecting our families today. To provide organization, they have been divided into two categories: *internal* factors and *external* factors.

This dual approach serves to keep us from oversimplifying the problem by bemoaning only the well-rehearsed distresses we all readily admit. Even so, those common and familiar problems are real, and ethnology continues to point to these as serious matters with which families must contend. For this reason, and because our nation's ever-changing demographics cause those difficulties to fester and mutate into more diverse expressions, we are duty bound to revisit them with a fresh perspective.

In addition, while acknowledging that there are sociocultural circumstances legitimately affecting homes from the outside in, there are also destructive realities imposed by individuals on themselves that affect all of those living under the same roof. As such, the crisis at the doorstep cannot be explained away by arguing that families are nothing more than helpless and passive entities being victimized by media and entertainment moguls in Hollywood, Washington, and New York, however destructive those things may be.

It also must be acknowledged that many of the crises families face are self-inflicted, irrespective of the gravitational pull imposed on them by culture. In effect, we are ministering to families who are simultaneously being assaulted from without and imploding from within. For this reason, gaining an acute understanding of these phenomena is a necessary part of formulating a theology of family ministry capable of helping others.

Internal Factors Affecting Families

The following factors represent key domains of internal family crises having specifically *intrapersonal* or *interpersonal* causes. In other words, these are internal issues caused by individual choices and conditions that cause dysfunction within those families rather than general cultural moods and mores that are acting on families from the outside. Three

---

[3] Barna Group, "Survey Reveals Challenges Faced by Young People" (September 10, 2007), http://www.barna.org/barna-update/article/15-familykids/96-survey-reveals-challenges-faced-by-young-people.

issues putting internal pressure on today's families will be the focus of our current discussion.

1. Breaking and Broken Homes. Social scientists of every stripe generally agree that the family is the fundamental and irreducible social unit in any civilization. In 1989 the United Nations offered its first formal recognition of the importance of the family in a landmark resolution that claimed 1994 as the inaugural International Year of the Family, whose motto was, "Building the smallest democracy at the heart of society."[4] In this effort, the General Assembly sought to emphasize to location, regional, and national governments the importance of the family and the possible societal consequences that the fragmentation and disintegration of the family unit posed.[5] Despite the diversity of that universal body, they affirmed each of the following maxims, among others:

- The family is the natural and fundamental group unit of society and is entitled to protection by society and the state.
- Various concepts of the family exist in different social, cultural, and political systems, but it is recognized that families are basic to the social structure and development of all societies.
- Families are the fullest reflection, at the grass-roots level, of the strengths and weaknesses of the social and developmental environment.
- Families, as basic units of social life, are major agents of sustainable development at all levels of society, and their contribution is crucial for its success.[6]

These grand remarks underscore the truism that the fate of culture, nations, and civilization is intrinsically linked to the well-being and flourishing of families. As such, various degrees of family dysfunction, leading up to and including divorce, are the ultimate problems being faced by today's families.

Broken Homes. Divorce causes broken homes. Divorce rates skyrocketed within the United States and many other parts of the world in the late twentieth century. Those statistics have declined since the 1980s, and

---

[4] United Nations Programme on the Family, *General Assembly Resolutions* (A/Res/44/82, December 15, 1989), http://www.un.org/esa/socdev/family/docs.html. See also http://daccess-dds-ny.un.org/doc/RESOLUTION/GEN/NR0/548/41/IMG/NR054841.pdf?OpenElement, 205–6.

[5] n.a., Encyclopedia of the Nations, http://www.nationsencyclopedia.com/United-Nations/Social-and-Humanitarian-Assistance-THE-FAMILY-SOCIETY-S-BUILDING-BLOCK.html.

[6] Ibid.

the most likely explanation for fewer divorces is the large percentages of unmarried people cohabitating; this is another way of saying "Fewer marriages mean fewer divorces."[7] Even with the decline, however, no one would be surprised to learn that the U.S. divorce rate is among the highest in the world. In fact, Americans are twice as likely to get divorced as couples in Australia or Canada and at least five times more likely than married people in Portugal, China, Greece, or Italy to suffer a marital breakup.[8] An estimated 40 percent of children born to married parents in the United States will experience their parents' divorce.[9]

The reality of divorce affects all demographic and ethnic categories, some more than others. According to a 2004 Census report, some 22 percent of the U.S. adult population has been divorced at least once.[10] Another 14 percent of the population has been married twice, and more than 3 percent has been married at least three times and divorced at least twice.[11] When divided by ethnicity, 24 percent of all whites, 19 percent of blacks, 13 percent of Hispanics, and 9 percent of Asian adults in the United States have been divorced.[12] Regarding ethnic children, 51 percent of black children live only with their mothers, whereas only 36 percent live with both parents.[13] Among Hispanic children, 64 percent live with both parents, and 74 percent of white children live with both parents.

The number of divorced couples leads to fewer children living with both parents. In 1960, 88 percent of children lived with both parents. Nearly 40 years later that number was down to 68 percent. When looking at children who live only with their mother, the percentage climbed from 8 percent in 1960 to nearly a quarter (23 percent) of all children in 1998.[14]

Although some smaller studies have infrequently suggested that significant percentages of children from families of divorce suffer no long-term effects,[15] the vast majority of research opposes those findings.[16] According to a landmark 25-year longitudinal study,

---

[7] C. Corry, "Marriage, Divorce, and Charges of Domestic Violence and Abuse," http://www.dvmen.org/dv-116.htm.

[8] n.a., NationMaster, http://www.nationmaster.com/graph/peo_div_rat-people-divorce-rate.

[9] E. M. Hetherington and M. Stanley-Hagan, "Parenting in Divorced and Remarried Families," in *Handbook of Parenting*, 2nd ed., vol. 3 (Mahwah, NJ: Erlbaum Publishers, 2002).

[10] U.S. Census Bureau, Housing and Household Economic Statistics Division, Fertility and Family Statistics Branch. *Detailed Tables-Number, Timing, and Duration of Marriages and Divorces, Table 3.* 2004 statistics published in 2007, http://www.census.gov/population/www/socdemo/marr-div/2004detailed_tables.html.

[11] U.S. Census Bureau. Population Division, Fertility and Family Statistics Branch. *Marital History for People 15 Years Old and Older by Age, Sex, Race, and Ethnicity: 2001,* http://www.census.gov/population/www/socdemo/marr-div/p70-97-tab01.html.

[12] U.S. Census Bureau, http://www.census.gov/population/www/socdemo/marr-div/2004detailed_tables.html.

[13] C. Russell, *Demographics of the U.S.: Trends and Projections* (Ithaca, NY: New Strategist Publications, 2000), 332.

[14] Ibid., 332.

[15] J. W. Santrock, *Life-Span Development,* 11th ed. (Boston:, McGraw Hill Higher Education, 2008), 296.

[16] Americans for Divorce Reform, http://divorcereform.org/all.html.

The Unexpected Legacy of Divorce, written by best-selling author and leading divorce authority Wallerstein, the effects of divorce are cumulative and crescendo once a child reaches adulthood.[17] She reports that the greatest impact of divorce on children is not felt until they reach their 20s and 30s, when those effects compound and strike with redoubled force.

Consistently research has indicated that the number of negative impacts of divorce on both adults and their children is incalculable. Statistics of this sort are well known and documented, but some of the more noteworthy examples include the following:

Selected Risk Factors of Children from Families of Divorce[18]

Poor adjustment	Anxiety	Dropping out of school
Academic problems	Depression	Premature sexual activity
Acting out	Social irresponsibility	Drug experimentation
Delinquency	Less intimate relationships	Poor friend choices
Low self-esteem	Insecurity in adulthood	More relational problems

Breaking Homes. Homes experiencing divorce are not the only ones that struggle. Some homes are not yet broken but may be in the process of breaking. For our purposes here, breaking homes are described as those dealing with passive, absentee, or conflicted parents or a combination of the three. These represent nuclear, blended, and other types of households that suffer from significant degrees of dysfunction.

The sources of family friction are innumerable: finances, lack of communication, moral dilemmas, sexual problems, interpersonal dynamics, poor health, and the list goes on. Each of these can cause varying degrees of stress that have an effect on marital happiness and satisfaction. Whether problems are external or internal in nature, they can,

---

[17] J. Wallerstein, Julia Lewis, and Sandra Blakeslee, *The Unexpected Legacy of Divorce: A 25-Year Landmark Study* (New York: Hyperion Publishers, 2001), 6, 29–31, 107–9.

[18] J. W. Santrock, *Lifespan Development*, 11th ed. (Boston: McGraw Hill Higher Education, 2008), 296.

and often do, cause frustration and conflict. Frustration often causes interpersonal conflict among family members. Conflict sometimes leads families to times of confrontation, and for some it leads to withdrawal.[19] If issues are not effectively addressed, parents can become passive or be plagued by conflict.

Having one or more parents absent from the home for several hours a day or several days a week affects families. Because of essential economic needs or materialistic wants, absenteeism is driven by realities such as day care, before- and after-school care, dual-income households, travel schedules, declining health of parents, and other time-consuming situations.[20]

Absenteeism can be a problem for even the most committed parents in our ministries. Christian believers are not exempt from pressures that would cause them to be physically or emotionally removed from their loved ones. A leader who comes immediately to mind is Billy Graham, the twentieth-century mega-evangelist. He frequently referred to his own struggles with good parenting in his writing and on televised interviews.[21]

One of Graham's most well-known children is his son, Franklin, the president of the Christian relief organization Samaritan's Purse. As documented in his autobiography, *Rebel with a Cause,* Franklin spent many of his earlier years in spiritual rebellion.[22] In a December 2009 interview, Franklin recalled his father spanning the globe for the cause of Christ, sometimes being gone for months at a time. He said:

> Travel was difficult back then and when my dad traveled to Asia, for example, he would visit as many Asian countries as he could while he was there. He felt it was being a good steward of the funds donated to him for ministry. I can recall one time when he was gone for six months.[23]

It is no wonder Franklin struggled with his absentee father. Many loving parents like Graham feel guilt similar to his as a result of being away from their children for hours or days at a time. Those absences represent precious moments and experiences that cannot be retrieved and that make the challenge of good parenting even greater.

---

[19] F. W. Kaslow and J. J. Magnavita, "A Relational Approach to Psychotherapy," *Comprehensive Handbook of Psychotherapy* (Hoboken, NJ: Wiley, 2002), 261.

[20] M. Eberstadt, "The Absentee Parent," *The Boston Globe* (September 12, 2005); opinion-editorial.

[21] B. Graham, "Billy Graham Pays Tribute to Ruth Graham," http://www.billygraham.org/News_Article.asp?ArticleID=163. In this article Dr. Graham writes, "Ruth also was a wonderful mother. Her task wasn't easy since I was away from home so much, but she handled our children with both great love and wise discipline. She felt it was her calling, and without her willingness to bear the major responsibility for raising our children, my work simply would not have been possible."

[22] F. Graham, *Rebel with a Cause: Finally Comfortable with Being Graham* (Nashville, TN: Thomas Nelson, 1995) 133–43.

[23] K. Virtue, "The Graham Family," *Pilot Challenge Magazine* (December 1, 2009), http://ptc-challenge.com/2009/12/the-graham-family.

Christian leaders and pastors are in an ideal position to minister to and equip families dealing with the stress of divorce, absenteeism, and passive or conflicted parenting. One not-so-obvious thing churches can do is to eliminate some of the extraneous or less-crucial ministry events scheduled on our annual calendars.[24] We can also identify intergenerational ministry events and activities where family unity can be fostered and nurtured. Equipping classes on parenting can be offered, as can sermon series on conflict resolution and ministries such as Divorce-Care or Celebrate Recovery.

2. Immature Parents and Hurried Children. The combined conventional wisdom of psychologists and sociologists produces generally accepted time lines for human development and behavior. These time lines stretch across the human life span from birth through late adulthood. Along these time lines are multiple layers of expected holistic maturation that should normally occur under given circumstances. These primary areas of maturity are physical, psychosocial, cognitive, moral, and faith development. Developmental tasks give broad guidelines as to what behaviors, abilities, competencies, and perspectives might be expected at each stage of human development. As such, for persons to be considered "normal" and functional within society and interpersonally, they are expected to reach certain assigned developmental tasks in each of these areas.[25] When people fail to meet those goals, they are said to be maladjusted or immature.[26]

Immature Young Adults and Parents. In past generations, when an individual reached physical maturity, the fullness of adult life was thrust upon them. In America today that is rarely the case. It is now widely agreed that merely "coming of age" and possessing identifiable traits of physical maturity do not make a male or female a mature man or woman. Indeed, it is not uncommon for a person to be well into his or her 20s, and even have a child or family, without showing consistent and substantial evidence of adult maturity.[27] Current research shows this delayed maturity to be a feature of Western culture that is not shared by other cultures, where exhibiting adult levels of responsibility, expectations, and maturity are commonplace by the early to mid-20s.[28]

---

[24] T. S. Rainer and Eric Geiger, *Simple Church: Returning to God's Process for Making Disciples* (Nashville, TN: B&H, 2006), 197–226.
[25] Santrock, *Lifespan Development*, 19–25.
[26] R. McGhee and R. J. Short, "The Prevalence of Social Maladjustment Among School-Age Children," *Psychology in the Schools*, Wiley Publications, vol. 28, no. 4 (2006): 285–89.
[27] J. Viegas, "Serious Study: Immaturity Levels Rising" (June 23, 2006), http://dsc.discovery.com/news/2006/06/23/immature_hum.html?category=human.
[28] L. Nelson, S. Badger, and B. Wu, "The Influence of Culture in Emerging Adulthood: Perspectives of Chinese College Students," *International Journal of Behavioral Development*, Sage Publications, vol. 28, no. 1 (2004): 26–36.

The differences between young adulthood in the United States and other parts of the world are partially because contemporary society in technologically advanced nations requires adults to have a higher level of postsecondary education, which serves to postpone many of the expectations of otherwise-mature adults.[29] Greater academic requirements allow for a type of suspended development and the elongation of adolescence, a season of life that has recently been identified as emerging adulthood.[30]

Along with this protracted season of adolescence has come the embrace of frivolity among some young people, resulting partially from the ever-changing indices of what constitutes "adulthood."[31] "Boomerang children" is the now-common occurrence for emerging adults to move back in with their parents after leaving home following high school or college. In years past it was a common expectation for adult children to be independent and to live on their own. Such a notion is now passé, as the Pew Research Center reports that some 11 percent of all adults age 18 to 34 currently live with their parents.[32] A full 30 percent of that group are 30 years or older. Statistics from the U.S. Census Bureau are consistent with the Pew report.[33]

Lifestyles and mentalities like these are part and parcel of at least a percentage of today's emerging adults, many of whom become spouses or parents long before they have developed the type of character and emotional intelligence needed to lead a family.

In the midst of these challenges, it is incumbent upon local churches actively to engage the culture and to intervene in the lives of single adults, young marrieds, and parents in general. Quality and compelling ministries that attract each of these target audiences are specific help that can be provided. Separate ministries for different demographic and affinity groups will ensure that life-stage needs are adequately addressed. Regular interaction with one another in semistructured fellowship environments where mature social competencies can be developed is also imperative.

---

[29] J. T. Mortimer and Reed W. Lawson, eds., "Macrostructural Trends and the Reshaping of Adolescent," *The Changing Adolescent Experience* (New York: Cambridge University Press, 2002), 1–5.

[30] J. Arnett, "2000. Emerging Adulthood," *American Psychologist* (55): 469–80.

[31] R. J. Glover, "Developmental Tasks of Adulthood: Implications for Counseling Community College Students," *Community College Journal of Research and Practice,* vol. 24, no. 6 (2000): 505–14.

[32] W. Wang and R. Morin, "Home for the Holidays . . . and Every Other Day" (November 24, 2009), http://pewsocialtrends.org/pubs/748/recession-brings-many-young-adults-back-to-the-nest#prc-jump.

[33] "Families and Living Arrangements (Current Population Survey Reports)," http://www.census.gov/population/www/socdemo/hh-fam.html.

Hurried Children. Nearly 30 years ago, during the turbulent times of latchkey kids in the 1980s, psychologist David Elkind coined a now-famous phrase—"the hurried child."[34] Perhaps no better term exists to describe the life of American preteens and adolescents. The hurried child refers to how today's youngsters are relentlessly pushed by parents, schools, and the media to mature to a premature adulthood in academics, social maturity, and sexuality. Although this phenomenon is the exact opposite problem of immature parenthood mentioned earlier, it represents the same dynamic of developmental dysfunction—where children are expected to be adults and adults act like children.[35]

A good deal of research has been done in recent years regarding how these pressures and other factors affecting children are contributing to the premature onset of puberty.[36] Research is also indicating that general stress, father absenteeism, and family conflict are particularly central to premature adulthood.[37] This condition, called precocious puberty, is when the appearance of physical and hormonal signs of pubertal development appear at a significantly earlier age than the average child (before age eight for girls and before age nine for boys).[38]

The typical age for the onset of puberty is 10½ years for girls and between 11½ and 12 years for boys.[39] Studies have shown that pushing children into puberty is both unnatural and unhealthy. Risk factors for early bloomers include increased potential for depression and other emotional problems, development of certain types of cancer, and the greater likelihood of underage alcohol consumption and illicit sexual activity.[40] Children who fit this description are commonly referred to as "tweens" because they fall between the developmental seasons of childhood and adolescence.

Marketers and the music and entertainment industry are targeting tweens or preteens in ways that make them vulnerable to exploitation in a variety of ways.[41] These factors also wreak havoc within our families and can lead to various dysfunctional conditions. Whether it is destructive

---

34 K. Ode, "Hurried Child Is Still with Us: The Extracurricular World Is Domain of Pushy Parents," *Star Tribune* (March 20, 1999): Variety Section. See also D. Elkind, *The Hurried Child,* 25th anniversary edition (Cambridge, MA: Decapo Press), 2001.

35 Anthony Campolo, *Growing Up in America: A Sociology of Youth Ministry,* (Grand Rapids, MI: Zondervan, 1989), 119.

36 B. Ellis and J. Garber, "Psychosocial Antecedents of Variation in Girls' Pubertal Timing," *Child Development,* vol. 71, no. 2 (March/April 2000): 485.

37 T. E. Moffitt, A. Caspi, J. Belsky, and P. A. Silva, "Childhood Experience and the Onset of Menarche," *Child Development,* vol. 63, no. 1 (February 1992): 47–58.

38 P. Kaplowitz, "Precocious Puberty" (June 30, 2009), http://emedicine.medscape.com/article/924002-overview.

39 V. Ianelli, "When Should Puberty Start? Learn the Signs of Early Puberty," http://pediatrics.about.com/cs/conditions/a/early_puberty.htm.

40 Ellis and Garber, "Psychosocial Antecedents of Variation in Girls' Pubertal Timing," 485.

41 K. Hymowitz, "Kids Today Are Growing Up Way Too Fast," *The Wall Street Journal* (October 28, 1998), http://www.manhattan-institute.org/html/_wsj-kids_today_are_growing.htm.

choices or challenges to parental authority in areas such as music, dress, language, entertainment options, or social and dating involvements, the hurried child is threatened and should be protected and nurtured.[42]

Christian congregations have a duty to contribute to the development of healthy and well-balanced students. Providing age-graded discipleship classes and age-group ministers for preteens, middle school, and high school is a great place to start. Ministers also can provide seminars with guest speakers on parenting topics and parent–student workshops to help facilitate communication and mutual understanding. There is no substitute for providing solid biblical counseling to these children and youth.

3. *Nonreligious or Nominal Faith Commitment.* Because matters of faith are so fundamental to our realities, one's worldview, and personal lifestyle choices, it is of little surprise that religious and faith convictions are so central to building healthy families. Incompatible religious beliefs within different family members can play a role in creating stress and misunderstandings that, in turn, lead to a crisis on the doorstep of the American family.

Nonreligious Families or Parents. In the United States there is a growing trend toward the embrace of atheism, agnosticism, and of having no particular religious affiliation. The most recent statistics suggest that some 11 percent, or more than 30 million Americans, now consider themselves irreligious or atheistic.[43] Because the personal convictions, moral choices, and ethical positions of the irreligious are sometimes markedly different than people of faith, one might expect families and children of atheist–agnostics to face greater challenges than many of those in more traditional and Christian families. Most notably, the nonreligious suffer significantly higher percentages of divorce than their committed Christian counterparts.[44] Atheists and irreligious people are also less likely to marry, more likely to cohabitate, and less likely to be involved in local church ministries.[45]

Nominal Christian Families or Parents. Most of the families to whom Christian churches minister are predominately Christian or are at some stage of considering a commitment to Christ and some degree of involvement in a local church. Among church attendees being affected by our congregations, a majority of them would consider themselves Christians.

---

[42] G. K. Olson, *Counseling Teenagers: The Complete Christian Guide to Understanding and Helping Adolescents* (Loveland, CO: Group Books, 1984), 74–88.

[43] G. Barna, *The Seven Faith Tribes: Who They Are, What They Believe, and Why They Matter* (Nashville, TN: BarnaBooks-Tyndale, 2009), 1–28. Because of the need to have consistency with these types of statistics and because George Barna represents one of the more trusted Christian researchers, he is relied on heavily in this section of the chapter.

[44] T. Hatch, "Christian Marriages Are Most Successful" (March 17, 2009), http://www.faithwriters.com/article-details.php?id=95893.

[45] Ibid.

Indeed, even when considering the population of the United States, two out of every three adults claim to be "Christian." This group includes Christians of all types: committed evangelicals and theologically nominal or minimally to moderately active born-again Christians.[46]

When it comes to exactly what "being a Christian" means, answers vary widely. In *Growing True Disciples,* researcher Barna indicates that 40 percent of those who attend Protestant church services on a typical weekend are not born again.[47] That is, 40 percent of Protestant church attendees would not agree to or would be uncomfortable with the idea that minimal "saving faith" requires an individual to make an ongoing personal commitment to Jesus Christ in which they confess their sins and accept Christ as their Savior.[48] That is the standard definition Barna has used for his research for the past two decades.

Statistics show that only those believers who live consistently within the principles of committed evangelical Christian discipleship exhibit a significant difference in lifestyle choices as compared to other self-described Christians or non-Christians.[49] For that reason one could assume that families who espouse these commitments may struggle less or be more victorious over many of the challenges being faced.

The failure to have solid theological convictions should not be minimized. Faithless families do not signify the absence of religious platitudes or ideological postulates that are only marginally important or even irrelevant to life. Biblical convictions are, after all, more than a side of kale garnishing a delicious meal on fine china. These types of convictions are rooted in understandings of the most fundamental levels of reality—beliefs that are consistent with revealed truth and that have direct consequences on choices and consequences in every domain of human life.

Thus, issues related to truth, ethics, morality, behavior, habits, and authority in particular are all intertwined with the issue of parental–familial faith commitments and their effects on family security, wellness, and harmony. Moreover, those who are involved in communities of faith have access to what has been described as "an unusually strong support

---

[46] Barna, *The Seven Faith Tribes*, 29–40.

[47] G. Barna, *Growing True Disciples: New Strategies for Producing Genuine Followers of Christ* (Colorado Springs, CO: Waterbrook Press, 2001), 60. Here respondents identified themselves along a continuum of theological commitments and personal beliefs, with "born-again" indicating they have made a personal commitment to Jesus Christ that is still important in their life today and in which they claim they will go to heaven after they die because they have confessed their sins and accepted Jesus Christ as their Savior.

[48] Barna Group, "One-Quarter of Self-Described Born Again Adults Rely on Means Other Than Grace to Get Them to Heaven" (November 29, 2005), http://www.barna.org/barna-update/article/5-barna-update/167-one-quarter-of-self-described-born-again-adults-rely-on-means-other-than-grace-to-get-to-heaven.

[49] Urban Youth Worker's Institute, "Faith Has a Limited Effect on Most People's Behavior" (May 24, 2004), http://www.urbanministry.org/wiki/faith-has-limited-effect-most-people%E2%80%99s-behavior.

network."[50] Not only are families of faith better supported during times of pain, but they also gain additional strength from sharing similar sets of beliefs about right and wrong, good and bad, and duty and responsibility.[51]

When it comes to children, homes without the strong foundation of faith have fewer and less clearly identified boundaries. This freedom can become a child's worst enemy because children and teens are vulnerable to all manner of emotional, social, physical, and spiritual threats.[52]

Vulnerable families need strong churches. They need Christian leaders who will step in and mentor and disciple them. Vulnerable children need advocates. Failing parents need older, successful parents with proven track records to shepherd them and hold them accountable. Churches can supplement these good and necessary efforts and organized ministries by launching ministries specific to men and women. Other targeted ministries such as MOPs (mothers of preschoolers) can provide training on important issues and offer godly support from older women and peers.

Lead pastors and age-group ministers can provide counsel to individual parents and students and offer a clarion call to commitment and character from their podiums and in their teaching. The development of lay leaders to supplement the work of these ministers by offering outstanding biblical instruction in small groups and Sunday schools is a must because this crisis is epidemic. Finally, churches can provide additional support by providing special discipleship classes that equip families in areas related to the Christian worldview, apologetics, and Christian ethics. To further assist families, they should allocate resources that provide college and seminary scholarship assistance to deserving students with demonstrated needs.

External Factors Affecting Families

Beyond these more covert or latent and less clamorous crises, other external forces are at work in our culture and add dysfunction in today's families. These artifacts have to do with broader social challenges and culturally bound phenomena bearing down on our children, youth, and parents. Although many such threats could be named, three leading external factors will be investigated.

1. Alcohol and Drug Abuse. The effects of substance and alcohol abuse are well-known and have been irrefutably documented. As time passes and as the use of different drugs becomes chic, however, updated information and statistical data are needed. With regard to the continued abuse

---

[50] E. M. Hetherington and J. Kelly, *For Better or For Worse: Divorce Reconsidered* (New York, W. W. Norton, 2002), 75–76.

[51] Ibid.

[52] D. Maglio, *Essential Parenting, Revitalizing and Remoralizing the Family in the 21st Century* (Spring Hill, FL: Wider Horizons, 2000), 48–72.

of alcohol and drugs among adults, youth, and even children, families continue to suffer from these problems in visible and invisible ways.

Alcohol Abuse. In a culture of high-school drinking parties and fraternity house escapades, some apparently forget that drinking alcohol is illegal for underage minors. Since 1984 the nationwide minimum legal drinking age (MLDA) has not changed. Prior to that time, individual states set their own laws on the legal limit, some being as young as age 18. The law was changed because of studies and statistics that had shown the increased number of automotive fatalities involving younger drivers who had consumed alcohol prior to or while driving. The national limit was set at 21, the same age identified at the end of prohibition in America.

Alcohol use among underage children and youth is not a harmless form of entertainment. Some research has shown that when Americans were compared with Europeans who had earlier legal access to drinking, they also had a greater statistical likelihood of alcohol-related diseases later in life.[53] Beyond health concerns and the danger of driving intoxicated, additional effects of underage alcohol use are seen in their behavior and personal judgment.

The National Council on Alcoholism and Drug Dependence reports a U.S. Department of Health and Human Services study, saying that the average person takes their first drink at age 13.[54] In addition, students who use alcohol before age 15 are four times more likely to become alcohol dependent than those who wait until the legal drinking age.[55] Also, alcohol was involved more than two-thirds of the time among those committing date rape and sexual crimes against high school and college-age students.[56]

The National Center for Health Statistics reports that 43 percent of U.S. adults, more than 76 million people, have been exposed to alcoholism in the family.[57] In other words, nearly half of all Americans adults grew up with or married an alcoholic or a problem drinker or had a blood relative who was an alcoholic or problem drinker. When the effects of alcohol and drug abuse are considered together, they become America's number-one health problem and a leading cause of dysfunctional families.[58]

---

[53] American Medical Association, "Facts About Youth and Alcohol."

[54] National Council on Alcoholism and Drug Dependence, "Facts About Underage Drinking," http://www.ncadd.org/facts/underaged_drinking.html.

[55] B. F. Grant and Deborah A. Dawson, "Age at Onset of Alcohol Use and Its Association with DSM-IV Alcohol Abuse and Dependence," *Journal of Substance Abuse,* vol. 9 (1997): 103–10.

[56] Office of Inspector General, U.S. Department of Health and Human Services, *Youth and Alcohol: Dangerous and Deadly Consequences* (1992), http://www.oig.hhs.gov/oei/reports/oei-09-92-00260.pdf, 5.

[57] National Center for Health Statistics (NCHS), *Advance Data,* United States Department of Health and Human Services, No. 205, 9/30/91, 1.

[58] See http://www.ncadd.org/facts/problems.html.

Drug Abuse. Drug use in the United States has reached epic proportions, and there are no signs of that changing. Controlled substances and illegal drugs are peddled from both within and outside American borders, and law enforcement of all types seems unequipped and underfunded in their ability to stop trafficking. Although valiant efforts are made by the authorities, their lack of manpower and the iron will of drug pushers make this an ongoing national crisis with enormous implications for families.

Modern drug lore has many developments that, at one time in America, would have been unthinkable. Take, for example, the enormous challenge to current law that would legalize marijuana. Other countries—including the Netherlands libertarian state in Scandinavia—are seeking to restrict its use and legalization.[59] Where I currently live in southern California, it is a common occurrence to see large demonstrations and to be personally approached by pot activists seeking signatures for petitions and legislative action. These efforts are despite the state having legalized "medical" marijuana and more than 800 reported dispensaries in California alone.[60] Ironically, a 1961 United Nations Convention on Narcotic Drugs classified it as a Schedule IV substance, which indicated that marijuana had little or no medicinal value.[61]

Because marijuana is considered a gateway drug to even harder types of illegal substances, the war against pot continues to be an important battle in American families. The National Institute on Drug Abuse reports that a 2009 study indicated that 14 percent of seventh graders and nearly 20 percent of high school seniors use drugs on at least a monthly basis.[62] In addition, 44 percent of high school students have experimented with pot, and 9 percent have tried cocaine.[63] The effects of illegal drugs are well known and may include physical ramifications, guilt, shame, remorse, illicit sexual activity and dysfunction, truancy, problem behaviors, depression, delinquency, and suicidal tendencies.[64]

Another surprising development in recent decades has been the increasing abuse of prescription drugs. According to studies conducted by the National Institute on Drug Abuse, an estimated 20 percent of

---

[59] "Stop the Drug War" (June 1, 2007), http://stopthedrugwar.org/chronicle/488/new_restrictions_dutch_cannabis_coffee_shops_marijuana. According to the Dutch news agency ANP, the move to restrict coffee shops in Rotterdam arose from concern about rising use of marijuana by school pupils and the problems caused by its sale and use.

[60] A December 2009 report by news agency CNN reported a mother–son family who had gone into business as marijuana farmers. See http://www.cnn.com/video/#/video/us/2009/12/12/spellman.marijuana.fam.business.cnn.

[61] European Legal Database on Drugs: UN Classification on Controlled Drugs, http://eldd.emcdda.europa.eu/html.cfm/index5622EN.html.

[62] National Institute on Drug Abuse, http://www.nida.nih.gov/MarijBroch/teenpg3-4.html#many.

[63] National Council on Alcoholism and Drug Dependence, http://www.ncadd.org/facts/youthalc.html.

[64] D. Korem, "Streetwise Parents, Foolproof Kids," in *Handbook on Counseling Youth,* ed. J. McDowell (Dallas: Word, 1996), 403.

all Americans have used prescription drugs for nonmedical purposes in their lifetimes.[65] The same report indicated that high school students were most likely to abuse the pain-killing medications Vicodin and OxyContin, with close to 10 percent of high school seniors occasionally using one or both without a prescription.[66] Other popular drugs such as antidepressants/sleep aids (Prozac, Valium, Ativan, Rozerem, and Ambien) or pain medications (Methadone, Fentanyl, Propoxyphene) that adults and young people are prescribed and sometimes abuse are powerful medications whose ease of availability is sobering.[67]

An increasingly popular practice among some risk-taking students is the practice of "pharming." Pharming is the practice of gaining access to and mixing various types of pills together in a container and then indiscriminately grabbing a pill or handful of pills and ingesting them to see what effect they will have.[68] When abused by single tablet or in groups, the purposes include reasons as diverse as boredom, artistic creativity, sexual enhancement, weight control, academic performance, and athletic endurance.[69]

The negative impact alcohol abuse and the drug culture are having on society, families, and among students is alarming and near pandemic in scope. Churches must act with resolve to provide families with the resources needed. They can provide support group and recovery help through ministries such as Celebrate Recovery, Narcotics Anonymous, Alcoholics Anonymous–type groups (e.g., Alcoholics Victorious), and Al-Anon–type support groups (for families of those affected by alcoholism). Churches can also offer personal and group counseling, professional Christian counseling and quality referrals, financial support for counseling fees, church staff counselors, alternative after-school and evening ministry programming, and educational ministries with medical health professionals targeting these problems.

2. Oversexed Society. If the 1960s were the Sexual Revolution, the 2000s have been the Sexual Devolution, and the 2010s may be our undoing. The culture in which we live is not only sex charged but also sex obsessed. Hundreds of formerly innocuous words have now been infused with sexual innuendos. It seems as though nearly everything that is heard on television or radio uses some type of double entendre. At a time when the age of information and scientific inquiry has yielded so much knowledge about

---

[65] N. Volkow, "National Institute on Drug Abuse, Prescription Drugs: Use and Addiction" (2005), http://www.nida.nih.gov/ResearchReports/Prescription/prescription.html.

[66] See http://www.nida.nih.gov/ResearchReports/Prescription/prescription.html.

[67] Drugs like these are prescribed to parents or sometimes their children for a host of symptoms (ADD, ADHD, anxiety, depression, etc.) but are abused for a host of other reasons listed elsewhere in this chapter.

[68] Substance Abuse and Mental Health Services Administration (March 7, 2003), http://ncadi.samhsa.gov/govpubs/prevalert/v6/4.aspx.

[69] See http://kidshealth.org/teen/drug_alcohol/drugs/prescription_drug_abuse.html.

our world, the irony is that we still do not know ourselves and, as a result, continue in our desperate struggle for identity, intimacy, and meaning.

In this matrix of existential lostness and our need for affection, our society is driven ever inward and compelled to explore the mystery of human sexuality. Unfortunately, because that search is bereft in its understanding of personhood and being, most miss the essence of love in their pursuit of pleasure. Yet that longing continues to plunge our society deeper into sexual dysfunction. Because of the varying types of sexual threats we are facing, it is hard to summarize them and their far-reaching effects. Perhaps presenting a laundry list of examples will alert us to the great challenges families and their children are facing.

Pornography. First, there is the normalization and popularization of pornography into the mainstream. In the early 2000s it was not uncommon to see teenagers wearing "porn star" T-shirts, and today discourse about pornography is literally everywhere. The statistics related to the porn industry are staggering by any account. It includes pornographic television networks, pay-per-view movies, Web sites, in-room hotel movies, phone sex, sex toys, conventions, magazines, DVDs, digital media for phones and other handheld electronic devices, and much more. This material is available everywhere an Internet connection can be found, including public and school libraries, homes, airports, hotels, restaurants, coffeehouses, and churches. It is so pervasive and insidious that obscenity and decency laws simply cannot govern or stay in front of it.

Sexual Activity. Beyond the viewing of sexually related materials is the actual participation in illicit sexual acts. Regarding sexually active teenagers, in 2003, 47 percent of students reported having had intercourse.[70] Data about students' sexual experiences beyond intercourse are less readily available, but a report from the mid-1990s and another after 2000 indicated that 11 percent of American teens (both boys and girls) had engaged in anal sex at least once, and half of all high school students (50%) said they had engaged in oral sex at least once.[71]

Another common teenage practice is that of "sexting," which involves the sharing of sexually explicit language, photos, or videos with someone via e-mail or text messages. In a large report by the National Campaign to Prevent Teen and Unplanned Pregnancy, the study indicated that one in five, or 20 percent, of teens reportedly sent or posted nude or seminude materials of themselves online or via some other form of digital electronic media.[72] Add this to general teen sexual involvement with people they

---

[70] CDC, Youth Risk Behavior Survey, http://www.kff.org/youthhivstds/upload/U-S-Teen-Sexual-Activity-Fact-Sheet.pdf.

[71] Guttmacher Institute study. See http://sexuality.about.com/od/sexinformation/a/teen_sex_stats.htm.

[72] See http://www.msnbc.msn.com/id/28679588.

know but have no ongoing relationship with in arrangements such as "friends with benefits" (FWB), sex buddies, and booty calls, and the crisis begins to be clearly seen for how serious it really is.

Teen Pregnancy and Sexually Transmitted Diseases. The high level of sexually active teenagers is a contributing factor to the number of teen pregnancies. Government statistics show that 33 percent of all girls will become pregnant at least once before age 20.[73] Of the 750,000 teen pregnancies in 2002, nearly a third (215,000) of those children were aborted.[74] Beyond pregnancies, the reality of the epidemic problems with sexually transmitted diseases (STDs) is undeniable. One of the most comprehensive and up-to-date documents that are available is the Sexually Transmitted Disease Surveillance 2008 from the U.S. Centers for Disease Control (CDC).[75]

According to medical doctor and researcher Meeker, author of *Epidemic: How Teen Sex Is Killing Our Kids,* the number of STDs has grown from two in 1960 to more than 30 different viral infections in 2010—only 50 years.[76] Among STDs, 20 percent of Americans over the age of 12 have genital herpes (a 500% increase since 1976). Moreover, the *New England Journal of Medicine* reports that the human papillomavirus (HPV) will infect 60 perent of all female students during their first four years of college. An estimated 80 percent of all U.S. women will be infected with HPV at some point during their lifetime, and this disease leads to virtually 100 percent of all types of cervical cancer in women.[77] With regard to HIV and AIDS, the CDC's 2007 statistics report that some 1.1 million Americans are HIV positive and about another one million have AIDS.[78]

Infidelity, Sexual Dysfunction, and Deviancy. The sex-sick culture in which we live continues to find ways to violate others' bodies and to corrupt minds with distortions of the divinely designed instrument of sexuality. At a fundamental level of the family, it involves the abuse of fidelity and the marriage vow. This was seen vividly in late 2009 as the sexual escapades of professional golfer Tiger Woods came to light. Long thought to be a committed family man, it was revealed that his five-year marriage had been riddled with serial adultery—nearing 20 different women only weeks after the story broke.[79]

---

[73] 4 Parents Gov Web site: http://www.4parents.gov/sexrisky/teen_preg/teen_preg.html.

[74] S. J. Ventura, J. C. Abma, W. D. Mosher, and S. K. Henshaw, "Recent Trends in Teenage Pregnancy in the United States (1990–2002)," *National Center for Health Statistics,* http://www.cdc.gov/nchs/products/pubs/pubd/hestats/teenpreg1990-2002/teenpreg1990-2002.htm.

[75] Download this full report/document at http://www.cdc.gov/std/stats08/surv2008-Complete.pdf.

[76] M. Meeker, *Epidemic: How Teen Sex Is Killing Our Kids* (Washington, DC: Lifeline Press, 2005), 12–50.

[77] HPV.com, http://www.hpv.com/index.html?WT.mc_id=GR06K.

[78] Centers for Disease Control, http://www.cdc.gov/hiv/topics/surveillance/basic.htm#hivest.

[79] See http://www.khabrein.info/index.php?option=com_content&task=view&id=30359&Itemid=60.

One activity that came to light with Woods and others, such as former New York Governor Spitzer, was the employment of call girls and the use of Internet-based prostitution rings.[80] A similar-but-different type of threat to families that is becoming more popular is the growth of discreet adult online dating sites. One such site, the Ashley Madison Agency, recently made headlines when it took out large ads in major newspapers using provocative phrases intended to make married men and women cheat on their spouses, like "We're all of the fun and none of the trouble" and "Life is short. Have an affair."[81]

Culture is constantly awash in these and other explicit forms of sexual deviancy. Interest in practices such as wife swapping, swingers' clubs, deviant sex, crimes against children, and self-made or secretly produced sex tapes is increasing. These and other scandalous practices are not as uncommon as one might dare to hope. A few years ago, a person I knew from school got wrapped up in "1-900" number sex chats. His marriage fractured and then fell through when he was not able to pay his family's mortgage because of a $1,200 monthly phone-sex bill.

I was once asked to provide initial counseling to a 12-year-old to whom school classmates had introduced pornography. He began acting out what he had seen on his younger siblings, who were in elementary school. To my knowledge he remains incarcerated today. Hearing these types of experiences shocks the conscience, but they represent the world as it is and not as we wish it were. The conscience of our culture is becoming increasingly calloused as the concept of "taboo" becomes passé and societal decency disintegrates.

It is paramount that Christian leaders model biblical relationships and healthy attitudes toward godly sexuality. Great care should be expended in promoting a healthy work and ministry environment with regard to sexual harassment and related policies. Families and students should be equipped about sexual sin and victory over sexual temptation. Churches should provide library resources and teaching on sexual themes and issues, including same-sex attraction. Christian educational programming should be provided for both parents and youth.

Children should be protected with security procedures and proper background checks and screening of volunteers. In addition, leaders must be activists in helping provide constructive ways to protect children and to meet the spiritual needs of child predators and offenders. Children also can be taught about avoiding harmful situations and the advances

[80] n.a., "Spitzer Is Linked to Prostitution Ring" (March 10, 2008), http://www.nytimes.com/2008/03/10/nyregion/10cnd-spitzer.html.

[81] S. Cochran, "'Life Is Short, Have an Affair,' Says Ashley Madison" (November 13, 2008), http://www.associatedcontent.com/article/1206394/life_is_short_have_an_affair_says_ashley.html.

of predators. Church leaders can suggest Internet protection software and home standards for Web use, and families can be taught how to monitor media and technology in their families.

3. Financial Insecurity. After an initial season of financial strength in the first part of the 2000s, the U.S. economy fell on hard times later in the decade. A sort of perfect storm hit major segments of the financial system in the country and continued to batter it for more than two successive years.[82] Because the U.S. economy is a macrocosm of family finances, the downfall of major quadrants of the nation's resources caused profound crises in the lives of American households.

Periods of strength in the American market generally have had a residual effect in the nation at large. As private business and industry sprawl, the influx of money into the free market feeds families and provides resources for government to provide essential services for safety and security. With this enormous blessing, however, has sometimes come a spiritual price tag.

During times like these, it is not uncommon for American ingenuity to produce in some people without character a degree of hubris and greed. This manifests itself in the form of materialism. Materialism can also negatively cultivate carnality in adults and children. Depending on whether one is the "have" or the "have not," an abundance of money cultivates the propensity toward envy, poor self-esteem, pride, angst, anger toward others who possess things a person may want, ingratitude, hopelessness, and any number of other negative emotions and dispositions. These factors also have the tendency to extinguish spiritual desire in the hearts of believers because it can cause family members to become enchanted with the world and invest less in more important familial relationships.

Financial instability creates insecurity in the one who has trusted in money as their god. In this sense there is a positive effect of the condition of need or material threat. There are also challenges and negative consequences. Such has been the case in the United States from 2007 to 2010.

The Dow Jones Industrial Average and the smaller but perhaps more accurate Standard and Poor's Index began falling in July 2007 and then got hammered with one leading index falling some 57 percent in value over a 20-month period ending in March 2009.[83] During the following months, the benchmark index for U.S. stocks surged some 61 percent, but the market was artificially stabilized and partially buoyed by an enormous investment on the part of the U.S. Treasury. Accordingly, consumer confidence was flat because of uncertainty about the signals the populace was receiving. In fact, the Consumer Confidence Index—the degree of confidence American

---

[82] B. Willis, "U.S. Recession Worst Since Great Depression, Revised Data Show" (August 1, 2009), http://www.bloomberg.com/apps/news?pid=20601087&sid=aNivTjr852TI.

[83] Bloomberg Financial, "Dow Ratio Signals Danger for U.S. Stocks" (December 9, 2009), http://www.bloomberg.com/apps/news?pid=20601103&sid5a0_HZI99gwnw.

businessmen and workers or "people" had in the economy—was near a 26-year low in late 2009 and only slightly up from a year before.[84]

Part of the crisis was a result of the excessive optimism and a type of unsustainable consumer debt and reckless financial speculation from decades of record domestic growth.[85] This led to loosened legislation regarding home loans and the availability of credit from large brokers such as Sallie Mae and Freddie Mac, in addition to excessive underwriting by insurance giant AIG. This, coupled with cutthroat lending policies and baseless jumbo loans being extended to unqualified buyers, led to overvaluing of homes and a housing bubble that ultimately burst.[86]

The housing bubble's burst led to a bailout and government takeover of those three major institutions' assets. As the crisis continued, banks underwriting those loans began to fail, which led to additional federal funds rescuing those banks, while still other banks became insolvent.[87] Once again the federal government stepped in with multiple bailout programs that included a so-called Troubled Assets Relief Program (TARP)[88] and an omnibus bill that calculated to more than $1 trillion of U.S. taxpayer money.[89] That degree of budget spending was enormous.

Economists reported that it took 233 years (from 1776 to 2009) for the nation to incur a $1.4 trillion debt. Since that time the national debt ceiling has reportedly increased to $12.3 trillion and is expected to continue to rise.[90] Meanwhile, at the end of 2009, while trying to come out of an economic recession, additional government spending bills went forward, and a national effort to create a government-run health care system through a national takeover of that industry was being waged.[91]

The economic situation in the United States at the end of 2009 was dire and had a significant impact on the American family. Because of the dynamics of national economics, whatever the causes, some 10.2 percent of all working Americans were out of work. During this time the

---

[84] The Conference Board, "Consumer Confidence Survey Release" (November 24, 2009), http://www.conference-board.org/economics/consumerConfidence.cfm.

[85] n.a., "Yearender: Year of Recession Leaves US Humbled on Global Stage," http://www.earthtimes.org/articles/show/299337,yearender-year-of-recession-leaves-us-humbled-on-global-stage.html.

[86] T. Sowell, "How Fannie Mae and Freddie Mac Sank in the Subprime Quicksand" (November 27, 2009), http://www.investors.com/NewsAndAnalysis/Article.aspx?id=513719.

[87] "Number of Banks Failing in 2009: 40" (June 19, 2009), http://www.huffingtonpost.com/2009/06/19/number-of-bank-failures-i_n_218343.html.

[88] "Another View: Redefining How to Repay TARP" (December 9, 2009), http://dealbook.blogs.nytimes.com/2009/12/14/redefining-how-to-repay-tarp-hfo-hfo.

[89] Reuters, "US Bailout Fund Left Many Problems Unsolved: Watchdog," http://economictimes.indiatimes.com/news/international-business/US-bailout-fund-left-many-problems-unsolved-Watchdog/articleshow/5318086.cms.

[90] A. de Borchgrave, "Commentary: President Petraeus?" *United Press International (UPI)* (December 14, 2009), http://www.upi.com/Top_News/Analysis/2009/12/14/Commentary-President-Petraeus/UPI-91471260795600/.

[91] S. Condon, "Healthcare Progress Report: *CBS News Healthcare Reform Special Report*" (December 14, 2009), http://www.cbsnews.com/stories/2009/12/14/politics/main5977451.shtml.

legislature was also working to pass a cap and trade tax, which President Barack Obama said would necessarily raise costs on the use of energy in a time many Americans could not afford it.[92]

This disheartened the American public and exacerbated an already-depressed financial situation.[93] Because of the lack of income for many families, the loss of jobs and less income on the part of most Americans, a national foreclosure crisis occurred because of the number of homeowners whose mortgage payments were in arrears.[94] In addition, crushing credit card debt and high interest rates on unsecured loans led to even greater strain. This led to 1.4 million bankruptcies being filed through 2009, which was one of the highest, if not the highest, year on record.[95]

Accordingly, families felt the crushing weight of financial stress. In addition to struggling with the basics of survival related to housing, energy, food, and the like, the economic crisis also threatened the American child. Children's materialism may have been challenged, but their personal security was also threatened during this time.[96] Many children felt the reality of financial stress and need, in addition to feeling as if many of their wants were unsatisfied. This contributed to a mood of unrest and challenge for families at the end of the first decade of 2000.

Churches generally step up in valiant ways during times of crisis. One way many churches can respond is by providing sound preaching and teaching on money, stewardship, materialism, and other financial issues as appropriate. They also can provide financial counseling and budget planning sessions and support groups. This would include ministries such as Financial Peace University, Crown Financial Ministries, and other similar services.

Many churches are in the position to offer job training and to coordinate local job fairs, including promoting position openings in appropriate ways through acceptable channels. As they have throughout church history, ministries can provide benevolence ministries that balance accountability with grace. They should establish food banks, clothes ministries, and low-cost or free furniture. Church leaders should encourage their memberships to assist parachurch ministries and other local churches that aid people in need in places that need volunteers for shelters and inner-city missions.

---

92 Video of Barack Obama's remarks on Cap and Trade tax, http://www.liveleak.com/view?i=80f_1246320700.

93 P. Goodman, "U.S. Unemployment Rate Hits 10.2%, Highest in 26 Years" (November 6, 2009), http://www.nytimes.com/2009/11/07/business/economy/07jobs.html.

94 F. Norris, "Americans Owe Less. That's Not All Good" (December 11, 2009), http://www.nytimes.com/2009/12/12/business/economy/12charts.html?_r=2.

95 See http://www.abiworld.org/statcharts/ConsumerDebt-Bankruptcy2009FINAL.pdf.

96 G. Barna, "Survey Reveals Challenges Felt by Young People" (September 10, 2007), http://www.barna.org/barna-update/article/15-familykids/96-survey-reveals-challenges-faced-by-young-people.

Conclusion

God cares about families. He cares about nuclear families, broken families, and households of all types. He wants His timeless principles to be applied to our lives so we can see the power of the living Christ break the cycles of bondage that affect moms, dads, sons, daughters, brothers, and sisters. Those of us who serve in ministry leadership positions in the church can no longer wait for those with broken families to come to the church for healing. Many feel insecure or ashamed. As a result, it is our responsibility to take the initiative to go into their world and offer them the message of salvation, hope, and reconciliation—both in a relationship with God and in their familial relationships. The God of second chances calls us to bring His message to our lost and needy world.

Churches who covenant to create family ministries that equip, train, and support households to whom they minister will place themselves in a position where they and the families they support will collide with the love and grace of God and usher in a new day of blessing and flourishing. It will not always be easy. In fact, it probably will be difficult, and you will be misunderstood by some. But when that day comes, count yourself fortunate because Jesus was often misunderstood in His ministry priorities too. They could not understand that He was called to minister to the broken and the sick. He had the deep and abiding peace that in so doing He was going about His Father's business. Such is your calling as well.

Unit 2

Forming a Biblical Theology of the Family

4 Old Testament Teachings on the Family

Michael S. Lawson
Dallas Theological Seminary

Introduction

Nibbling a cookie's edge! What else would describe a one-chapter summary of the Old Testament's teaching on the family? After all, family belongs at the center of God's creation. God crowns creation with man but not man exclusively as male. He creates man as male and female and, perhaps more important, man as family. God binds up the male and the female in His plan to procreate and replenish the earth. From Genesis to Malachi stories, histories, genealogies, instructions, regulations, songs, wisdom, and warnings testify to God's ongoing concern for His human family.[1]

Genesis records how God made the first two humans from exactly the same material and designed them to serve as His coregents over His earth. Their willful disobedience immediately affected their primary relationship and bore excruciating results in their immediate family. We now know that the sin nature took up permanent residence in the human family. The only remedy for this predicament rested with God. He provided a simple promise to the woman. Her offspring, as a true member of the human family, would rescue them from eternal disaster.[2] So the Old Testament opens with the family created, in trouble, and hopeful.

Family issues also saturate the final chapters of the Old Testament. In these final chapters the burning issues are a family matter. God,

---

[1] Unless otherwise noted, Scripture references are cited from the NIV.

[2] In hindsight, it is rather curious that the promise is limited to the woman and not to both Adam and Eve. The Savior most certainly came from Mary but not from Joseph. Although some discussion has been raised about whether this passage really anticipates the Savior, the majority historically has viewed the passage with a prophetic element. Cf. NET Bible.

through Malachi, accuses leaders of failing to honor Him as Father. Further, God chooses to ignore the prayers of those men who break faith with their marriage partner. He hates the divorce they use as an excuse to destroy their marriage covenant. As the prophet anticipates the great and dreadful Day of the Lord, Elijah promises a family intervention as he turns the hearts of the fathers to their children and the hearts of the children to their fathers. In that day the so-called "natural bonds" of family appear to have completely collapsed. One cannot escape the obvious connection between failing to honor God as Father and failing to honor marriage covenants or being tenderhearted toward children.

Perhaps we would be wise to allow the massive weight of material to weigh on our minds before condensing it into manageable portions. We should remember that no summary could ever do justice to the implications of all the direct and indirect references to family in the Old Testament. From Genesis to Malachi and everywhere in between, God works with families. But how do we condense so much material?

Although a number of approaches present themselves, the literary categories of Pentateuch, Historical Books, Wisdom Literature, and Prophetic Literature[3] could provide a helpful structure. I have decided to review the terms that define core family relationships. The selection of passages was mine alone. The following list of terms outlines the discussion in the remainder of the chapter: *family*, *husbands and wives*, *parents*, *children* (sons/daughters), *relatives* (near and far), and *exceptions* (widows and orphans).

Family

Any beginning thoughts about the Old Testament's teaching on family require removal of our twenty-first-century glasses. Two thousand years of church history, the industrial age, and modern census techniques have accustomed us to think in terms of *family units*. By that we usually mean a husband, wife, child/children, and perhaps an occasional loose relative attached for a brief time. Therefore, when we think of family ministry, we often think of ministering to that kind of family unit. But the Old Testament characters and writers did not think that way. In those days, family relations defined people so completely that "the concept of the individual and individual identity did not yet exist."[4]

---

[3] For an excellent treatment in this form, see R. S. Hess and M. D. Carroll R., *Family in the Bible* (Grand Rapids: Baker Books, 2003), Part 1. In some Western societies the term *family* encompasses individuals with no blood or covenant connection living in the same household.

[4] L. G. Perdue, J. Blenkinsopp, J. J. Collins, C. Meyers, *Families in Ancient Israel* (Louisville: Westminster John Knox Press, 1997), 21. This jaundices the twenty-first-century reader who is accustomed to hearing about individual human rights.

"Family" in the English text of the Old Testament shows up many times.[5] An exact count will vary with each translation because our English term has only rough equivalents in the Hebrew text.[6] Translators vary in the exact translation from passage to passage. Three Hebrew words appear to describe relationships moving from closest to most distant relatives, but relationship and connection always remain in view. Of the three terms—"father's house," "clan," and "tribe,"—"father's house" comes closest to our modern concept.[7] Even there, the concept includes a broader understanding that at times involves multiple generations and servants.[8] One oversimplified way to think of family from an Old Testament point of view is concentric circles depicting distance in relationships (see figure).

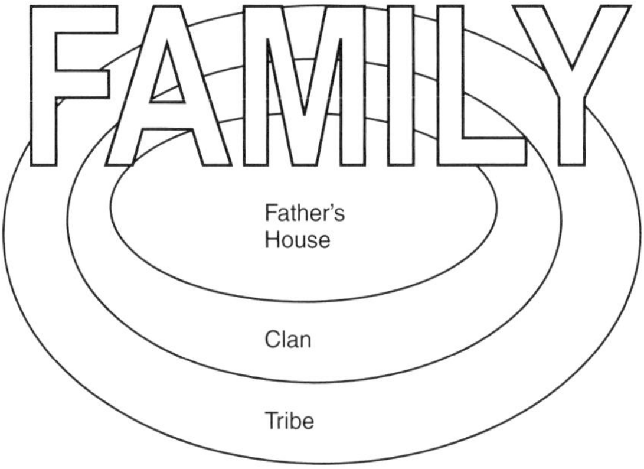

This picture brings us closer to their ideas than our modern understanding of the term *family*. "Father's house" would identify those nearest to our immediate family; "clan" would range through our near relatives; and "tribe" would connect us to our most distant relatives. But any and all of these terms could be and were thought of as *family* in the Old Testament sense.

Those who accept the Bible as true also accept the idea that the whole human family descended from one set of parents before the flood and one set of parents after the flood. Although we may not all be children

---

[5] The term *family* or its cognates appear 264 times in the NIV, whereas it appears 296 times in the KJV.

[6] For a helpful summary of three Hebrew terms used, see J. Rogerson, "The Family and Structures of Grace in the Old Testament," in *The Family in Theological Perspective,* ed. S. G. Barton (Edinburgh, Scotland: T&T Clark, 1996), 29–33. Although he dismisses the term *shevet* as an equivalent for *family*, the tribes of Israel had one common ancestor and could in that sense still be thought of as "family."

[7] For an extended discussion of this term, see *Theological Wordbook of the Old Testament,* Note 241, 105 found in Libronix Digital Library.

[8] That certainly is the sense in Gen 50:22, where the NIV translates the term "father's family," which numbered 70 according to Gen 46:27.

of Israel, we are all children of Noah and Adam. So significant is this larger sense of family that Luke's genealogy traces Jesus not just to His Jewish ancestors but all the way back to Adam. Jesus' true family was both Jewish and human.[9]

Today, few of us really feel any connection to those who lived "a long time ago in a land far away." When we think of ourselves or our families, we rarely connect our thoughts or behaviors to those distant ancestors. In contrast, Old Testament characters always thought in those connected rather than individualistic terms.

Although not generally true in America, some people still think in those terms today. A few years ago in Oklahoma City, I asked a tailor to hem a pair of slacks in preparation for a trip to Israel. When I shared the purpose of my trip, he disclosed his Palestinian Christian heritage and his hometown of Jerusalem. We launched into an exhilarating conversation that concluded with his invitation to see something special in the back room. I followed him to a wall covered with a curtain, which he pulled back. The round graphic with Arabic letters looked roughly three feet in diameter. Most of the lettering was in blue ink, but one section a short distance from the center was in black. My lack of enthusiasm must have been visibly displayed on my face because the kind tailor asked, "Do you know what this is?" I apologized for my obvious ignorance. He then said, "This is my family dating back to the first century." His ancestors were among the first converts to Christianity as Arabs. He went on to explain, "The names in blue were all Christians, and the names in black designated the part of the family that converted to Islam." He saw himself connected to his family dating back 2,000 years and still connected to those who embraced a different faith.

This tailor's understanding of family appears close to the Old Testament perspective. The Old Testament characters certainly saw themselves related to their "father's house," "clan," and "tribe" in time and space, but they also saw themselves intimately connected to their ancestors in history.[10] Passage after passage in the Old Testament documents these ancestral family connections. Even the term "son of" blurs in our modern vision because it can and often does span a number of generations. "Who's your daddy?" was not a casual question in the Old Testament and probably called forth an ancestral litany.[11]

---

[9] This would add weight to Matthew's tracing Jesus back through David to Abraham and more significance to Luke's tracing Jesus past Abraham to Adam and ultimately to God. The designation of Adam as "son of God" then connects everyone to God's family. This would also help us understand how the critics of Jesus could claim, "Abraham is our father!" (John 8:39).

[10] For an excellent treatment of the importance of the genealogies, see P. W. Crannell, " Genealogy," in *The International Standard Bible Encyclopedia,* ed. J. Orr II (Grand Rapids: Eerdmans, 1939), 1183–96.

[11] In many societies today, "Who is your father?" replaces "What do you do?" as the second question in an introduction.

Not only did the Old Testament characters and writers think about family in ever-expanding and historical connections, but God also turned their eyes forward to their ancestors in life after death. Although the phrases "rested with his fathers" or "gathered to his people" most certainly are euphemistic for death, they nevertheless carry a reality with them.[12] The sense of family thinking in the Old Testament extended beyond the grave. Even if the average rural Israelite failed to think this way, it seems that the obvious intent of the Scriptures always pointed men and women backward to God through their family lineage and forward to their family experience with God in life after death. They should never lose sight of their connections through family to God.[13]

What student of marriage, ancient or modern, has not wondered, "So, what was God thinking when He invented marriage?"[14] In the beginning God's thoughts resulted in action. He created the man and the woman from identical material and in His likeness. Both bore the image of God. Distinguished clearly from the animals, they were living images of God in every way. As they interacted with each other in the conversations and activities of everyday gardening, each one would see the image of God lived out in the other. After God's creation of them, they were to procreate other little images. God connected this collection of living images by blood and flesh. They formed a family of living images. Of course, we do not think of family in these terms today. But that is what God created "in the beginning."

When sin blurred man's vision of the image, the desire to see God's living image in one another also faded. Would Cain really have killed his little brother if he had thought deeply about destroying God's image? Genesis 9:6 indicates that one really good reason not to take a human life is that God created man in His image. Although Genesis 9 describes events after the fall, nevertheless, man still bears God's image in ways we do not fully understand. No wonder God forbade graven images of Himself and called for the destruction of all the images created by the Canaanites. God had filled the family with living images! What would happen if family members considered carefully how their words and actions affected someone in God's image?[15]

---

[12] In Luke 11, Jesus pictures Lazarus reclining with Abraham. A helpful discussion of these terms can be found in W. C. Kaiser Jr., P. H. Davids, F. F. Bruce, M. T. Brauch, *Hard Sayings of the Bible* (Downers Grove, IL: Intervarsity Press, 1996), 227.

[13] Jesus embodies this continued connection to God in John 13:3, which reads, "Jesus knew . . . that he had come from God and was returning to God."

[14] Problems in marriage transcend culture and time. Yet Jesus points everyone back to Genesis when discussing divorce in Matt 19:8, where He says, "Moses permitted you to divorce your wives because your hearts were hard. But it was not this way from the beginning."

[15] Sin blurs our ability to evaluate ourselves clearly but enables us to justify successfully our choice of words and action (Prov 21:2).

God not only created the family; He also preserved the family. When men degenerated into continued evil thinking, God saved Noah and his *family* from judgment. God could have completely started over or just preserved Noah and created a new Mrs. Noah as He had created Eve. Instead, He chose to preserve male and female representatives of humankind along with their sons and daughters-in-law. This family of eight would once again replenish the earth as all other family lines were cut off in judgment.

God demonstrates His interest in and commitment to the family in more ways than just saving Noah's family. In Gen 12:3 God made a covenant with Abraham. The covenant promises belong to Abraham and his family, but the blessings extend beyond Abraham's "father's house," "clan," or "tribe." These blessings extend to all the earthly families. In other words, all these families may expect blessings from God's promise to Abraham. Today we understand Abraham's blessing to come through Jesus Christ.

From a human perspective the whole concept of family in the Old Testament differs from our modern one. The connections resemble a chain-link fence. Pick a link and you can trace how it is somehow connected to each and every other link anywhere on the fence. Current thinking misses this interrelatedness that pervades the Old Testament. In addition, God's specific creation of the original family unit, His preservation of a single family from judgment, and His intended blessing of families through Abraham's seed point out how central families are in the purposes of God.

So many modern theological categories intersect with the family. Perhaps the following list would be a good starting place for a revised family ministry curriculum.

- Eschatology should help families think through how they come from God and will return to God.
- Anthropology should help families learn to see the image of God in one another and reorient their conversations and conduct.
- Hamartiology should help families understand the corrosive nature of sin when one family member injures another with words or actions.
- Theology proper should help families think more deeply about what it means to damage the image of God and make "the fear of the Lord" a reality in the family. Certainly we are not far from the central purposes of God when we turn the family's affection first toward their Creator and then toward one another.

Husbands and Wives

After Adam and Eve, every family begins with a husband who "leaves his father and mother and cleaves unto his wife."[16] These two will now become one flesh. As with many of the opening words in Genesis the significance of this idea unfolds with the progressive revelation of Scripture. Too often, these words are explained in exclusively sexual terms without further discussion.[17] However, the phrase has deeper and broader implications.

First, what was physically true for Adam and Eve now *becomes* true for succeeding husbands and wives. After all, God actually refashioned and enlivened a portion of Adam's flesh and bone into Eve. Adam expresses that exact thought when he declares the obvious: "[S]he is bone of my bone; flesh of my flesh." If this one thought dominated every husband's thinking, women would find themselves cared for differently than they have experienced throughout history. As I age, I find more illustrations of how this was intended to work.

I now have aches and pains in places where I did not know I had places. My arthritic hip contributes a constant reminder that I am not 35. But, when it hurts (which is all the time), I do not hit it, gouge it with a knife, shoot it with a pistol, or even talk ugly to it. Instead, I step over to the cabinet and take an Advil. I rub it with ointments, soak it in warm water, and buy an expensive mattress to sleep on. This is *my* flesh, and it hurts me so I take care of it. Should I not think of my wife in these same terms?

Malachi 2:15 seems to expand the idea of "one" even further.[18] Genesis 2 indicates that the two shall become one flesh but does not say how. In Malachi we find that *God* has created one out of two through the marriage covenant.[19] What God did literally and physically in the garden, He now does through covenant. God did not perform surgery on me to create my wife. However, we are one flesh because God made us one flesh through the marriage covenant. In the biblical text all of us inherit Adam's flesh. In the marriage covenant God makes two into one. Then He serves as an ongoing covenant witness *for* those who remain faithful and *against* those who break faith with their marriage partner. The prophet warns anyone who fails to take God's "recreation" seriously or interferes with that new union.

---

[16] The Old Testament knows nothing of homosexual marriages.

[17] This approach is justified because the apostle Paul uses the phrase in this way to warn against a sexual union with a prostitute (1 Cor 6:16). The mistake is to assume this is the full explanation.

[18] Even though this verse is extremely difficult to translate, the scholars of the NIV seem to catch the sense intended. God has in fact turned two into one. In Jesus' interpretation of Genesis 2, He appears to emphasize this idea when He says, "What God has joined together, let no one separate!" (Matt 19:6).

[19] Malachi is the first to introduce the notion that marriage was indeed a covenant. However, Jehovah and Israel as marriage partners, united by covenant, appear everywhere in the Old Testament. Malachi's warning would have little meaning unless a marriage covenant was indeed the expected and common practice.

In between Genesis and Malachi, God presents a plan to protect Israel from the sexual chaos of the ancient world. He intended Israel's sexual purity and marriage fidelity to provide a living contrast to the practices of the day. In Leviticus 18, God takes great pains to surround the married couple's sexual purity with clear boundaries.[20] By articulating this shield of forbidden practices, God also condemns the accepted practices of Egypt and Canaan. Among other things, God prohibits homosexuality and bestiality. If married couples stayed within this perimeter, they would avoid the sins that brought judgment on the Egyptians and Canaanites. Instead of unrestrained sexual behavior with unlimited partners, God presents the picture of an ageless devotion and delight in each other as lifelong marriage partners (Prov 5:18).

Of course, everywhere in Scripture God prohibits sex outside of marriage. Words like *adultery*, *fornication*, *prostitution*, and *rape* describe other unlawful practices. The assumed progressive sexual revolution of the 1970s in the United States actually turned America back toward the sexual chaos of the ancient world. The social sciences have begun to question whether this was really a good idea. Coalitions such as Smartmarriage.com have emerged to restate the case for fidelity in marriage. They build their case on solid sociological research, which seems to be more persuasive to Americans than the Bible.

We applaud their efforts. They have discovered what the Bible has presented all along. "Marriage as a social institution is regarded throughout Scripture as the cornerstone of all other structures, and hence its purity and integrity must be protected at all times."[21]

Just because God joins two people in marriage and makes them one flesh does not mean they always function as one. The Old Testament provides many examples of two people in marriage functioning as individuals without regard for the other. Abraham protects himself while risking Sarah's moral integrity. Leah survives as the unloved marriage partner of Jacob, a bigamist. Hosea pursues his unfaithful wife.

Functioning as one requires both time and practice. Applying the principles of three-legged racing or ballroom dancing might help couples understand how husbands and wives practice functioning as one. Both of these require considerable practice to be done well. Functioning as one flesh in marriage also requires practice.

No section on husbands and wives in the Old Testament would be complete without some treatment of the Song of Solomon. The Song of Solomon appears suddenly in the Old Testament without any

---

[20] God directs this section mostly to male behavior because women had fewer options or opportunities. The Old Testament presents some unruly women in Potiphar's wife, Lot's daughters, and Jezebel.

[21] R. K. Harrison, *Leviticus*, Tyndale Old Testament Commentaries series (Downers Grove, IL: InterVarsity Press, 1980), 186, as cited by T. Constable, *Tom Constable's Expository Notes on the Bible* (Lev 18:6), Galaxie Software (2003).

introduction or stated purpose. Its presence teases and haunts even the most skillful scholars.[22] Untangling the Song's structure has created a parade of ideas.[23] Idealists want to make Solomon and the Shulamite a model for marriage. Unfortunately, Solomon was a polygamist. The book's sensuous rhetoric caused many ancient rabbis to prohibit young men from even reading it. Whether we misunderstand it or ignore it, the Song of Solomon remains permanently in both the Jewish and Christian canon.

How can it be used? What was it supposed to teach us about love and marriage, if anything? At the most obvious level, we could simply accept it as an inspired love song without eulogizing the lives of those who wrote it.[24] Perhaps God intended those particular moments and events to reflect appropriate feelings and conversations.[25] As a love poem, we know it would require the writers to:

- Contemplate and reflect on each other's beauty.
- Select the most exquisitely descriptive metaphors and words.
- Edit the words and phrases to fit poetic form.
- Set the lyrics to music appropriate for a romantic song.
- Select an appropriate occasion to sing to one another. (After all, if this is the Song of Songs—its alternate title—shouldn't we assume someone sang it?)

Perhaps the best lesson from this Song comes from the time Solomon and the Shulamite spent reflecting, selecting, editing, and singing to one another. This Song of all Songs yields rich material for those wishing to show husbands and wives how to think about and communicate with each other.[26] What if couples routinely rehearsed and used the most exquisite words on each other both in private and in public?

---

[22] See G. Johnson's excellent trilogy in *Bibliotheca Sacra* (2009), where he traces the history of approaches and then offers a wonderful analysis of the structure that fits the text. Johnson's thoughtful work reminds us how helpful scholarship can be. G. H. Johnston, "The Enigmatic Genre and Structure of the Song of Songs, Part 1," *Bibliotheca Sacra* 166 (January–March 2009): 36–52; "The Enigmatic Genre and Structure of the Song of Songs, Part 2," *Bibliotheca Sacra* 166 (April–June 2009): 163–80; "The Enigmatic Genre and Structure of the Song of Songs, Part 3," *Bibliotheca Sacra* 166 (July–September 2009): 289–305.

[23] A simple Amazon search renders more than 17,000 hits.

[24] We accept the prophecy of Caiphas without endorsing his character. Perhaps the Holy Spirit lifted these lovely interludes, thoughts, and conversations from the lives of Solomon and the Shulamite without endorsing Solomon's polygamy.

[25] God accepted Psalms from David, the man after God's own heart, in spite of his adultery and premeditated murder.

[26] Could the Song of Solomon be Exhibit A for Phil 4:6–9 applied to a marriage?

This lovely song shines more brightly when set against its contemporary context. Readers should contrast the delicate words of the Song of Solomon with the rampant crude immorality of the day. The worship of Baal, Ashera, and Molech had much in common with each other but nothing in common with this song.[27] These pasty substitutes for God in the area promoted disgusting acts of brutality and sexuality. Their appeal to lust twisted and distorted God's beautiful design for sex in marriage.[28] Perhaps God lifted this song out of Solomon's and the Shulamite's experience simply to demonstrate how couples ought to think, speak, and treat each other as they moved toward and engaged in marriage. What if husbands and wives were taught to think and speak more often with such wonderful language? Who has the courage to suggest that husbands and wives sing to each other? Because the Song is in the Bible and we affirm its presence by the Holy Spirit's direction, perhaps we should find ways to use it more generally in family ministries.

Parents

Even before the words of Genesis 2 declare that the two shall become one, God connects their creation in His image with the command to be fruitful and multiply and replenish the earth. Husband and wife now have new roles as father and mother. Being a good husband and wife is the first step toward being a good father and mother. The deepest need of every child is to see mother and father working lovingly together as husband and wife. Critical remarks cut deep into the soul of a child who feels the need to connect with both parents. Children enduring divorce hopelessly fantasize various ways for mom and dad to reconcile.

But the Bible expects parents to provide more than an emotionally secure marriage environment. In the Old Testament, parents are educators in the finest and purest sense of the word. These two image bearers raise children who encounter God's image in their parents and hear God's voice in their teaching. As parents explain God to their children, they reconfirm their own understanding and faith. All good teachers know the axiom, "I always learn more when I teach." No parent can be excused from this responsibility for biblical and practical reasons.

The wonder of the Old Testament Levitical system lies in the intrinsic educational mechanisms that support parental teaching. Everyone notices the practical nature of the mandate in Deuteronomy 6. The ongoing

---

[27] A. T. Clay, "Baal," in *The International Standard Bible Encyclopedia*, ed. J. Orr (Grand Rapids: Eerdmans, 1939), 1:345–50; A. H. Sayce, "Ashtaroth," in *The International Standard Bible Encyclopedia*, ed. J. Orr (Grand Rapids: Eerdmans, 1939), 1:268–69; T. Nicol, "Molech," in *The International Standard Bible Encyclopedia*, ed. James Orr (Grand Rapids: Eerdmans, 1939), 1:2074–75.

[28] A wholesome theology of sex can be found in C. West, *Theology of the Body for Beginners* (West Chester, PA: Ascension Press, 2004).

conversations about God, His love for us, and our duty and pleasure in returning His love with all our being creates the best pedagogical instruction. Lessons learned from loving parents and reinforced over and over again can never be forgotten. The whole Levitical system offered even more to the devoted Jewish parent. Consider how the following behaviors might affect children when reverently enacted over decades of growing up:

- Resting together one full day each week
- Resting from planting and harvesting for a whole year once every seven years (an unheard-of practice anywhere else in the Ancient Near East)[29]
- Preparing every meal thoughtfully (not mixing certain things together, not eating certain tasty foods, etc.)
- Associating certain tastes with national history (bitter herbs at Passover as a reminder of slavery in Egypt, etc.)
- Traveling on holiday trips to Jerusalem or Shiloh for festivals
- Enjoying the larger gatherings of relatives and their children
- Selecting appropriate clothing
- Restricting certain cosmetics
- Regulating personal hygiene
- Circumcising personal flesh
- Visiting national shrines (such as Gilgal)
- Singing the praises of God, the history of Israel, and the prayers of the heart
- And who could forget the Tabernacle where everything embodied a lesson of some sort?[30]

Best of all, everything connected with God and love for Him in one way or another for the devout family. No one has ever devised a more

---

[29] "In spite of the extensive efforts of more than a century of study into extra-Israelite sabbath origins, it is still shrouded in mystery. No hypothesis whether astrological, menological, sociological, etymological, or cultic commands the respect of a scholarly consensus. Each hypothesis or combination of hypotheses has insurmountable problems. The quest for the origin of the sabbath outside of the OT cannot be pronounced to have been successful." D. N. Freedman, *The Anchor Bible Dictionary* (New York: Doubleday, 1996, © 1992), 5:851.

[30] Imagine the stimulation of a small child's curiosity when coming to the tabernacle and the endless stream of "What is that for?" and the necessity of the thoughtful parent providing a truthful answer.

comprehensive education system to empower parents in their responsibility to raise children.

God gave more than a mandate to parents. He provided essential infrastructure for meaningful conversations in daily and weekly routines and the annual rhythms of rural life. No one knows how many godly parents took advantage of this rich soil in which to nurture faith and love for God. We know that as a nation Israel drifted away from God. But some faithful families raised children like Joseph, Mary, Elizabeth, Zechariah, Simeon, Anna, and "all who were looking forward to the redemption of Jerusalem" (Luke 2:38).

In the Old Testament, God permeated family life. He was not conveniently relegated to Sunday morning. Nothing escaped His concern or presence. For those loyal followers of God, theological education was a family experience. Theological education was normal—not exceptional or special. Theological education connected truth and living, moment by moment, as life happened rather than a cognitive encounter in a classroom. If we could catch the spirit of the Old Testament, perhaps we would think of "theological units" rather than "family units." Although the family was certainly the centerpiece of God's creation, God Himself expected to be the centerpiece of the family in the Old Testament.

In addition to a stable emotional context provided through a healthy marriage and an environmentally saturated theological education, parents in the Old Testament were supposed to give correction and discipline. These measures varied in degree from verbal correction to corporal punishment. Uncontrollable and unrepentant youth who dishonored their parents could find themselves facing a death penalty administered by the community (Lev 20:9).

One infamous example comes through King David. Although arguably the greatest king in Israel's history, David may not have been the greatest parent. His sons were notorious problems. The author of 1 Kings inserts the curious note about Adonijah in chapter 1, verse 6a which says, "His father had never interfered with him by asking, 'Why do you behave as you do?'" David's passive approach to Adonijah may have characterized his style with other sons as well. After all, he did nothing when Amnon raped Dinah or when Absalom murdered Amnon in revenge. For a man of action, David appears paralyzed when dealing with his children. Rape, murder, or revolt should elicit some kind of a parental reprimand at least.

The advice of Proverbs stands in stark contrast to David's experience. Over and over again, the writer calls parents to discipline and correct their children. Who can escape the Lord's expectations when verses like these appear again and again?

- For these commands are a lamp, this teaching is a light, and the corrections of discipline are the way to life (Prov 6:23).
- He who spares the rod hates his son, but he who loves him is careful to discipline him (Prov 13:24).
- Discipline your son, for in that there is hope; do not be a willing party to his death (Prov 19:18).
- Folly is bound up in the heart of a child, but the rod of discipline will drive it far from him (Prov 22:15).
- Do not withhold discipline from a child; if you punish him with the rod, he will not die (Prov 23:13).
- Discipline your son, and he will give you peace; he will bring delight to your soul (Prov 29:17).

Of course some of these verses have been used to excuse severe beatings or even abuse. However, discipline and even corporal punishment need to be administered by consistently affectionate and caring parents. The teaching about discipline must be couched within the overall teaching on family. The model to follow is God the Father Himself. Unfortunately many parents see God as exclusively harsh and judgmental while failing to see His patient, providential care and love as He calls His human family and especially Israel's family back to the wholesome life He designed for them.

Discipline as envisioned in Proverbs contains an instructive ingredient. Proverbs links discipline with the path to wise living. The most natural conclusion from the collection of passages in Proverbs sees wisdom as the product of discipline. Stated another way, discipline has done her true work when the child has learned to make right choices.

- For these commands are a lamp, this teaching is a light, and the corrections of discipline are the way to life (Prov 6:23).
- He who heeds discipline shows the way to life, but whoever ignores correction leads others astray (Prov 10:17).
- Whoever loves discipline loves knowledge, but he who hates correction is stupid (Prov 12:1).
- He who ignores discipline despises himself, but whoever heeds correction gains understanding (Prov 15:32).
- Buy the truth and do not sell it; get wisdom, discipline and understanding (Prov 23:23).

Surprising to some, Job envisions God's discipline as God's blessing (5:17). The psalmist echoes His perspective in Ps 94:12. In Prov 3:11 we hear the true heart of God as the writer proclaims,

> My son, do not despise the LORD's discipline
> and do not resent his rebuke,
> because the LORD disciplines those he loves,
> as a father the son he delights in.

In other words, the Lord's loving delight surrounds discipline. The most powerful correction always comes from someone who genuinely cares about us. The Lord Himself models this central principle of discipline.

If family is truly the centerpiece of creation, then taking care of "family business" has to be a top priority. Being loyal marriage partners, theological educators, and caring disciplinarians forms essential pieces in the will of God for families. Performing these successfully depends on a healthy devotion to God who works in and through us. No wonder the first commandment is the *first* commandment. Somehow these priorities have given way to careers, accumulation of possessions, and personal amusements.

Children

Once again, to appreciate God's perspective revealed in the Old Testament, we need to divest ourselves of modern thinking as much as possible. Contemporary attitudes consider children as strictly optional. Family planning has become the standard in Western societies. Although not condoned by the Roman Catholic Church, the practice of contraception among Christians has become a common practice. Hardly anyone outside the Roman Catholic Church questions it. With modern techniques, couples choose when, where, or whether to birth little ones. If doctors suspect genetic defects, the child may face the consequences of abortion on demand.[31]

Many cultures in the ancient world had a similar casual view toward the life or death of children. Canaanite worship involved the sacrifice of children to Molech. This disgusting practice, among others, justified God's extermination of their nation and culture (Lev 18:21–25).[32] God warned Israel that she would share a similar judgment if she followed

---

[31] Statistics vary but some estimate 3,000 babies are aborted daily in the United States alone. If true, more than 1 million babies meet a premature death each year. By all descriptions, they experience a painful and merciless death. I am personally persuaded that God hears their cry and holds everyone at any level of participation or permission responsible.

[32] Of course, modern scholars question whether God justly exterminates nations. In their opinion, God is free to do anything "good" that He pleases but is unjustified to pronounce any form of judgment. They ignore His justified destruction in the worldwide flood and His final judgment upon the return of Christ.

those practices. The warning in Lev 20:2–3 calls for the death penalty for any native or alien in Israel who offers a child to Molech. Further, those who turn a blind eye to anyone who offers children to Molech find God their personal adversary. Israel ignored this threat, demonstrating they had no "fear of the Lord" in them.

Despite this warning, Solomon built an altar to Molech on a hill east of Jerusalem (1 Kgs 11:7). We do not know if he offered any of his children to Molech, but he so angered God that the kingdom would never be united after his death. First Ahaz (2 Kgs 16:3), then Manasseh (2 Kgs 21:6), offered their children as sacrifices to this moribund lifeless relic. Little Josiah stems the tide of infanticide for awhile by destroying the altars set up by Solomon (2 Kgs 23:8). Unfortunately, this practice persisted at least until the Babylonian captivity. Who can really explain why this inexcusable, revolting sacrifice continued to be popular? Isaiah, Jeremiah, and Ezekiel all regard its presence as just cause for God's judgment.

The Canaanites and the Israelites were not alone in their disdain for the helpless. Newborns in Sparta had to pass inspection by the leaders. Any baby considered unfit for any reason was simply dumped in a canyon or left in the open to be killed and eaten or to die of exposure. Modern reconstructions of Spartan society from Plutarch's *Life in Lykourgos* indicate that "Spartan babies were inspected by elders, who ordered weaklings to be cast out."[33] Romans put that same decision in the hands of the father.[34] This practice was widespread in Rome itself until Christians began taking the babies in and raising them. "Christians, however, did more than just condemn child abandonment. They frequently took such human castaways into their homes and adopted them. Callistus of Rome gave refuge to abandoned children by placing them in Christian homes."[35]

The harsh treatment of children in ancient cultures paints a dark contrast to the Genesis account of creation. From God's point of view, creation unfolds as an ongoing process. God placed within every living thing the power of "procreation." Adam and Eve were no exception, but just in case they did not pick up on the clues, God mandates,

> God blessed them and said to them, "Be fruitful and increase in number; fill the earth and subdue it. Rule over the fish of the sea and the birds of the air and over every living creature that moves on the ground." (Gen 1:28)

---

[33] A. Powell, *Athens and Sparta* (Portland, OR: Areopagitica Press, 1988), 219.

[34] "A *paterfamilias* even had . . . the right of life and death over the members of his *familia*" and they "might decline to accept a newborn child into the *familia*." E. M. Lassen, "The Roman Family: Ideal and Metaphor," in *Constructing Early Christian Families*, ed. H. Moxnes (London: Routledge, 1997), 105.

[35] A. J. Schmidt, *Under the Influence: How Christianity Transformed Civilization* (Grand Rapids: Zondervan, 2001), 53.

As surprising as it may appear to the modern mind, bearing numerous children was the individual will of God for Adam and Eve. The expected result of intercourse was conception, pregnancy, and childbirth. Intercourse, conception, pregnancy, and childbirth formed an unbroken sequence until modern times. The exception to this was childlessness, which was considered embarrassing or even a curse from God in biblical times. The Bible expresses the notion that children are a blessing *from God* (Psalms 128 and 144).

God's mandate to be fruitful and multiply precedes, but connects to, Adam and Eve's responsibility as regents over the earth. Unlike our contemporary preoccupation with career and recreation, children come first in the Genesis account. Notice the order of the words. Everyone realizes that unless God provided further instruction, that first baby must have created more than a little confusion. Could Adam and Eve have looked at each other and wondered out loud, "Now what do we do?"

Birth pain is intense but brief when compared to the challenge of raising a child to maturity. Of all living creatures, humans have the longest maturation time. Human children require seemingly endless amounts of parental guidance and attention over the entire experience. Some never mature. Conscientious parents experience a constant drain of emotional and physical energy.

After the opening chapters, Genesis provides little information about where children fit in the family experience. As God's plan for man unfolds and narrows its focus to Jacob's family, children emerge out of the shadows to center stage. Israel's theocracy places children and family in proper perspective. Although everywhere in the background, certain passages pull children fully into the spotlight. References to "little ones" and "my son" abound.

Today, after nearly 3,500 years, even barely religious Jews observe Passover. In many ways Passover would be considered the central feast in Israel. In significance, only the Day of Atonement would be considered an equal. The sacrifices for the Day of Atonement were offered at the central sanctuary and mostly out of plain sight, however, and the feast of Passover was conducted in and by each family. The home required special cleansing, prescribed clothing, and particular foods specially prepared and consumed. All of these activities were designed to stir up the curiosity of small children and embed the Lord's deliverance in the minds of everyone (Exod 12:27).

The Passover meal itself occurred on one evening, but a great deal led up to this meal. Children could, should, and would be involved in the whole process. Consider the impact of the annual rehearsal of each of the following activities on children:

- Anticipating the feast, which marked the beginning of the Jewish New Year

- Perhaps helping select a perfect little lamb or goat on the tenth day of the month
- Cleansing the home from every trace of yeast on the fourteenth day
- Watching fathers kill the little lamb on the front porch at sundown on the fourteenth
- Watching fathers smear the lamb's blood over the lintel and doorposts with a hyssop branch
- Watching as the lamb/goat was roasted (burned with fire) because it could not be boiled or eaten raw
- Eating the lamb with bitter herbs and bread without yeast
- Wearing special traveling clothes
- Burning all the leftovers in the cooking fire
- Eating the meal in a hurry
- Eating only bread without yeast for seven days following
- Having father's full attention because he was not working during these days
- Enjoying other meals, which could be prepared and cooked, as family
- Anticipating the festival (party) to the Lord, which concluded these special days

At every point you can almost hear the little "whys?" echoing through the homes of Israelites. With no work to be done, there was time to retell the story in detail along with its significance. Did every child cheerfully eat the bitter herbs? Were no complaints heard about the "bad bread"? Did butchering the prize lamb on the front porch and smearing its blood around the door offend tender hearts? No wonder God expects Israelite children to ask, "What does this ceremony mean to you?" (Exod 12:26). God emphasizes the educational aspect of both Passover and unleavened bread once more in Exod 13:8. God intended to provoke conversations and affirmations about Himself in the family. If the child failed to ask the right question for some reason, the father was to initiate the conversation.

The Passover ceremony was not the only indicator of God's connection to children. He singled out the firstborn as uniquely belonging to Him. In fact, families had to redeem the firstborn sons and male animals.

This sacrifice also called forth questions from children (Exod 13:14). Somewhere along the line, a father would need to explain how he bought his firstborn son back from the Lord. No doubt, the conversation was repeated every time he had to yield up the firstborn from his flock or herd. What child ever wanted to hear a story told just one time?

In addition to the annual Passover feast and redeeming the firstborn, the central affirmation of Israel found in the *Shema* was permanently attached to teaching children in the family. Everyone cites Deut 6:4–9 as the single most important text related to parenting. God was *the* topic of conversation, as pointed out in the previous section. Neglecting these conversations annulled God's intention to communicate His interest and involvement in every aspect of life to the next generation.

> The reason for this emphasis on the children is clear. Deuteronomy is always aimed at the next generation. It takes the present (next) generation back to the past and brings the past afresh into the present. The children are now the ones before whom all the choices are laid, and some day their children will be there and the divine instruction will confront them (e.g., 30:2). Can they learn afresh what it means to love the Lord wholeheartedly?[36]

Although the Ten Commandments are often marginalized as a mere list of do's and don'ts, the *Shema* looks way beyond perfunctory compliance. Here in this opening injunction, God invites Israel to enter into a wholehearted love relationship with Him. Jesus would later emphasize how everything hangs on this one command and its close relative (Matt 22:40). This deep, penetrating, and pervasive love for God provided motivation for everything else. Nothing makes any sense whatsoever without it. But the passionate, all-consuming love for God expected in the *Shema* cannot be impressed on any child without residing first in the parent. Sooner or later children see the hypocrisy. However, the love of parents who devote themselves to a loving God becomes contagious. We do not see this often, but when we do, we find children naturally drawn to those who possess it. Perhaps true theology was always intended to be absorbed by observation and conversation prior to formal instruction.[37]

---

[36] P. D. Miller, *Deuteronomy*, Interpretation series (Louisville: John Knox Press, 1990), 107, as cited in T. Constable, *Tom Constable's Expository Notes on the Bible* (Duet 6:6), Galaxie Software (2003).

[37] I wrote *Grandpa Mike Talks About God* in an attempt to bring God back into family conversations. In reality, this volume written directly to children is a theology proper exploring 34 different aspects of God's nature. Two 17-week semesters were in view when the 34 aspects were chosen. Each aspect is explored through story, Scripture, explanation, experimentation, and open-ended questions. Five features were chosen with a school week in mind so that the child could focus on one aspect of God's nature in five different ways. Michael S., Lawson, *Grandpa Mike Talks About God* (Ross-shire, UK: Christian Focus Publications, 2007).

One final place where children are clearly in view appears in Joshua 4:5–6. The historic crossing of Jordan would forever be connected to Passover. Forty years after their release from Egypt, on the exact day the lambs were selected (tenth day, first month), Israel entered Canaan and began their Passover preparations. Once again children are brought into the limelight as 12 large stones emerge from the riverbed and take their place as a national monument.

> The purpose of the stones was clearly pedagogical: to remind Israel for generations to come that it was *God* who brought them through the *Jordan* (cf. vv. 6–7) just as He had taken their fathers through the *Red Sea.* But how were the *future* generations to know what the stones meant? The answer is clear. Parents were to teach God's ways and works to their children (cf. Deut 6:4–7). A Jewish father was not to send his inquisitive child to a Levite for answers to his questions. The father was to answer them himself.[38]

What can we say about children in the Old Testament?

1. In creation they are the fruit of a couple bound together in one flesh by God.
2. In Psalms they are specifically a blessing from God.
3. In annual ceremony they are central participants in the Passover feast.
4. In birth order the first had to be bought back from God.
5. In the Commandments they benefit from parents who embrace the great *Shema.*
6. In history they inherit symbols of God's mighty miracles in Israel.
7. In regulation they are protected from abuse.

If that were not enough, the prophets remind Israel about God's view of children in the Old Testament. Earlier we referred to Ezekiel's condemnation of child sacrifice along with Isaiah and Jeremiah. God speaks directly through Ezekiel in no uncertain terms. Ezekiel 16:2–21 quotes God:

> And you took your sons and daughters whom you bore to me and sacrificed them as food to the idols. Was your

---

[38] J. F. Walvoord, R. B. Zuck, Dallas Theological Seminary, *The Bible Knowledge Commentary: An Exposition of the Scriptures* (Wheaton: Victor Books, 1983), 1:336.

> prostitution not enough? You slaughtered my children and sacrificed them to the idols. (vv. 20–21)

Israel may wonder why God inflicted such harsh judgment on them through the Babylonians. Did anyone besides the prophets beg for mercy on the children? Did the priests and leaders impose the death penalty called for in the law? Even those who simply ignored their neighbor's crime could not escape their responsibility to God.

In these words God shows that He maintains His fatherly connection to children in the family. Israel's children in particular, but ultimately all children, are His children because He is the Father of all mankind. Children belong to Him. Parents are not free to deal with children as they wish. Rather, they serve as trustees and guardians of little ones who belong first and always to God. Therefore, to kill one, abuse one, or mistreat one directly confronts and defies God.[39] Furthermore, as trustees, failure to provide proper nurture, education, and discipline is a breach of duty.

On a happier note, God reveals His delight with children in a neglected text in Zechariah. At the time Zechariah writes, Israel had returned from their exile in Babylon. But Jerusalem and the temple had not returned to their former glory. Further, God's prophets were still admonishing the people for their lackluster obedience to the law.

Zechariah 8:5 opens with God's declaration of His jealous love for Zion. He promises personally to return and dwell there. Jerusalem will take on two distinctively new features because of His presence. First, old people will be safe in the streets. Second, "The city streets will be filled with boys and girls playing there." Playing children are not a nuisance in this picture. God must hold them in special regard because He fills the streets of His city with them. The giggling, squealing, laughing sounds of children apparently appeal to God Himself.

Exceptions

Family is such a powerful and central feature of the Old Testament that those who find themselves without family are considered worthy of special mention and special care. Given God's husbandly and fatherly nature, we expect widows and orphans to find special protection under the law. God's concern extends beyond them to include servants in the household and foreigners living in the land.

Exodus 22 sets the standard high, firm, and straightforward. No exegetical footwork is needed to understand God's intention. He very plainly says:

---

[39] Ultimately Jesus would reinforce these words with His comments about the millstone (Matt 18:6) and their angels (Matt 18:10). Note that Jesus' purpose in John's Gospel is to reveal the Father—a family term and specifically a term implying children.

> "Do not mistreat an alien or oppress him, for you were aliens in Egypt. "Do not take advantage of a widow or an orphan. If you do and they cry out to me, I will certainly hear their cry. My anger will be aroused, and I will kill you with the sword; your wives will become widows and your children fatherless. (vv. 21–24)

As with many other regulations, Israel generally failed to observe these instructions and warnings. Hundreds of years after Moses, the prophets Isaiah and Jeremiah are still complaining about the mistreatment of widows, orphans, and aliens in the land. The abuse extended to all ranks of society, but the wealthy leaders bore particular guilt. Their position provided special opportunities, and the effects of their example permeated and spoiled the culture. Even after the exile Zechariah and Malachi issue warnings. God's call for the protection of the helpless went consistently ignored.

As with the Song of Solomon, the book of Ruth provides a lovely contrast to the apparent practices of the day. Ruth herself embodied the lowest social rank as both widow and alien from Moab. Boaz displays the God-intended grace of an Israelite landowner. Not only does he follow the legal requirement to provide the edges of his field for gleaning widows, but he also instructs his harvesters to leave extra (2:15–16). As a kinsman–redeemer, Boaz and Naomi were linked, although he was not considered first in line. His redeemer obligation to a Moabite widow would have been considered discretionary at best. This happy story results in a direct link to Jesus Christ. One can only wonder at the destiny of Israel had she embraced and practiced the values of Boaz. Could anyone reading this lovely little book miss the fact that God's Spirit used this as an example of how to observe the law?

Families formed the basic economic unit under the Old Testament legal system. As God parceled out the land of Canaan to the tribes and families, their produce provided for their own needs and their offerings to God. Although offered to God, families consumed the offerings at the central sanctuary in a festival celebration of God's goodness. Those without families (widows, orphans, men servants, maid servants, and even foreigners) were invited to the feast even though they came with empty hands. In other words, those with families became a blessing to those without a family.

In addition to this annual tithe and feast, every third and sixth year required special offerings to be collected and stored in the various towns and villages. God used these offerings for the Levites who owned no land and for the widows and orphans. The words of Psalm 146 come alive when we think carefully about these provisions: "The LORD watches over the alien and sustains the fatherless and the widow" (v. 9). This was not an empty promise.

Deuteronomy 16 describes the regulations for various festivals. God draws the Levites (who did not have a land inheritance), those without means (the widows and the orphans), and foreigners into the central worship and festivals that celebrated the blessings from God, since the Passover is essentially a family feast.[40] When Israel divided up into families for the Passover, what became of the Levite, the widow, the orphan, and the foreigner? Those outside the family units became special guests and full participants in a family unit. This central feast pulled everyone into a family celebration. Thus, each family became a source of blessing and a worship center.

Summary

Research for this chapter revealed many attempts to describe how ancient families actually lived, but few wrestled with the incredible volume of information found in the Old Testament itself. In our modern information explosion, books and points of view become obsolete almost as quickly as they are written. The average marriage and family manual of the 1950s is almost a novelty item 60 years later. In contrast, the Old Testament's multiple authors wrote their documents over roughly 1,000 years, yet they present a consistent picture of God's concern for and protection of the family. The Old Testament standards never vary in spite of cultural pressures from Egypt, Canaan, Assyria, and Babylon to name only a few. Nor are errant practices condoned although they persist over that same period.

At the end of the Old Testament, 400 years of silence separate the voices of Malachi and Jesus. Although divorce and remarriage have mostly replaced polygamy, abuse of women and neglect of children abound. One might wonder whether God has finally given up any hope for healthy families. When confronted with the current practice of "divorce for any cause," Jesus acknowledges Moses' permission as a result of their hard hearts. Then, to punctuate the conversation, He reminds them of God's unchanging point of view when He says, "It was not this way from the beginning" (Matt 19:8).

---

[40] G. J. Wenham, J. A. Motyer, D. A. Carson, R. T. France, eds., *New Bible Commentary: 21st Century Edition*, 4th ed. (Downers Grove, IL: InterVarsity, 1994).

5 New Testament Teachings on the Family

Richard Melick Jr.
Golden Gate Baptist Theological Seminary

"About one-third of my congregation is single and plan to be so for life," a friend told me, discussing the church he pastors. It is a rapidly growing, young but large and significant church with many singles and young families. Knowing many of them are successful professional people, I asked him why. It was simple—even though they are committed Christians, they have "never" seen a marriage work. Marriage brings pain and harm. Not wanting to inflict that on themselves, their friends (of either sex), and potentially on their children, they are disillusioned.

Families are in trouble today. People feel it intuitively, and most contemporary polls confirm their feelings. Many have never seen a properly functioning family and feel inadequate to serve as role models. Christians must address this problem. For a variety of reasons, God reveals Himself in the family context, and, conversely, He uses the institution of family to explain His relationships to His people. As we live out our lives in the context of a family relationship, we give testimony to those around us that God wants to live in fellowship with us. This chapter addresses the problem by providing a theology of family drawn from the New Testament. In it we will present some preliminary concerns, then address the family in the New Testament.

Preliminary Concerns

Before addressing the theology of family, it will help to speak to some important preliminary concerns.

Family in the Old Testament Compared to the New Testament

Teaching about the family occurs in both the Old and the New Testaments. Because the previous chapter focused on Old Testament teachings about the family, we should make some observations about the similarities and differences between the testaments.

Points of Similarity. First, both affirm the origins and basis of marriage and family. Genesis 2:24, describes the origins of marriage and is the first editorial about the meaning of marriage. God expected that man and woman would "leave father and mother, cleave to themselves, and become one flesh." The basic truth about family units stems from this verse: Man and woman are to commit to each other and build their families out of that commitment. The New Testament echoes this teaching. For example, in discussing divorce, Jesus stated that Moses commanded a bill of divorcement because of the sinfulness of society. Quoting Gen 2:24, He explained that God never intended divorce but rather permanent and committed marriage relationships.[1]

Second, both the Old and New Testaments use the same imagery for God's relationship to His people when they strayed from Him. Frequently, God used adultery to explain Israel's unfaithfulness. Perhaps the most explicit embodiment of this is Hosea, the prophet instructed to marry "a promiscuous wife and have children of promiscuity."[2] God even told Hosea to name his children symbolically, further identifying the people's unfaithfulness and God's attitude toward them.[3] The picture continues in the New Testament. For example, James addressed some of his readers as adulterers.[4]

Points of Difference. First, perhaps the most notable difference is the way the testaments handle genealogies. In the Old Testament, genealogy supersedes almost everything. Once again, this begins in Genesis. After the fall into sin and God's provision for covering it, God pronounced the course of redemptive history, saying, "I will put hostility between you and the woman, and between your seed and her seed. He will strike your head, and you will strike his heel" (Gen 3:15).[5] From that time forward, the book of Genesis records the differences between the line of Satan (those who followed the tempter) and the line of Seth (those who followed God's will). In addition to other functions,[6] genealogy served

---

[1] Matthew 19:1–9. Particularly, it should be noted that Jesus referred to Gen 2:24 for His argument. Note: All Scripture quotations, unless otherwise indicated, will be from the *Holman Christian Standard Bible.*

[2] Students of the Old Testament recognize a significant discussion exists about whether Hosea's wife, Gomer, was a prostitute before or after he married her. It matters little for this point of our argument.

[3] The children are, therefore, named "no mercy" (Hebrew *lo ruhumah),* 1:6; "no people" (Hebrew *lo ammi),* 1:9.

[4] James 4:4–6. James wrote to warn Christians of attitudes and actions inconsistent with their Christian profession.

[5] Most obviously, this promises redemption. It is often called the *proto evangeliorum,* or the "first good news."

[6] "Genealogies established individual identity; reflected, established, or legitimated social structures, status, and entitlements to office; functioned as modes of praise or delineations of character or even as basis of exhortation . . . Historical or biographical interest was important at times, but not at all uniformly so . . ." J. Nolland, vol. 35A, *Word Biblical Commentary: Luke 1:1–9:20,* Word Biblical Commentary (Dallas: Word, 2002), 169.

to connect families to the promised Redeemer. For example, much later (700 BC), God spoke through Isaiah that "the virgin will conceive, have a son" (Isa 7:14). No doubt devout women of every generation, and of the appropriate genealogical line, asked if one of their daughters might be "that virgin."[7]

The New Testament departs from the primacy of genealogy. It contains only two extended genealogies, both of which connect Jesus to antiquity.[8] For obvious reasons Jesus' genealogy had ultimate importance. Among other things it qualified Him to be Messiah.

Jesus fulfilled the law through His death. After that, Jewish genealogical matters had little importance. Historically, the Jewish genealogies have been lost in the myriads of political and geographical changes that so disrupted their national interests. Furthermore, no New Testament writer mentions genealogy in a way that suggests it has importance to spiritual life.[9]

The lack of genealogical focus suggests that the family exists for something other than succession. While Paul commends Eunice and Lois for providing a spiritual heritage for Timothy (2 Tim 1:5) and speaks approvingly of his own heritage (2 Tim 1:3), the family's relationship to Christ matters most. In the Old Testament saving faith had a dual perspective. It looked ahead to the coming Savior, trusting that God *will someday* provide for sins. It also looked within, trusting that God *is providing* the Savior through the genealogical succession of those in the promised line. In the New Testament, Jesus' death fulfilled that expectation.

Second, national and ethnic identity have less significance. Closely related to the issue of genealogy, this issue speaks to the need to become part of Israel's faith for salvation. God promised to bless the world through Israel (Gen 12:1–3). Individual families took that in a deeply personal way and taught their children the national and ethnocentric importance of the nation. In the New Testament, as the result of Jesus' death, the gospel message goes out without national and ethnic obligations.

Overview of Teachings Related to Family in the New Testament

Christians often look to the Old Testament for instructions about family life. The New Testament has a paucity of explicit information about it. Covenant theology represents the most systematized integration of family

---

[7] Significantly, the LXX, the earliest translation of the Hebrew Old Testament, used an articular noun for this text, making it "the virgin." Quoting the LXX after the angel appeared to Joseph, Matthew, the distinctively "Jewish Gospel" writer, wrote of Jesus' fulfillment of this promise (Matt 1:23).

[8] Matthew 1:2–16 connects Jesus to Abraham through Joseph; Luke 3:23–38 connects Jesus to Adam. The differences in the two genealogies have been much discussed. Interested readers could consult D. L. Bock, *Luke Volume 1: 1:1–9:50*, Baker Exegetical Commentary on the New Testament (Grand Rapids: Baker Books, 1994), 351–60, who explains the differences well. See also Nolland, *Luke 1:1–9:20*, 169–70 for common attempts at harmonization of the genealogies.

[9] Paul even warned Titus about preoccupation with genealogies (Titus 3:9).

and Scripture. In it, most of the patterns for family life are drawn from the Old Testament.[10] The New Testament contains almost no direct teaching on the specifics of how to raise children or the rituals that hold families together. Buswell suggests, "One reason why it is not explicitly described in the New Testament is evidently that it was so clearly understood."[11] It might be helpful to survey some of the teachings related to family.

Vocabulary. A few terms predominate when searching the New Testament teaching on family.

1. Family. The most obvious term is *family*. The Greek word *family (patria)* comes from the word root for *father (patēr)*.[12] The term can be used broadly for "family house, tribe, race, nation, or more specifically the family tree."[13] It occurs only three times in the New Testament and has multiple meanings among the three.

> Luke 2:4: Joseph took Mary to Bethlehem because "he was of the house and family line *[patria]* of David."
>
> Acts 3:25: Alluding to Gen 12:3, Peter referred to God's promise to Abraham "[a]nd in your seed all the families of the earth will be blessed." The plural word "families" translates the Greek. The meaning is wider than Luke 2:4, suggesting something more like "races" or "nationalities."
>
> Ephesians 3:15: Speaking to the issue of Jew and Gentile unity, Paul expressed his conviction that from God "every family in heaven and on earth is named." Scholars differ as to whether this means that in Christ there is one family composed of Jew and Gentile[14] or it refers to human families, all of whom derive their existence and character from God the ultimate Father.[15] It seems best to understand it as describing God as the model for every *human family*. That does not mean, of course,

---

[10] For example, the children being brought into a covenant of grace is symbolized by infant baptism, based on the Old Testament and Jewish patterns of child circumcision. Although dated, one of the best explanations of children in covenant theology occurs in J. O. Buswell, *A Systematic Theology of the Christian Religion*, vol. 2, *Soteriology and Eschatology* (Grand Rapids: Zondervan, 1962), 257–66.

[11] Ibid., 262.

[12] G. Kittel, G. Friedrich, G. W. Bromiley, *Theological Dictionary of the New Testament* (Grand Rapids: Eerdmans, 1995), 815.

[13] Ibid.

[14] "That the apostle is still writing about The Church Glorious is very clear. In fact, he supplies us with a double description of the concept *church*, calling it, first, 'the whole family in heaven and on earth,' and afterward, 'you [Ephesian believers] together with all the saints.'" W. Hendriksen and S. J. Kistemaker, vol. 7, *New Testament Commentary: Exposition of Ephesians*, New Testament Commentary (Grand Rapids: Baker, 1953–2001), 165.

[15] Lincoln states, "Here in Ephesians, 'every family on earth' should be taken straightforwardly as a general reference to family groupings, and thus to the basic relationship structures of human existence." A. T. Lincoln, vol. 42, *Word Biblical Commentary: Ephesians*, Word Biblical Commentary (Dallas: Word, 2002), 203.

> that every human family follows its model, God. It does mean that every human family should seek to live up to its model, God.

The three references to family identify three different nuances of the Greek *patria.* This last, however, has the specific reference of individual families and thus has immediate value to our study.

2. *House or household.* The most common Greek word we associate with family is "house," sometimes translated properly as "household" (*oikos).* It occurs commonly, 114 times in 106 verses. Like other words it carries different nuances of meaning in the New Testament. It can mean "(a) house, temple, (b) family, (c) lineage, (d) property."[16] The primary meaning for our purposes is a household, consisting of those who are related naturally and by marriage and slaves for whom they are responsible.[17]

Romans organized society by households, usually known by the name of a patriarch. Thus they spoke of the house(hold) of "someone." The organization correlated with the authority of the father. Frequently entire households turned to Christ in baptism, and at times the churches met in houses named by the householder.

This appears in the New Testament multiple times—for example, Cornelius at Caesarea (Acts 10:7, 24), Lydia's household and that of the jailer (Acts 16:15, 31–34), "the first converts in Achaia" were the household of Stephanas (1 Cor 16:15), Crispus the ruler of the synagogue and the hospitable Gaius (Acts 18:8; 1 Cor 1:14–16; Rom 16:23), Prisca and Aquila (at Ephesus, 1 Cor 16:19; Rom 16:5), Onesiphorus (at Ephesus, 2 Tim 1:16; 4:19), Philemon (at Colossae, Phlm 1–2), Nymphas or Nympha (at Laodicea, Col 4:15), and Asyncritus and Philologus (at Rome [?], Rom 16:14–15). Apparently households received instruction in the faith (Acts 5:42; 20:20). When the father converted to a new religion, often the entire household converted with him. Naturally the father and his household were foundational to the spread of Christianity.

3. *Father.* The Greek word for father, *patēr,* occurs 413 times in the New Testament. It predominates in the Gospels (273 times), where it is used primarily in John describing God as Father. Paul uses the term 63 times, again primarily of God.[18] The tension between a human father and God as Father points to a significant theology in the New Testament.

4. *Mother.* The Greek word for mother, *matēr,* occurs 32 times. It normally carries the meaning of a literal mother.

---

[16] J. P. Louw and E. A. Nida, vol. 2, *Greek-English Lexicon of the New Testament: Based on Semantic Domains,* electronic ed. of the 2nd edition (New York: United Bible Societies, 1996), 173.

[17] Occasionally, the derivative word *oikia* can also mean family.

[18] These numbers are based on calculations from the *Logos Bible Software, version 4* (Bellingham, WA).

In addition to texts using the vocabulary of family, a study of family in the New Testament must focus on imagery. The writers of Scripture use the institution of family consistently to describe the relationships between two of the Godhead: particularly Father and Son. They also frequently use the imagery of marriage to express the various truths of the relationships between Christ and the church.

This use of language points us in two directions. First, it reveals the usefulness of family terms to describe difficult and complex theology. Second, it reveals the usefulness of the created institutions of marriage and family to reveal theology. Thus the imagery illustrates and reveals.

Family in the First-Century Mediterranean World

The New Testament reflects its contexts, incorporating or challenging many "first-century" patterns. Many think of the first-century cultures as monolithic. The search for proper backgrounds often becomes an improper reading of one cultural situation as though it applied to all. The first century, however, contained significant and varied multicultural situations—perhaps more than any culture up to modern times.

The Roman Empire included vastly different peoples and cultures. First, because they conquered the Greeks and appreciate the Greek values of art and thought, the Romans assumed much of Greek culture and built on it. Greek "culture" incorporated a variety of cultures, but because of Alexander the Great, the empire developed a common language, architecture, and education. Rome inherited this complexity. Additionally, Rome's economy depended on conquest. The tremendous resources necessary for supporting Rome's infrastructure came largely through war. Borders kept expanding. As the frontiers moved farther from Italy, increasingly more cultures came into the Roman Empire, each with its own distinctive patterns. Because most of the New Testament is written to a Gentile setting, the pluralism of the Roman Empire characterized the young churches also.

Jewish culture remained more monolithic largely as a result of a deep commitment to the Old Testament Scriptures. Even so, the years of foreign dominance and the Jewish *diaspora* brought significant cultural challenges. Judaism remained strong because of the strength of its families. Perhaps no culture so totally integrated every aspect of life so that the family gained strength from the culture and, in turn, the culture strengthened the families.

That is not to say that Jewish families remained pure. Challenges came from the dangers of syncretism, attraction to the athletic and economic ways of the Gentile world, and the pressure to conform.[19] Furthermore,

---

[19] People like Timothy were increasingly common. Timothy's mother was Jewish, but his father was Greek (Acts 16:1).

conflict often raged between Jewish and Gentile cultures. The early church divided over whether Gentile cultural patterns or Jewish best represented Christianity.

This realization leads to an important point about the New Testament in general and Christian families in particular. When Paul addressed family issues, he did so with sensitivity to the larger questions of culture(s) and the theological heritage that brought Christianity. Thus, the New Testament does not speak to family issues in the same way as that of the Old Testament or even the other primarily Jewish documents. Non-Jewish Christians needed to know how to raise Christian families in their own cultural settings. It is important, therefore, to know specifically what questions the churches raised in order to know how to answer. Paul and others sought to meet these problems with a deep commitment to the Old Testament as understood by the resurrection of Jesus and, therefore, the lordship of Jesus.

Roman culture struggled to preserve the integrity of family. By the time of the first century, various influences produced a mosaic of ideas and related philosophies. Traditionally, the husband ruled. Under the Republic, before Christ, marriages took one of three forms, all of which fed into the hands of the husband's authority, placing the wife under the husband's hand *(manus)*. The most elaborate and solemn form, the *confarreatio,* might be considered the "most traditional" of forms. The *coemptio* involved the sale of a woman to her husband. The *usus,* living together uninterruptedly in a man's house for a year, also formed a legal bond.[20] Later, by the time of the empire, largely occasioned by woman's equality, marriage *sine manus* (without *manus*) replaced the others. Marriage *sine manus* enabled a woman to remain a part of her father's family instead of belonging to her husband's. In the earliest years it required a "legal guardianship" of males who oversaw her interests in such things as her father's inheritance. By the first century the emperor had replaced the "legal guardianship."[21]

By the end of the first century AD, family life had radically changed. Along with the traditionalists, numerous examples of more "liberated" marriages prevail. Regarding wives,

> some evaded the duties of maternity for fear of losing their good looks; some took a pride in being behind their husbands in no sphere of activity, and vied with them in tests of strength which their sex would have seemed to forbid;

---

[20] E. Ferguson, *Backgrounds of Early Christianity* (Grand Rapids: Eerdmans, 1993), 66–67.

[21] J. Carcopino, *Daily Life in Ancient Rome: The People and the City at the Height of the Empire,* trans. E. O. Lorimer (New Haven: Yale University Press, 1940), 84. Although this book is dated, its almost total dependence on primary Greek sources makes it invaluable.

> some were not content to live their lives by their husband's side, but carried on another life without him at the price of betrayals and surrenders for which they did not even trouble to blush.[22]

The decline in marriage and family was dramatic.

> Then, the woman was strictly subjected to the authority of her lord and master; now, she is his equal, his rival, if not his imperatrix. Then, husband and wife had all things in common; now, their property is almost entirely separate. Then, she took pride in her own fertility; now she fears it. Then, she was faithful; now, she is capricious and depraved. Divorces then were rare; now they follow so close on each other's heels that, as Martial says, marriage has become merely a form of legalized adultery. "She who marries so often does not marry; she is an adultress [*sic*] by form of law: *Quae nubit totiens, non nubit: adultera lege est*."[23]

Father's authority (*pater familias*) gave the father absolute control. The Royal Laws of Rome originally gave the father the right of life or death over his children.[24] Theoretically, that right remained during the time of the New Testament. Infanticide dominated in Roman life. The father had complete control over which infants lived at birth, giving preference to boys over girls. Refusing to accept an infant forced "exposure," casting the unwanted child on a garbage heap until it died. Often, because the unwanted children were girls, sex traders took in the discarded babies and raised them for prostitution.[25] The Roman answer to the age-old question of when a life is to be protected by law was simple: when the father acknowledged it. Abortions and exposure mattered little to many Romans.[26] Furthermore, if an infant did survive infancy, it had few rights until it reached adulthood.

The husband's loss of control over his wife also brought repercussions in the remainder of the family. The most dominant characteristic of family life, father's authority, gave way to anarchy. For various reasons, fathers "emancipated" their children, giving them an early inheritance and separating them from the family. As pressures exerted themselves, the literature reveals many examples of "fathers of families whose *patria potestas* was betrayed only in the indulgence shown to their children and of children

---

[22] Ibid., 90.
[23] Ibid., 100.
[24] Ibid., 77.
[25] Ferguson, *Backgrounds of Early Christianity*, 70.
[26] Ibid.

who in their father's presence behaved as they pleased, as though they were completely their own masters. . . . Having given up the habit of controlling their children, they let the children govern them, and took pleasure in bleeding themselves white to gratify the expensive whims of their offspring. The result was that they were succeeded by a generation of idlers and wastrels."[27]

Of course, not all families should be characterized in these ways. The point is that an increasing number were. That caused concern for many of the moralists, including the writers of the New Testament who sought to reinforce God's order in a world of flux.

Jewish life, however, more successfully preserved traditional family life. Even in the days of the New Testament, strict laws governed marriage and family. Ultimately marriage represented a contract between two families. As indicated in the New Testament, marriage involved two stages: betrothal and the ceremony. Rabbis discouraged couples' living together. At the ceremony the couple exchanged vows of what they intend to "do" in marriage, and they agree on a financial settlement in the case of the marriage dissolving.[28]

Similarly, they valued families. The situation requires little comment because the Old Testament sets the direction for the patterns of marriage and family in Jewish life. *The Mishnah* states:

> No man may abstain from keeping the law *Be [sic] fruitful and multiply,* unless he already has children: according to the School of Shammai, two sons; according to the School of Hillel, a son and a daughter, for it is written, *Male and female created he them.*[29]

Family life in the first century was obviously complex. This survey brings considerable historical interest, but it also paves the way for understanding the various texts of the New Testament. In determining the instructions given by the New Testament writers, the reader must be aware of the specific situation addressed. Readers must ask such questions as: Is this primarily a Jewish or a Gentile setting? Is this related to a libertarian situation in family life, or is the writer seeking to encourage more individuality in family members? Is a distinctively Christian perspective ascertainable by understanding the cultural and ethnic backgrounds? How do the various teachings have relevance to modern families and their problems? Both questions and answers require serious study.

---

[27] Carcopino, *Daily Life in Ancient Rome*, 78–79.
[28] Rather extensive "laws" and interpretations on the subject may be found in H. Danby, *The Mishnah: Translated from the Hebrew with Introduction and Brief Explanatory Notes* (London: Oxford University Press, 1933), 218–329.
[29] Ibid., 227.

Toward a Theology of Family in the New Testament

Approaching the subject in limited space requires addressing representative passages in support of general truths. Thus, although more can be said, the remainder of this chapter seeks to integrate the New Testament teaching with various parts of the preliminary observations mentioned earlier and to suggest basic directions for a theology.

Gospels

On first reading we may assume the Gospels contain extensive teaching about the family. As noted in the overview of vocabulary, however, such is not the case. The general teaching of the Gospels can be observed in two primary types of texts. First, we learn from Jesus' relationship to His family. Second, Jesus' teaching informs us of God's intent in organizing society in family units.

1. Jesus' Relationship to His Family. The Gospels reveal Jesus' attitudes of appreciation and distance. The tension requires careful thought lest one mistake one side of Jesus' teaching as the primary and move in a tangential direction.

In appreciation Jesus honored family. In debate Jesus quoted the Commandments, including honoring one's father and mother (Matt 19:18). Like the other commands, Jesus expected this one to guide relationships with human parents and, through treating them properly, to please God. Similarly, at the time of His personal physical, emotional, and spiritual crisis, He remembered His mother (John 19:25–27). In death, He thought about the needs of those who loved Him most and to whom He was most indebted on a human level. At a deeper level, however, John's record of Jesus' actions reveals his concern that Jesus could not leave this life without carrying out His first responsibility, that to His parents.

The circumstances of His life may reveal more about His concern for His family than a cursory reading of the texts provide. For example, after Jesus' appearance at the temple at age 12, His father Joseph disappears from the gospel story. The Gospel writers resume Jesus' life with Him headquartered in Capernaum rather than in His boyhood home, Nazareth. Further, Jesus had at least four brothers and some sisters.[30] Most likely, Jesus, the oldest Son, assumed responsibility for His family after the premature death of His earthly Father, Joseph.[31] Without doubt, Jesus honored the Commandments and patterned His own life after them. He respected His family.

---

[30] Matthew 13:55. The early church debated the relationship of Jesus to these named "brothers and sisters" in part because of the desire to preserve the perpetual virginity of Mary. There is no need for such exegesis because there is no concern about Mary's remaining a virgin after Jesus' birth. More to the point, these should be understood as "half brothers and half sisters" because they had a different father.

[31] Given Jesus' siblings included at least six, and probably more, Jesus' care for them may explain from a human perspective why He did not begin His ministry until He was 30 years of age. (Jesus would have been in His 20s before the youngest grew to be a teenager.)

However, Jesus distanced Himself from His family. At His visit to the temple, He explained to Joseph that He must be about His [real] Father's business.[32] At the first recorded miracle, He carefully told His mother that He had not come to fulfill her expectations of Messiahship. His hour had not come (John 2:4). Many question the way Jesus related to His mother on this occasion, but the Greek text is not as harsh as many today read into the scene.[33] Jesus had a higher obligation than doing what His mother asked.[34]

2. Jesus' Teaching about Family. In His teaching Jesus also indicated that His relationship to God took priority over family relationships. Once His mother and brothers wanted to meet with Him, apparently to dissuade Him from the intensity of His ministry. He replied, "My mother and My brothers are those who hear and do the word of God" (Luke 8:21). Similarly, Jesus knew His ministry had a divisive—and unifying—element. He would divide "father against son, son against father, mother against daughter, daughter against mother" (Luke 12:53).

Other texts reveal this tension, but these suffice. The point made is theological, found in the tension illustrated earlier. Those who do not care for their families fail to honor God and His commandments. However, those who fail to honor God's will for their lives regardless of cost, even to family, fail to enter the kingdom of God. The Gospels reveal a higher concern than family. The kingdom of God must have top priority. Even family relationships, as important as they are, should not deter one from fulfilling God's plan.

As an extension of Jesus' teaching, we should consider the many parables about family life. Parables describe earthly situations to teach about God's kingdom. The parables instruct in two ways. First, they teach us how to honor God—to be a part of His family. Second, they instruct by illustrating what family life should be like through both positive and negative pictures. For example, the Prodigal Son (Luke 15:11–32) demonstrates the Father's heart for erring children in spite of the prevailing Jewish cultural demands that a father sever relationships with one who so disrespected Jewish life. We should read the parables for both kinds of instruction: what it is like in heaven and what it should be like on earth.

Epistles

Although written by various authors, the epistles contain a uniform teaching about the family. The nature of epistles makes them particularly important in forming a theology. They are "answers to questions,"

---

[32] Luke 2:49.

[33] Literally, it reads, "What to me and you?" This construction asks on what basis Mary is asking Jesus for help.

[34] In this light, three times "hour" occurs in John, each with significance. Here and in John 7:1, Jesus indicates that He operates on His Father's "clock," not theirs. In John 13:1 Jesus realized that His hour had come.

theoretical or actual, posed by the readers.[35] Three primary texts address family relationships, although others contribute significantly.[36] Each of these makes a strong emphasis in different areas. For an overview of family relationships, the most extended and detailed passages are Eph 5:22–32 and Col 3:18–22.

Ephesians and Colossians contain almost identical content. They follow a similar format, although each puts emphasis on different relationships. One interprets the other and vice versa.

The passages cover more than modern readers expect. Three sets of relationships occur. Contemporary readers expect to see husbands and wives and parents and children. Masters and slaves occur as well. The ancient world completely understood grouping these three into a family. "The family consisted of the entire household, including husband, wife, children, sometimes other relatives, and slaves."[37] Proper family relationships involved caring well for all three mentioned in these epistles.[38]

Several introductory comments help put the passage in proper context. First, the passages continue the major thought Paul began earlier (Eph 5:18; Col 3:16).[39] The domestic codes directly relate to the "filling of the Spirit" and "the Word of Christ dwelling richly within." Thus proper family relationships express, in part, a vibrant relationship with God. In Ephesians Paul reveals that such relationships are demanded as part of proper submission to God's economy, whereas in Colossians he explicitly states that wives should submit. In other words, proper family relationships evidence God's economy within the church and to the world outside.

Second, the three couplets of the domestic code follow an exact pattern in both texts. In each case and in both epistles, Paul addressed the hierarchically inferior first (thus "wives . . . children . . . slaves"). His concern is for proper order. Each occurs in parallel with the hierarchically superior (thus "husbands . . . parents . . . masters"). He clearly has instructions for the hierarchically superior because they often receive the longer and more pointed, instruction.

Third, the writing contains remarkable balance. The law of the "first mention" carries significant weight in terms of the primary commands to wives, children, and slaves, but the law of "length of address" brings

---

[35] One of the best and most readable books addressing this and other genre of the Bible is G. D. Fee and D. Stuart, *How to Read the Bible for All Its Worth* (Grand Rapids: Zondervan, 2003).

[36] Ephesians 5:22–32; Col 3:18–4:2; 1 Pet 3:1–7.

[37] Ferguson, *Backgrounds of Early Christianity*, 65.

[38] Paul does not include relatives in his list, but the fact that slaves occur reminds us of the first-century context. Slavery dominated the economy. Although it is unlikely that many Christians owned slaves, some certainly did as evidenced in the Philemon/Onesimus relationship.

[39] The writing style of each differs. Ephesians contains one long sentence introducing the domestic code. Colossians makes several independent sentences.

balances to the weight of the text. Structurally and in content, Paul accepts a hierarchy, but he also recognizes equality.

1. Wife/Husband Relationships.[40] In this most extended discussion about husbands and wives, Paul reveals his ultimate concern. Because chapter 6 in this book specifically addresses the theology of marriage, only a few comments occur here.

This passage speaks to the heart of marriage relationships. Because of the chiastic structure of the passage, the "center member" of the construction receives emphasis.[41] Verse 32 expresses that central point: Paul has Christ and the church in mind. Genesis 2:24 states, "[F]or this reason a man will leave his father and mother and be united to his wife and they will become one flesh." "Leaving" and "cleaving" express commitment to each other. "Becoming one flesh" identifies the sexual relationship but certainly involves more. Sexual expression always involves more than the physical act (1 Cor 6:13, 18). With this Old Testament text at the center of the passage, Paul explains that marriage pictures Christ and the church. When asked, "Why marriage?" the answer was "Christ and the church." Marriage reveals truths otherwise not so easily grasped. Properly functioning marriages best reveal how Christ relates to His people (sometimes even called His bride).

The commands to each member of the relationship have deep significance. Addressing wives, Paul commands them to "submit" (Ephesians infers this from an immediately preceding participle; Col 3:18 makes it definite). Addressing husbands, Paul commands them to love in such a way as to bring the wife to her total life fulfillment ("holy and blameless"). The greatest joy of a husband is the fulfillment of his wife.

Many remark about the magnificence of this passage. Higher words and concepts cannot be found. They are the essential guidelines for a proper, and happy, relationship. Yet Paul's commands also address concerns of the Gentile culture to which he wrote (Ephesus and Colossae). Earlier we described the tension in Roman families during this time. The changing culture challenged the *patria potestas* (authority) of the father. Although it is uncertain how—or even if—some of the tensions described there actually apply to these specific contexts, clearly some assumptions are legitimate. Potentially, some wives sought independence. They saw their husbands as roadblocks to their total fulfillment as persons. At the least some thought they should have independent standing in the world and the church. Paul countered this attitude by explaining the need to submit.

---

[40] This and the next three headings follow the order of the biblical texts.

[41] Chiasms are named for the Greek letter "X." In literature it represents a structure where two themes are addressed in four [or more] statements, two [or more] of which are parallel. Here the structure is A [wives]; B [husbands]; C [Christ and the church]; B′ [husbands]; and A′ [wives]. The parallel statements are interrupted by a center member, C, which because it is singular, receives special emphasis.

Three elements in the passage explain submission. First, the word *hupotassō* ("submit") implies a voluntary submission for the sake of order. It is normally used in a "task" context where individuals have different roles to play. The voluntary element of a wife's submission is that she accepts God's plan and organization for the family, including her husband's headship. Her submission is "in the Lord."[42] Second, her submission has a different character from the others in the domestic code. Children and slaves are to "obey" (*hupakouō*). The word suggests a more comprehensive attitude of "servitude." Third, the wife's role pictures that of the church, whose primary responsibility is to follow Christ who loves them so. It is a high and holy calling in both cases.

However, husbands may long for the days of *patria potestas*. They may blame modern life for the decline in family order and assume God wishes to correct it by authoritarianism. Such is *not* the case. Although clearly the husband bears the responsibility for the wife and family, he is the head,[43] his focus is more to enable than to rule. Like Christ, he gives serious attention to his wife's being what she should be. Thus he must love with a truly "Christian" love.

The passage displays a perfect balance of emphasis both theologically and culturally. Theologically, marriage reveals Christ and the church. There is no higher calling and responsibility for Christian people. If and when marriages fail, the world loses its most available picture of Christ and the church.

2. Child/Parent Relationships. The second set of relationships is parent/child. Once again, child relationships challenged the authority of the father.[44] As usual in these sections, the subordinate receives the first command: obey. In Ephesians the textual support drawn from the Ten Commandments reinforces Paul's charge. The commandment comes with a promise—according to Paul it is the first one to do so. Honoring father and mother bring personal satisfaction ("it may go well with you") and long life ("you may have a long life in the land"). Here Paul follows the LXX rather than the Hebrew text of Exod 20:12. The LXX adds these two promises to the original command, thereby providing the earliest interpretation of the Hebrew text. Most likely the promises are like proverbs. They are axioms so that,

---

[42] Ephesians says somewhat ambiguously "as to the Lord," leading some naïvely to interpret this as "when my husband acts like the Lord." This is a gross misinterpretation, as Col 3:18 clarifies: "as is fitting in the Lord."

[43] Of particular help in defining this term is G. W. Knight III, *Role Relationships Among Men and Women: New Testament Teaching* (Phillipsburg, NJ: P&R Publishing, 1989). See also J. Piper, W. Grudem, *Recovering Biblical Manhood and Womanhood: A Response to Evangelical Feminism* (Wheaton: Crossway, 2006), and A. Köstenberger, *God, Marriage, and Family: Rebuilding the Biblical Foundation* (Wheaton: Crossway, 2004). Many of the resources of Council on Biblical Manhood and Womanhood also discuss these issues.

[44] Hoehner points out that the Greek word with its article probably means these are beyond infancy and certainly able to exert a choice to obey. H. W. Hoehner, *Ephesians: An Exegetical Commentary* (Grand Rapids: Baker Academic, 2002), 786.

if kept, there is a greater likelihood of blessing. "As a general rule, obedience and honor foster self-discipline, which in turn bring stability, longevity, and well-being; disobedience and dishonor promote a lack of discipline, which in turn bring instability, a shortened life, and a lack of well-being."[45]

In turn, parents are cautioned against provoking anger in their children. The plural word "fathers" suggests Paul includes mother and father here, although as in general in Scripture, the husband bears the responsibility for the family. The form of "making angry" carries the nuance of unnecessary anger. No parent can keep a child from being mad on occasion. Fathers must, however, treat children in such a way that they have no reason to be angry at the parents. Colossians indicates the potential of discouragement as a result of the fathers' ill-treatment of their children.

Fathers must educate and correct them in the things of the Lord. The passage suggests that the fathers serve as agents of the Lord in accomplishing His purposes.[46] Clearly children need both positive instruction and loving correction.[47] Childhood education should be within the sphere of the Lord—that is, it must be thoroughly Christian. Fathers only accomplish this because of their relationship to the Spirit (Eph 5:18) and God's Word (Col 3:16). The contrast between drunkenness and the Spirit in Ephesians suggests that the fathers have learned the difference between spiritual and natural sources of satisfaction. They order the family out of their own self-discipline in matters of the Spirit and the Word (Eph 5:18 and Col 3:16 together). Thus fathers treat children the way they have been treated by the Lord and, step by step, encourage their children to walk with God.

Every age faces tensions caused by a clash of generations. The first century was no different. The idea of family faced new challenges from both wives and children. Fathers and husbands had to take seriously their charge to be like Christ in holding order together. The order of God's creation should characterize the church. That means maintaining balance between authority and liberty, between structure and freedom. The theological principle found here is that God holds the father responsible for the family. A wise father recognizes both his stewardship of the lives entrusted him and the necessity of preserving God's plan for society through the home.

3. Servant/Master Relationships. Finally, Paul included servants in the household. Such was common in the first century, although it is likely that few Christians could afford slaves. Slaves are to obey. They do so from the heart. Their obedience ultimately is to God rather than their masters, and

---

[45] Ibid., 792.
[46] Ibid., 798–99.
[47] The two words occur together here: *paideia* is Greek for "training." The other word, *nouthesia*, suggests correction.

thus the command comes with spiritual importance. Indeed, it, too, is the outworking of the presence of the Spirit and the Word.

Conversely, masters must treat slaves as they would wish to be treated in the same circumstances. Consideration that they have their own Heavenly Master, and are therefore slaves themselves, creates humility and a sense of equality. Significantly, the biblical writers did not advocate the abolition of slavery directly.[48] Rather, Paul's encouragement took a relational, spiritual, and theological direction. As he reminded Philemon, the slave Onesimus was his brother. The implications of that relationship correct all others.[49]

Because modern family life does not include slaves, little need be said about this portion of the house code. Two comments deserve mention, however. First, in modern life we do not find an actual parallel to this situation. Some have applied it to the workplace, yet the principles generally do not apply because of the freedom employees have. All Christians should work enthusiastically and from the heart as a stewardship of life, which Paul commends in these verses, but these principles also occur elsewhere in the Bible. Second, the pattern of this instruction follows that of the others and has the same goal: order in the family. Wise masters recognize the tensions imposed by the economic situation (slavery) and the dignity of all human life, and seek to preserve order harmoniously. However, slaves must recognize these same economic conditions and, acknowledging the sovereignty of God, seek to be true to their Heavenly Master as they expend their life energies on earth.

4. Other Texts. Other passages in the epistles correlate well with these. Some extend the principles into specific cultural situations, and some assume the theology taught here. For example, in the Pastoral Epistles Paul addressed family life in light of the cultural libertarianism. In both Timothy (1 Tim 3:4) and Titus (2:1–10) Paul recognized the difficulty of developing the church in cultural confusion. Timothy pastored in Ephesus and Titus in Crete. Both epistles reveal specific cultural inroads into the church that threatened church and family order. Everyone knew the "freedoms" of Crete where people gave themselves to liberty, licentiousness, and luxury (Titus 1:10–14). The settings provided unique challenges to the gospel. They also threatened the integrity and dignity of human life, especially expressed in the family and the church.

Paul addressed the problems on two levels. First, there were theological concerns because the libertarian lifestyles came from errant teaching.

---

[48] To do so would have likely encouraged a slave revolt. Prior slave revolts ended in the slaughter of thousands of people, primarily slaves.

[49] For further information on the slave/master relationship, see R. R. Melick Jr., *Philippians, Colossians, Philemon*, vol 32, The New American Commentary: An Exegetical and Theological Exposition of Holy Scripture (Nashville: Broadman, 1991), 315–20, 341–43. Paul provided three motivations for heartfelt service to the masters: (1) the Lord will reward them; (2) they are ultimately serving the Lord; and (3) anyone who does wrong will be paid for their wrong. Of course, the attitude of Scripture is clearly against the practice of slavery.

> The false teachers, in addition to their recruitment of younger widows (5:13), may also have targeted households where, according to Greek and Roman custom, a man held formal authority, but which were in disarray. They seem to have preyed on houses where the women were already corrupt (2 Tim 3:6) and failed to take care of their relatives (1 Tim 5:4, 8,16). They were also successful in households where unorthodox teaching went unchallenged (2 Tim 3:6; Titus 1:11).[50]

Proper Christian theology taught the opposite of these social manifestations encouraged by heresy and the prevailing philosophies. The answers provided consistently reflect the more extended teaching of Eph 5:22ff.

Second, Paul had concerns that the church not disqualify itself in the eyes of society. Society expects Christians to live in accord with the highest and best principles. Indeed, many turn to Christ after experiencing the bankruptcy of non-Christian approaches to life. The church as the representative of Christ on earth must maintain proper order first because of its very nature and second because of its witness. This was a major concern of early Christians.[51]

> If women and slaves are insubordinate, the message about God's saving work in Christ Jesus will be lost to those outside the church who will not be able to see beyond the threat that Christianity poses to their positions of power and privilege. Paul believes that Christians must look beyond their own, often subordinate, social positions, to the overriding need of everyone for the gospel.[52]

Thus two major theological principles emerge, as evidenced in the teaching about family. First, the Christian home should express the order God expected when He created us and put us into family units. Second, for Christian witness, the family should be ordered God's way in spite of the often prevailing cultural winds to the contrary.

This discussion leads to one final relevant and crucial point. The family pictures God. We may well ask the question of marriage and family: Why did God create us and organize us into family units? The answer may be given on two fronts. First, the properly functioning family brings the greatest human joys imaginable. At the same time, the family provides the greatest opportunity to develop personally and spiritually into complete

---

[50] F. Thielman, *Theology of the New Testament: A Canonical and Synthetic Approach* (Grand Rapids: Zondervan, 2005), 421.

[51] See for example these biblical texts, which contain a strong sense of witness to the world: 1 Cor 11:13–16; 1 Thess 4:9–12; and Acts 15:19–21 (for witness to the Jews).

[52] Thielman, *Theology of the New Testament*, 428. Thielman also points out that the domestic codes are similar to Greek philosophy but with some major differences. The philosophers were valued for their insights about the greatest good for the individual and society and the expectations for family life. See also Thielman, 383–85, 420.

maturity and fulfillment. Second, the properly functioning family reveals God. The first point witnesses to the fact that God is found in the family. The second speaks to the fact that God reveals Himself to the world through the family.

Both of these point to the importance of family life. If families fail, people fail. If families fail, people have a much harder time understanding God and coming to Him. Out of failure we approach God with a lack of trust, a fear of being hurt, reservations about commitment, and a focus on individual survival disregarding human community. When families succeed, it is an easy and natural movement from the family on earth to the family of God. The apostle Paul suggested as much when he wrote that it is from the Father that "every family in heaven and on earth is named" (Eph 3:15).[53] Every family bears the responsibility of looking like God.

Conclusion

In this chapter we have tried to present the contours of a theology of family. We have suggested the following axioms:

- There is far less material on the family in the New Testament than the Old Testament.
- The New Testament applies the theology of family rather than addresses the specific duties of family members.
- Family members must honor other family members, as Jesus showed and taught us.
- The kingdom of God may bring separation from family members. The family of God takes precedent over human families.
- Proper order in the family is God's will. It expresses God's will in the creation of the family, and it bears powerful Christian witness to the world.
- The Christian family must take seriously its calling to represent God on earth. This includes proper order and function of all family relationships.

Much more could and should be said. The battle to keep family life what God intended passes from generation to generation. It is necessary, therefore, that each generation of Christians knows God's instructions about family life. Through the instruction of the Word of God and the power of the Spirit, families can be what God intended.

---

[53] Note the previous brief discussion of this verse. Whereas many understand it to speak of the church, the spiritual family, many others take it to mean each earthly family.

6 A Theology of Marriage

Curt Hamner
Between Two Trees Ministry

Introduction

Who would have thought just 50 years ago that the Supreme Court of so many countries would be wrapped in controversy over something so basic as the definition of marriage? Many European countries have succumbed to the postmodern position of redefining it to fit into a more political or socioeconomical definition, one that does not leave anyone out and allows for wider boundaries. The problem with such politically correct positions is that they are based on presuppositions that are anything but biblical. What a farce to think that the one who designed and created the institution of marriage itself is left out of its definition altogether.

Our study of the theology of marriage is based on God's Word and His intent for the institution. It certainly stands in juxtaposition to what secular authorities espouse because ours carries the potential of illuminating our relationships and the study of our relationships was meant to illuminate our understanding of God. Every time a couple walks back up the aisle after completing their vows to one another, they begin a theological adventure that unfolds the greatest of eternal mysteries. With big smiles and thrilled countenance, they make their way up the aisle, out the door, and into the future "for better or worse, for richer or poorer, in sickness and in health." On each side of the aisle a collection of family and friends cheers them on. Many are cynics, however—not so much about that couple but about marriage itself. Statistically, more than half of the audience has been there themselves only to see it crash and burn. Others have watched from the sidelines or are children of divorce. They all hope it is happily ever after, but too many have deep questions. Inside and outside the church there are many questions about the vitality and sustainable of marriage.

The state of marriage in Western culture is in need of a reformation, a call back to the biblical foundations that have been part of our Judeo-Christian culture since the days of our country's independence. A theology of marriage upon which a family, church, and society is built is critical to our survival. The church needs a worldview of marriage that is anchored in the Scriptures and not derailed by those with a postmodern agenda.

The Need for a Theology of Marriage

The necessity of a theology of marriage is critical to not only the family ministry of a church but also to the church at large. Many theologies are polemic in nature and written as a response to a doctrinal lapse or a cultural hot button. The most helpful are written to establish the foundation of right thinking (orthodoxy) and right living (orthopraxis). Although there are many theological challenges to marriage in the church and culture at the beginning of the twenty-first century, it is my desire to establish a theological foundation for creating healthy marriages in the church, extending into the culture. There is a tension in the church today as to whether marriages are in need of more propositional information or the tools to apply existing biblical truth to their relationships. The intention of this chapter is to provide the background for both. Out of a sound theological base, leaders will design and evaluate programs that will begin to reform our divorce-prone culture.

When the divorce rate of the American culture is equal to that which is found in the church, we have a tragedy. It is indeed a social dilemma, but even more so it is a theological travesty. From the beginning of time, the marriage relationship has been central to God's revelation of Himself as a God of community and a God of redemption. It is a theological statement. From the Genesis account, when God declared the creation of man as male and female as being "very good," to the marriage supper of the Lamb recorded in the book of Revelation, the image of marriage serves to reveal both the *imago dei* and God's divine work of redemption. It is such a strong and repeated analogy that many refer to marriage as having a sacramental impact.[1] Augustine, in his work *On the Good of Marriage,* listed sacrament as the third of the benefits of marriage. His use of "sacramental" was in the mode of reflecting divine grace, displayed in marriage as it depicts the relationship of Christ and his church.[2] Similarly, it correlates with the relationship between husband and wife.

---

[1] R. Jolley, "Marriage," an unpublished sermon in the series Sacraments (Santa Barbara Community Church, 2008).

[2] Augustine, "On the Good of Marriage (De bono Conjugali)" in *The Nicene and Post Nicene Fathers,* ed. P. Schaff, first series vol. 3 (Grand Rapids, MI: Eerdmans, 1980), 397–413.

As a social institution throughout global cultures, marriage may take on a variety of forms (e.g., monogamy, serial monogamy, polygamy, etc.). However, God's original design has always been one man and one woman joined together for life. Years since its inception, mankind has sought to redefine this arrangement and confuse God's original intent. Over the centuries marriage has taken the sociological intent of propagation of the race; reproduction of a workforce; the security of faithful sexual purity; or, as in Western culture of the twenty-first century, personal happiness and fulfillment. From the beginning God ordained marriage with a revelatory purpose: to display the glory of the triune God in community as a God of gracious redemption. Although marriage has evolved into an important social institution, at its core it is a theological expression by the God of creation and human redemption.

If marriage is not held in high esteem in the church as a theological expression, it will never hope to have a positive impact within culture. The church still maintains the strongest position for defining and protecting marriage in its theological context. Central to this stewardship is the starting point of marriage, the wedding ceremony. Although the church is often disregarded or marginalized by our culture at large, weddings are still regarded as being primarily ecclesiastical events because research shows that 80 percent of weddings are still held in churches and officiated by clergy.[3] The theologically astute, culturally aware church must make marriage ministries a significant priority in their programming efforts. Furthermore, healthy marriages are directly associated with spiritual maturity and should be a clear initiative of biblical discipleship. It is no mistake that included in the qualifications for an elder is the "husband of one wife." Church leaders should have exemplary marriages demonstrating spiritual maturity and devotion. Giving consideration to the marriages of their leaders and the premarital preparation of couples who marry in their church should be the minimum consideration of programmed marriage ministries.

Although it may sound archaic to those who are not from its denominational persuasion, the Anglican *Common Book of Prayer* gives grave but theologically sound warning to those who enter into holy matrimony as a theological institution:

> Dearly beloved, we are gathered together here in the sight of God, and in the face of this congregation, to join together this man and this woman in holy matrimony; which is an honourable estate, instituted of God in the time of man's innocence, signifying unto us the mystical union that is betwixt Christ and his Church; which holy estate Christ adorned and beautified with his presence, and

[3] P. Hart, *Research for Human Rights Campaign* (Washington, DC: Hart Research, 2003).

> first miracle that he wrought, in Cana of Galilee; and is commended of Saint Paul to be honourable among all men: and therefore is not by any to be enterprised, nor taken in hand, unadvisedly, lightly, or wantonly, to satisfy men's carnal lusts and appetites, like brute beasts that have no understanding; but reverently, discreetly, advisedly, soberly, and in the fear of God; duly considering the causes for which Matrimony was ordained.[4]

Weddings and marriage ministry are the work of the church. It is in "holy matrimony; which is an honourable estate, instituted of God in the time of man's innocence, signifying unto us the mystical union that is betwixt Christ and his Church."[5] That statement ought to be on the mind of every wedding coordinator, marriage mentor, and pastor. It should also be clearly stated to every couple who enters our churches.

The Institution of Marriage

Throughout the history of the Scripture, the marriage relationship is central to the story of the Bible; it is the story of passion, fidelity, and oneness. It all begins with the love story of God, flows through the first couple in the garden, and continues in the analogy of the community of faith (e.g., Israel in the Old Testament and the Church in the New Testament). The story is refreshed and renewed at every wedding as a man and woman are drawn together, committing themselves to become one, as husband and wife.

The Marriage Analogy in the Old Testament

The marriage analogy of God's redeeming love for Israel in the Old Testament is a recurring theme. Early in the history of the nation, God declares why He loves the nation and has chosen it as His own. Clearly in the prophets He declares His love like a husband for His chosen wife. Isaiah 54:5 states, "For your husband is your Maker, Whose name is the Lord of hosts; And your Redeemer is the Holy One of Israel, Who is called the God of all the earth" (NASB). In the days of Solomon, the King wrote to his lover of his passionate pursuing love, which has been seen through the ages, at least in part, as a celebration of Yahweh's love for Israel.[6] The marriage analogy is drawn most clearly in the infidelity of Israel in pursuing other lovers (foreign deities). Like a betrayed husband, The Lord remembers the days of Israel's faithfulness. In Jer 2:2 we read, "Go and proclaim in the ears of Jerusalem, saying, Thus says the Lord, 'I remember concerning you the devotion of your youth, the love of your

---

[4] Church of England, *The Common Book of Prayer* (London: Everyman's Library, 1999, 1662), 424.
[5] Ibid.
[6] M. H. Pope, *Song of Songs*, The Anchor Yale Bible Commentaries (New Haven, CT: Yale University Press, 1995), 89.

betrothals, Your following after me in the wilderness, Through a land not sown'" (NASB). But Israel took no regard to the covenant and the one who loved her like a bride and faithfully pursued her even in her disobedience, as she pursued other deities. Ezekiel 16:32 declares, "You adulterous wife! You prefer strangers to your own husband!" (NIV).

Perhaps nowhere is it clearer than in the assignment given to Hosea to illustrate to the people the grave impact of their unfaithfulness when he is told to take a prostitute as his wife and to continue to pursue her in her infidelity and bring her back as his wife. Isaiah declared, "For your husband is your Maker . . . For the LORD has called you, like a wife deserted and wounded in spirit, a wife of one's youth when she is rejected, says your God." "I deserted you for a brief moment, but I will take you back with great compassion" (Isa 54:5–7 NASB). Through a variety of passages in the Old Testament, God declares His passionate, faithful love for his beloved Israel. The analogy cannot be missed or overestimated.

The Marriage Analogy in the New Testament

With the clarity of this Old Testament imagery in mind, John the Baptist, as the forerunner of Jesus, draws on the marriage/wedding analogy in John 3:29. "In light of the Old Testament background where Israel is depicted as 'the bride of Yahweh' (cf., e.g., Isa 62:4–5; Jer 2:2; Hos 2:16–20 . . .), [John] the Baptist is suggesting that Jesus is Israel's awaited king and Messiah. The main focus, therefore, is upon Christ as the bridegroom with John simply being his friend whose task it is to assist him."[7] John was the "best man," securing the rightful place for the bridegroom. Throughout His ministry, Jesus correlates His person and ministry to the bridegroom, continuing the marriage/wedding analogy into the New Testament. Even His prophetic words of His own return both in parable and by analogy (e.g., Matt 25:5–7; Mark 2:19–21) are of the coming of the bridegroom for his bride.

The apostle Paul continues this thought when teaching on the intimate relationship between the submitting church and Christ as its loving head. He leans so heavily on the marriage analogy that he clarifies, "I am speaking with reference to Christ and the church" but finishes by exhorting the Ephesian husbands and wives to apply what he has said to their marriage relationship. Both Paul and Jesus use the Genesis account as the foundation for their teaching of marriage—Paul, when he speaks of the "roles" of husband and wife in illustrating the church's relationship to Christ (Eph 5:31), and Jesus, when confronted with the question of the permanence of marriage in the divorce debate. He responds, "Have you not read, that He, who created them from the beginning made them male and female" (Matt 19:4). Finally, at the end of time, the apostle John prophesies of the

---

[7] A. J. Köstenberger, "John," in *Commentary on the New Testament Use of the Old Testament*, ed. G. K. Beale and D. A. Carson (Grand Rapids, MI: Baker, 2007), 437.

return of Christ for His church, the bride (Rev 21:9), and the coming marriage supper of the lamb (Rev 19:7–9).

The apostle Paul is clear that the purpose and definition of marriage are tied to the historical creation of man in the garden and directly related to the redemptive work of Jesus Christ on the cross, turning back the curse of Genesis 3. However, it is also clear that there is an inscrutable mystery in marriage. That mystery is tied both to the origins of marriage, as the revelation of God in the creation of man and woman, and to living out that analogy in the daily promises that make up a marriage relationship. The purpose of marriage then is to glorify God, revealing Him as a God of relationship and redemption. Marriage can then be defined as "an exclusive heterosexual covenant between one man and one woman ordained and sealed by God preceded by a public leaving of parents, consummated by sexual union issuing in a permanently mutually supportive partnership."[8] Given this high view of marriage, the application to our own lives and ministry in the local church is of critical concern.

New Testament Teaching on Marriage

Although the previous chapter dealt in detail regarding this topic, suffice it here to say that the centrality of the marriage relationship appears to be a significant element of spiritual formation and discipleship to the writers of the New Testament. The question of how to live as Christ followers in marriage, pursuing sexual purity, roles, and responsibilities, not to mention the significant nonmarriage-specific New Testament principles of relationship, applied to this closest of relational ties. It is evidenced to a greater degree when the issue of spiritual maturity is delineated for choosing elders. The "above reproach" kind of a leader is "the husband of one wife," which most believe relates more to the godly character of the leader, as a faithful husband, than it does to his relationship to divorce or polygamy.[9]

The clarity of the New Testament teaching on the marriage relationship must be seen in context to its theological background, the divine work of creation and redemption. The complexity of this assignment is seen in Paul's entangled and entwined parallel of the husband/wife relationship reflecting the redemptive and responsive nature of Christ and His church. The great obstacle in communicating and applying this passage in Western culture in the early part of this century is the exhortation submission (Eph 5:12). In the lingering wake of the twentieth century, the women's movement, and the radical individualism of modern

---

[8] J. R. W. Stott, "Marriage and Divorce," in *Involvement: Social and Sexual Relationships in a Modern World* (Old Tappan, NJ: Revell, 1984), 163.

[9] A. J. Köstenberger, *God, Marriage and Family* (Wheaton, IL: Crossway, 2004), 261.

rationalism, submission has become an almost unspeakable "dirty word." However, if we understand the New Testament marriage analogy in the light of a Trinitarian theology, it would assist us in our comprehensive understanding. Beginning with the image of God revealed in the intimate oneness of husband and wife, we begin to understand a clearer image of the godhead.

Understand the divine members of the godhead as distinct "equal persons" in relationship to one another with a clear biblical sense of priority in the hierarchy. The Scripture clearly teaches of the submission of Jesus, the Son to the Father, and the subordination of the work of the Spirit to the Son—all without loss of unity, fidelity, or passion. This is clearly seen in the high priestly prayer of Jesus (John 17) as He reflects on the accomplished work He was given to do by the Father, His passionate desire to return to the Father, and His great purpose in seeing those who believed on Him to be one, even as He and the Father were one.

In the New Testament when spouses are called to submit to one another, both husband and wife can reflect on the Trinity as the example to follow. As each fulfills their designated role (e.g., for husbands to love their wives and wives to submit to their husbands), it is seen as a reflection of the dynamic that operates in the godhead itself. Each of the members of the godhead operate as distinct and equal persons in relationship to each another with a clear biblical sense of priority. So it is in the marriage relationship—the husband's loving sacrifice creates an open, vulnerable posture before his wife and the wife as she willing submits to her husband's leadership is accepting of his oversight. This vulnerability allowed the first couple (and every couple since) to experience the kind of intimacy for which they were created—that they might genuinely become "one flesh."

Mason explores the depth of this kind of naked vulnerability in his book *The Mystery of Marriage,* where he states:

> For to be naked with another person is a sort of picture or symbolic demonstration of perfect trust, perfect giving and commitment. If the heart is not naked along with the body, then the whole action becomes a lie and a mockery. It becomes an involvement in an absurd and tragic contradiction the giving of the body but the withholding of the self. . . . It is in effect, the very last step in human relations and therefore never one to be taken lightly. It is not a step that established deep intimacy but one which presupposes it.[10]

This kind of vulnerability is imprudent outside of a trusting relationship marked by lifelong faithfulness in marriage. The one flesh reality of

---

[10] M. Mason, *The Mystery of Marriage* (Portland, OR: Multnomah Press, 1985), 117.

marital sexual intercourse is a physical, spiritual image of the mystery of "two becoming one." It is the enigma of a reality and mystery tied into a single experience. It is the restoration of the scene in Genesis 2 in which Adam and Eve are living naked and unashamed, as they become one flesh. The flow in the narrative naturally moves from the initial encounter to their mystical, physical, spiritual union separated by the divine narrative of verse 24. God gives editorial comment, directing that in this first marriage and every marriage to follow ". . . the man shall leave his father and mother and cleave to his wife and they shall become one flesh" (Gen 2:23–25 NKJV). This is the idea of the necessity of separation, permanence, and intimacy to provide the only legitimate environment for nakedness and ultimate vulnerability. It is this progression from passion (v. 23) to intimacy (v. 25). The route to achieve that kind of intimacy is through vulnerability (nakedness), yet the only environment safe enough to risk that kind of vulnerability is in the security of lifelong fidelity (Gen 2:24).

It is in this context of nakedness that the biblical roles of husbands and wives in marriage must be considered. Both Paul and Peter delineate the roles of both mates in the marriage relationship. Husbands are clearly called to love their wives as Christ loved the church and gave Himself for her. Wives are called to submit to their husbands as the church submits to the leadership of Christ in the church. Both of these postures require an authentic vulnerability before the other.

When a husband is called lovingly to lead, it is in the tenor of the sacrifice of Christ for the church. Paul's own description of the submissive "attitude of Christ" in this act is clearly displayed in his letter to the Philippians, where we read: "Your attitude should be the same as that of Christ Jesus: Who, being in very nature God, did not consider equality with God something to be grasped, but made himself nothing, taking the very nature of a servant, being made in human likeness. And being found in appearance as a man, he humbled himself and became obedient to death—even death on a cross!" (Phil 2:5–8 NASB).

In all three significant New Testament citations of marital submission, it is in a context of communal relationships that have some sense of reciprocal submission—husbands and wives, children and parents, slaves and master. Every citation is a reflection of the submission of Jesus to the Father. All three draw upon the believer's responsibility to submit first to Christ and then the outworking of submitting to one another. Therefore, when husbands are called to love their wives as Christ loved the church and wives are directed to submit to their husband's leadership, it is a reflection of the original intent of the Creator redeeming the image He designed in the prototype of the garden.

On leadership, the practice of mutual submission and equality does not infringe on the New Testament teaching of male leadership in the marriage relationship. As is seen in the relationship of the Trinity, there is a sense of divine hierarchy. There is no doubt as to the submission of Jesus, the Son, to the authority of the Father, perhaps most clearly seen in the ultimate confession in the garden of Gethsemane, "Never the less not my will but yours be done." At no time during his earthly experience did the Son ever lose his equality with the Father. Nor did He at any point do anything but what the Father directed Him to do (John 5:19). There is within marriage, as there is in the godhead, a distinct sense of priority of leadership without superiority.

In the marriage relationship, as the reflection of the Trinity, the responsibility of leadership has fallen to the husband. The motif of the creation account carries a strong sense of governance, representative rule expressed in a co-regency of both man and woman. "By placing his image on the man and the woman and by placing them in particular environment, therefore, God assigns to the mandate of representative rule."[11] When the apostle Paul speaks of wives submitting to their husbands, he refers to the husbands as the "head" of the relationship as Christ is the head of the church. Paul's position is clearly expressed in his teaching on order in the church in 1 Cor 11:5–16 and 1 Tim 2:12–15.[12] The order of creation, the man and then the woman in Paul's position, and evidence from Ancient Near East literature provide adequate proof to place clearly a biblical expectation of leadership in the marriage relationship originating from the husband and directed toward the wife. In this context the godly husband is to provide vision and leadership in line with biblical teaching on leadership with the attitude, which was in Christ Jesus. And the wife is to submit to her husband's sacrificial, loving leadership with the attitude of the church toward the headship of Christ. In this experience both husband and wife enter into a position of risk that reflects the naked and unashamed vulnerability of Adam and Eve.

Sex and Marriage

The Scripture speaks of the beauty of sexuality in the purest and most organic terms. From the poetry of King Solomon's Song of Songs to the frankness of Paul's encouragement of frequent sexual activity in marriage, sex is blessed, encouraged, and protected by the Creator. The writer of Hebrews declares that the marriage bed is not to be defiled (Heb 13:4). Sexual intimacy was created by God for marriage to be enjoyed and appreciated and for the procreation of children.

---

[11] A. J. Köstenberger, *God, Marriage and Family* (Wheaton, IL: Crossway, 2004), 33.

[12] Both of these passages are directly related to authority in the church, but many believe they have bearing on the use of headship in the home because of its grounding in the Genesis creation story.

Although sexuality itself is a dynamic component of masculinity and femininity, its ultimate expression in intercourse is reserved for marriage and is to be protected by marriage. As previously stated, only in marriage do the two people find the secure fidelity to enter into such deep physical and spiritual oneness. There is something mysterious in the coming together of a man and a woman in sexual intercourse that, even outside of marriage, is defined as a one-flesh experience (1 Cor 6:16). This is the grounds for the significant protected prohibitions in Scripture, restricting sexual intercourse exclusively for a marriage relationship.

This has profound implications in a marriage relationship. Paul addresses the Corinthian believer in 1 Cor 7:1 with an introduction that rings of contemporary authenticity, "[B]ecause of immoralities" (in the culture and in the church). He then touches on the responsibilities of husbands and wives to pay close attention to their sexual relationship with each other. The Scripture does not speak often about the sexual relationship between a husband and wife, so when it does, we should pay close attention. The passage is so clear that even some 2,000 years later, in a completely different time and culture, the realities of regular, exclusive sexual intercourse is to be the practice of husbands and wives, recognizing that our bodies are to be shared with each other freely.

When Scripture speaks about the sexual relationship between a husband and wife, it is not reserved or shy, but bold and free. The Song of Songs in the Old Testament is such a frank expression of young married love that some rabbis restricted young Jewish boys from reading it. However, in its poetic fashion it draws on the sensual desire of the bride and bridegroom for each other fulfilled in the exclusivity of their fidelity. The explicit language, although at times awkward to the modern lover, is clearly an expression of the beauty of passionate sexual expression in the pages of Holy Writ.

The clearest expression of understanding of marital sexual relations in the Scripture is the exclusivity of sex in the security of the marriage covenant. There are boundaries around sex, which protect marriage and affirm that sex is reserved for those who are married. The prohibitions of fornication and adultery throughout the Bible are expanded by Jesus' interpretation of the law to include the thought life of a person. "But I tell you that anyone who looks at a woman lustfully has already committed adultery with her in his heart" (Matt 5:28 NIV). Protecting the fidelity of the sexual component of the marriage is central to protecting the security of the oneness and intimacy of the relationship. The analogy of sexual adultery, infidelity, and spiritual infidelity in both the Old and New Testaments draws a clear correlation between the faithfulness in marriage and faithfulness in relationship to God for both Israel and the church. It is as close as one can come to terminating the covenant.

The Challenge of Divorce

While taking care not to create a polemic argument for marriage by addressing the issue of divorce, no theological work on marriage would be complete without addressing the issue of divorce. Divorce is a legal accommodation altering a theological covenant because of the hardness of the human heart (Deut 24:1–4; Matt 19:8). That is the cold truth. Statistically and experientially, we know divorce to be so much more. No one has to look too broadly to see the destruction of divorce culturally or personally. The pain of divorce is hard to describe and looks different in every relationship. The pain and the controversy of divorce are real, and many of the questions that Moses and Jesus faced are the questions we face today.

Moses wrote on the origins and conditions of divorce (Deut 24:1–4), Jesus clarified the parameters (Matt 19:3–12; Mark 10:2–12), and pastors have attempted to understand the biblical position on divorce for centuries. What is clear is this: Divorce is contrary to God's original design for marriage, which was "A man shall leave his father and mother and cleave to his wife and the two shall become one flesh" (Gen 2:24 KJV). In fact, God abhors divorce (Mal 2:14–16). This strong language may be understood in context with the Sixth Commandment (prohibition of taking human life); it is a violation of the *imago dei in* every man. If marriage is the clearest expression of the *imago dei,* in "two becoming one," separating that union would be a distinct detraction of the image of God. If the purpose of marriage were to reveal the glory of God, dissolving a marriage would be denigrating that image.

However, in both the Old and New Testament, God by his grace has made exceptions to the prohibition of divorce based on the hardness of men's hearts (Deut 24:1; Matt 19:8). Although God abhors divorce, the clarity of the gospel is the all-sufficient work of Christ's death on the cross to forgive sin. The sin of divorce is not the unpardonable sin.

There is much to determine in applying the biblical teachings regarding divorce and must be understood by those within the leadership of the church. It has never been an easy issue and has deep theological, moral, and personal ramifications. As one sorts through the implications of divorce, one must also understand the nature of the care for the widow and the orphan and the concern of the New Testament Church for these people (Jas 1:27). Divorce is a theological, cultural, and legal issue, and there are always genuine victims of this malady.

Implications for the Church

A great responsibility rests on the Church in the decades to come to increase the percentage of healthy marriages in the church and our community as a whole. The church, like no other institution, has the leverage and resources to make a difference, not to mention the responsibility to steward the truth. Like always, it must begin with right thinking. Rescuing a drowning culture is never easy, but if anyone has a foot on the dry shore to send out a lifeline, it is the church. We must think biblically and theologically about marriage and about what we are teaching as we transform people into fully devoted followers of Jesus. Marriage is a clear and dominant metaphor throughout the teaching of the Scripture, revealing the image of God and the work of redemption. It is theology in our home every day. It is evangelism in our neighborhood week by week.

The teaching ministry of the church both from the pulpit and in every setting should include instruction on marriage that is biblical, relevant, authentic, and gracious. It begins with a sound theology of marriage. The Roman Catholic Church is miles ahead of Protestants in this field. Although the field of marriage literature is extensive, the number of books that give a biblical theology of marriage is few. There must be clear teaching from the pulpit setting the standard for marriage education in the church. The theology of marriage should be a part of preparing couples in premarital training and in marriage enrichment and counseling ministries.

Alongside strong theological training in marriage, practical skills–based training cannot be overlooked. Bringing together two sinners to live faithfully as husband and wife will take more than correct theology; it will require relational skills unique to marriage. Communication skills, working together on understanding family finance, and conflict resolution do not come naturally to most of us. The sexual relationship is a natural skill, but in our sex-charged culture, many couples need to learn *the art of making love.* Far too many couples are dealing with the consequences of past sexual experiences and have no clue how to navigate the challenges that lay before them. Many couples who want a healthy biblical marriage feel unprepared and ill-equipped for what the Scriptures require of us. Biblical parenting is too distant a goal and hard to grasp.

In our divorce-filled culture, the number of children who will grow up in a home that is not headed by their biological parents still married to each other is staggering. The growing number of couples who cohabit to avoid the pain of divorce also must be considered. This is a segment of the next generation that will never have seen mom and dad's wedding picture because there never was a wedding. Skills-based marriage education will only grow in its need as a tool of discipleship and family ministries.

Pastors need to receive greater attention to marriage preservation as part of their seminary training, and leaders who are struggling in their marriage are not ready for the responsibility of leading the church of God. Churches need to take seriously the health of the marriages of their leaders, understanding the unique strain on ministry marriages in the contemporary church culture. Far too many church leaders break under the strain of this tension, and the collateral damage can overwhelm a church. Churches and seminaries must provide care to the marriages of the pastors. Although much of the responsibility falls on the leadership couple, creating a safe place for these husbands and wives to authentically share their needs and care for their marriage is essential.

Leaders are *not* expected to have perfect marriages, but they should have marriages that are exemplary and biblically healthy and that provide instruction, modeling, and mentoring. There is direct instruction to older women to teach younger women to love their husbands (1 Timothy 2), and the model of older men mentoring younger men is clear throughout the Scripture. The attitude of this kind of exhortation is seen in Peter's letters to fellow elders (1 Peter 5). Marriage mentoring ought to be a part of family ministry not only at the critical stage of premarital but also throughout the seasons of life. Mentor training and the presence of a marriage mentoring program will often raise the bar, creating an environment where mentoring is an organic outcome of healthy marriages in the church.

Conclusion

Throughout the Bible marriage is used as the most sublime metaphor for the relationship between God and man—"a good Christian marriage, indeed, is more than a religious metaphor," it is a tangible and visible and "most glorious fruit of the Kingdom of God."[13]

Marriage is more than a legal social institution or a covenant between two lovers—it is the foundation for healthy families. The church of today has a greater responsibility than ever before to strengthen healthy marriages, turning the tide of the infiltration of the divorce culture into the church. We also must be salt and light to a culture that is deeply affected by the demise of healthy marriages and the avoidance of marriage in the wave of cohabiting couples. We must restore the sanctity of marriage, as a portrait of the Creator/Redeemer God, as we provide truth and practical tools to help couples survive the onslaught of their own sin and the breakdown of the culture.

While we attempt to understand the great mystery of marriage, by creating a theology of marriage and by designing programmed ministries to teach and train Christ followers the skills of living with one another in a mutually submissive way, we must never lose sight of the mystery. As Miroslav Volf puts it, "[A] model with which we seek to approach the mystery of the triune God, not in order to comprehend God completely, but rather in order to worship God as the unfathomable and to imitate God in our own, creaturely way."[14]

---

[13] M. Mason, *The Mystery of Marriage* (Portland, OR: Multnomah Press, 1985), 24.
[14] M. Volf, *After Our Likeness: The Church as the Image of the Trinity* (Grand Rapids, MI: Eerdmans, 1998), 198.

7 Spiritual Markers in the Life of a Child

Leon M. Blanchette Jr.
Olivet Nazarene Theological Seminary

Spiritual Milestones

Spiritual milestones serve the Christian in much the same way a scrapbook serves as a reminder of important moments in one's life. Pictures and mementos of significant moments of life are recorded for future remembrance. A lock of hair from a child's first haircut, a picture with a group of friends on a retreat, the love note from a dear friend, and the Bible given by your grandparents all serve as reminders of moments that are never to be forgotten. These scrapbook items may have little intrinsic value to anyone else, but to the person who experienced the events they serve as a road map of moments that have contributed to shaping one's life. These mementos remind children who they are and where they are from. They serve as reminders of God's faithfulness through tough times and good.

The same is true for spiritual milestones. There are key moments in the spiritual life of a child. These moments have the potential to change the trajectory of a child's journey for a lifetime. Significant moments not only serve as milestones on the journey with God but also serve as a way for parents and the church to gauge the spiritual development of their children. As children participate in key biblical milestones, they create mementos that are placed in the spiritual scrapbook of their lives. These moments in time are captured in these scrapbooks as reminders of their journey with God and serve as an encouragement to continue the faithful journey with Christ. In those moments of discouragement, despair, and doubt, this scrapbook of biblical milestones will be the encouragement that challenges them to continue on the journey with Christ.

Measuring Faith in a Child

What is taught to children and how we worship, in the context of Christian faith, should affect what they believe and what they believe should govern how they live. The goal of every Christian parent and every local church congregation should be to help their children know God and to live in a faith-filled relationship with Him—to journey with Christ. The question then is: How do parents and the church know when they are being successful in achieving this goal?

The ancient church believed there is a direct relationship between how one worships, what one believes, and how one lives. The relationship between doctrine and worship is a life lived that is consistent with both. As beliefs of the church are taught to children and these beliefs affect the rituals and practices of the church community, the result should be children who practice these truths in their daily lives. By looking at these outward expressions of children, a glimpse of what the children believe is possible.

Outward expressions provide a glimpse into the hearts of children. Although outward expressions do not necessarily demonstrate Christian maturity, they do provide a sense of the heart of children. It is possible to have outward signs without any inward change, and it is even possible to have inward change without outward signs, but because of the cognitive limitations and the lack of developed verbal skills, not to mention the struggles adults have trying to express in words what is happening to them spiritually, it seems the best way of measuring what is happening inwardly in the life of a child is to look at what is happening outwardly. This approach to understanding what is taking place within a child is supported by the social-learning theory, which proposes that some things, such as faith, are more "caught" than "taught." One way of determining what is caught is to observe the outward expressions and activities of children.

By observing the outwardly expressed spiritual milestones in a child's life, the parent and church community can determine if the ultimate goal of transformation is occurring. By following biblical examples found in both the Old and New Testaments, parents and the church community can know both how to train children for spiritual transformation and what to look for to determine if transformation is taking place. Every event and activity in the lives of children, whether in a formal setting or in everyday life events, provides opportunities for transformation to take place. Within those formal and informal teaching moments are significant events that one looks for to confirm that transformation is taking place. These biblical milestones serve as spiritual snapshots in the life of the maturing Christian child. The five biblical milestones discussed in this chapter are somewhat unique to children but are consistent with the biblical instruction found in the Old and New Testaments for guiding a child to a transformed life.

Biblical Call to Nurture Children

Although the number of references to children and their spiritual nurture are somewhat limited in the Scriptures, those texts that do address the topic demonstrate a clear and consistent model of the parent passing on faith to the child. From the earliest days of recorded biblical history, parents and other family members shared the stories of the love and faithfulness of Yahweh with the children of the family. The telling of these stories was viewed as an important venue for passing on the faith. Many of these stories can be found in both Old and New Testaments and are helpful in understanding the way children are to be viewed within the faith community and how they are to be reared in that faith for a lifetime of faithfulness to God. Two texts will be the focus of the mandate to rear children in the faith so that their story will become a part of God's story.

> ***Shema***
> Hear, O Israel: The LORD our God, the LORD is one. Love the LORD your God with all your heart and with all your soul and with all your strength. These commandments that I give you today are to be upon your hearts. Impress them on your children. Talk about them when you sit at home and when you walk along the road, when you lie down and when you get up. Tie them as symbols on your hands and bind them on your foreheads. Write them on the doorframes of your house and on your gates. (Deut 6:4–9 NIV)

The *Shema* is one of the most sacred and well-known texts in ancient Jewish tradition because in it is found the central theme of the book of Deuteronomy: to love God. As a part of Moses' final words to the community of Israel, he presents a model for loving God and passing that love on to future generations through the spiritual nurture of the community, the family, and children. He essentially restates the first commandment, later referred to in the book of Mark as the Greatest Commandment, reminding the community that while others may worship many gods, they are to remain loyal to the one, true God with their full devotion and love. The call to love God serves as the central theme of the book.

The focus of Moses' instruction is obedience to the words of God, and that obedience comes when one knows and understands God's Word. As a way of demonstrating their love for God, Moses challenges the people to hide God's words in their hearts so that the way they live their lives will match up with what they understand and confess with their mouths; so they will be obedient. After parents have loved God with all their being and have hidden God's commands in their own hearts, then they are ready to teach them diligently to their children. The implication of verses 6 through 9 is that teaching obedience to God's commands is to be done at all times, in all places, with intention, as parents are being obedient to God's commands.

The basic meaning of the verb *shāma`* is "to hear," but when it is associated with such words as "commandment," as it is in Deut 6:4–9, the meaning takes on the additional command "to obey."[1] Therefore, when the commandments of God are being taught by parents or other teachers, children are not only to be taught for cognitive understanding, but also for obedience. If children are taught the commandments of God and they are not obedient to those commandments, it could be said that they did not really learn them. The ultimate goal then is not the acquisition of information but learning for the purpose of obedience.

The teaching of one's children is to take place in both formal in informal teaching moments. Teaching obedience is to take place in informal moments as life is being lived (v. 7) and in formal ways as described by the binding of the law on one's body and the posting of the law within one's territory (vv. 8–9). Formal teaching is best described by the typical classroom setting where the teacher is the deliverer of knowledge and the student is the recipient; the setting is controlled and curriculum is tightly organized. The weakness of formal education is that it is possible for the student to learn the data isolated from life experiences. The strength of formal teaching is that specific outcomes can be identified and competency can be measured.

Whereas formal teaching plays an important role in education of children, informal teaching moments produce learning occasions that produce life change. Opportunities for informal teaching occur more often than those of formal teaching, and these moments allow for practical application at the level the child is ready to learn. The setting is unstructured and focuses on learning through the experiences of life. The weakness of informal learning is that it is mostly based on experience, which is also its strength.

Many scholars recognize that education in general, but specifically religious education, is best learned by the model of "walking in the shadow of parents who live out their teachings."[2] In a similar way that one's first language is learned not by intentional formal teaching but through observing, mimicking, and imitating in everyday life, much of Christian education is learned through the everyday opportunities of experiencing life together as a family. Donald Joy adds that if one had to choose between the formal approach to education provided through public and private schools and the informal education provided by parents as life is experienced, the schools would lose out every time.[3]

---

[1] L. R. Harris, G. L. Archer Jr., B. K. Waltke, eds., *Theological Wordbook of the Old Testament* (Chicago: Moody Press, 1980), 938.
[2] D. Joy, "Why Reach and Teach Children?" in *Childhood Education in the Church*, ed. R. E. Clark, J. Brubaker, and R. B. Zuck (Chicago: Moody, 1986), 6.
[3] Ibid.

Although modes of teaching the faith are extremely effective in transforming the lives of students, there must also be intentional formal educating of the Word of God as described in the *Shema*. It is clear by the biblical examples of Jesus' teaching ministry that there is no single way to teach and that both formal and informal forms of education benefit the believer in their spiritual nurture. Formal education is important for teaching doctrine, data, and facts, and informal education is important for bringing about life transformation. Together these two approaches provide a balanced prescription for the spiritual nurture of children.

Several significant truths are revealed in a summary of the Old Testament passages that address the spiritual nurture of children. The role of the faith community is significant in the spiritual nurture of the child; however, it is secondary to the role of the parent(s). The faith community is to function as a support system to parents as they teach the commandments and ordinances of God to their children. Children are to be taught to love God, which is demonstrated in the life of the child by obedience to God. Teaching is to be conducted using a variety of techniques, which include formal and informal teaching, modeling, relationship building, and immersion. A test of the level of success in teaching a children is by determining if they have learned the information, which is gauged by their level of obedience. Teaching, learning, loving, and obeying go hand in hand.

> **The Great Commission**
> Therefore go and make disciples of all nations, baptizing them in the name of the Father and of the Son and of the Holy Spirit, and teaching them to obey everything I have commanded you. (Matt 28:19–20a NIV)

Although a number of Scriptures in the New Testament call parents and the church to nurture their children spiritually, and several examples when Jesus sets children among the people to express their importance in the kingdom, there is no more comprehensive New Testament text in defining the outward expressions desired and the responsibilities of the faithful follower of God than the Great Commission. In this text is found an exhaustive list of characteristics that Jesus identifies as the essence of a Christian's life. The five milestones that will be discussed in this chapter can be found in the Great Commission in both implicit and explicit ways.

The heart of this passage is found in the words "make disciples." The focus of the text is a command to make disciples and a description of how it is to be done. Wilkins notes that making disciples is "both a call to and the process of becoming a disciple."[4] Wilkins means that this text functions as the call of all Christians to make disciples and at the same time describes the process for becoming a disciple. The verb *mathēteuō,* which means "to make disciples," is an imperative that calls "individuals to absolute commitment to the person of Jesus as one's sole master and Lord."[5] The "how to" make disciples is found in the three subordinate terms that go with making disciples: *go, baptize,* and *teach.* These terms both describe what should take place in the life of a disciple and the process for making disciples.

The first subordinate term, "go," has an evangelistic connotation. Although the term is not purely evangelistic, it has a clear call to lead the unbeliever to conversion and an ongoing transformation through a life committed to Jesus in discipleship. The intention is to go into the entire world to make disciples. This call includes all people no matter their social status, race, gender, or age. Children are clearly intended to be included in this list. As persons who are included in the mandate to make disciples, children are not only to be made into disciples; they also are to be ones that "go."

As disciples are made, they are to be baptized. This second subordinate is a public proclamation of breaking from allegiance to the world to devotion to God for a lifetime. The public proclamation is to be shouted loudly as the baptismal candidate is an active participant in the symbolic act of the old self dying and being buried in the water and subsequently being raised to new life in Christ. Of course, this act is symbolic of what has already taken place in the life of this believer. This act of obedience becomes another significant moment in the disciple-making process.

Teaching for obedience is an ongoing process in the life of the disciple that begins prior to baptism and continues for a lifetime. It is significant that Christ's command to teach includes the phrase "to obey all I have commanded." According to Hagner, the word *disciple* means "learner" or "pupil" and implies that true learning is to take place when teaching is done.[6] The purpose of teaching is for obedience. This understanding is contrary to much of the teaching that takes place in the church today. Effective teaching is often evaluated by the ability of the student to parrot back to the teacher the information that was taught. Too few times success in teaching is determined by whether the students became more obedient as a result of what has been taught. Perhaps the way teachers teach their material would change if the focus was obedience rather than knowledge for the sake of knowledge. Obedience must always be the goal of teaching.

---

[4] M. J. Wilkins, *Matthew,* The NIV Application Commentary (Grand Rapids, MI: Zondervan, 2004), 952.
[5] Ibid.
[6] D. A. Hagner, *Matthew 14–28,* Word Biblical Commentary (Dallas: Word, 1995), 887.

Becoming a disciple or making others into disciples is not an option. Wilkins says, "Everyone who has become a disciple of Jesus is to be involved in the process of discipleship."[7] This means two things should happen in the life of every child that enters into a relationship with Christ. First, children should be discipled so they can become more like Christ and live in a life-changing relationship with Him. Second, every child should be trained to be a disciple to others. Although being a child disciple might look a bit different from an adult disciple, the difference does not indicate any less value. In fact, Christ Himself said, "[U]nless you change and become like children, you will never enter the kingdom of heaven" (Matt 18:3 NIV).

Spiritual Markers

Scripture is clear about the importance of passing down the faith to our children. It is such a critically important role of parents and the church that God has not left it to chance. Scripture is clear what spiritual formation in the life of the child should look like and how to help children grow in their relationship with God. Certain characteristics have been identified that one looks for in the life of the child on the journey with God. This scrapbook of a Christian child's life should include snapshots of the following biblical milestones, moments that are significant in the spiritual development of a child and moments that show that spiritual nurture is occurring.

> **Confession of Faith: Conversion**
> If you confess with your mouth, "Jesus is Lord," and believe in your heart that God raised him from the dead, you will be saved. (Rom 10:9 NIV)

Spiritual Capacity. The theological question that must be asked is: At what point is a child capable of entering the journey to life? Bushnell responds to this question with his earth-shaking proclamation: "[T]he child is to grow up a Christian, and never know himself as being otherwise."[8] Bushnell's response clearly communicates his belief that children are capable of entering this journey at a young age. Bushnell abhorred the modern idea that children should grow up in sin and be converted at a more "mature age."[9] Although some accuse Bushnell of not taking the conversion process seriously, his intention is to champion the cause for children's ability to love God from a young age and to walk the journey with Christ. Wesley recognized this same truth within many of the children he encountered. Throughout his journals Wesley notes

---

[7] Wilkins, *Matthew*, 956.
[8] H. Bushnell, *Christian Nurture*, 5th ed. (New Haven: Yale University Press, 1953), 4.
[9] Ibid.

instances when, apparently to his initial surprise, he observed spiritual maturity among young children. In one such journal entry he wrote the following:

> Sat. 28, 1746—I inquired more particularly of Mrs. Nowens, concerning her little son. She said, he appeared to have a continual fear of God, and an awful sense of his presence; that he frequently went to prayers by himself, and prayed for his father, and many others by name; that he had an exceeding great tenderness of conscience, being sensible of the least sin, and crying and refusing to be comforted, when he thought he had in anything displeased God. . . . When the Holy Ghost teaches, is there any delay in learning? This child was then just three years old! A year or two after he died in peace.[10]

Wesley believed that children were capable of a real relationship with Christ at a young age and was so serious about this matter that he required that his ministers "preach to and instruct children, whether or not they felt gifted to do so."[11]

Second-Generation Christians. Children who grow up in strong Christian families often have unique conversion experiences. Gordon Smith, dean at Regent College in Vancouver, Canada, and professor of spiritual theology, refers to children who are reared in Christian families as "second-generation Christians" and believes that their spiritual status is unique. This uniqueness occurs because these children are reared in a family that at their center is a relationship with Christ. Smith is adamant that "conversion for first- and second-generation Christians is *not* the same; it *is* possible to 'grow up in the faith.'"[12] He is concerned that there has been undue pressure on these children to "become" Christian, in large part from a misunderstanding of the conversion process in the life of these second-generation Christians. He notes that one common characteristic of these second-generation Christians is that they often have difficulty identifying the date and time of their conversion.[13] This may be in part because their journeys often begin at birth and continue into adulthood without a clear distinction of a "salvation moment." Smith notes that commonly heard phrases from these children include, "I have always believed in God" or "I have always loved Jesus."[14] Walter Brueggemann supports

---

[10] J. Wesley, *The Works of John Wesley*, vol. 2, 3rd ed. (London: Wesleyan Methodist Book Room, 1872; reprint, Kansas City, MO: Beacon Hill Press, 1986), 16.
[11] Ibid., vol. 8.
[12] G. T. Smith, *Beginning Well: Christian Conversion and Authentic Transformation* (Downers Grove, IL: InterVarsity, 2001), 207.
[13] Ibid, 212.
[14] Ibid.

this understanding when he states, "It is clear that there is no single, decisive meeting which will suit such children. . . . But an ongoing conversation, whereby the child-en-route-to-adult begins, a little at a time at one's own pace, to affirm and claim the 'news' which defines the community."[15] Often these children have a number of significant events—snapshots that are included in their scrapbook of life—that identify significant moments of response to God's promptings.

Authentic Conversion Process. The conversion process in second-generation Christians often occurs as life is lived within the Christian community. Children that are reared in a faithful Christian community often make what appears to be a natural decision to follow Christ. The *Shema,* Deut 6:4–9, anticipates this reality as parents faithfully immerse their children in the faith. It is as if the child says, "What else would I do? I have loved Jesus since I can remember. I must give my life to Jesus and accept His gift of forgiveness and salvation." This process, in many cases, is a natural movement for these children. There is an expectation among parents and the faith community that these children will respond to the message that has been taught to them from a young age.

Smith proposes that "for both theological and developmental reasons we should avoid pressing young people to make a decision, or be baptized, or acknowledge adult faith before they are intellectually, emotionally and socially ready to do so."[16] This does not mean that children should not be trained in the faith or, as Bushnell implies, immersed in the faith. In fact, Smith argues just the opposite. He believes that rather than pressuring children about what they should experience, adults should be in conversation with children about what they are experiencing as they encounter God. Adults should nurture children in the faith and allow them to respond in their own time, thereby allowing for an authentic conversion that will be demonstrated by the faith of their parents becoming their own faith and their faith experience leading them to a life that is transformed.[17] This conversion may occur in a moment in time, but in the case of many second-generation Christians, conversion is an affirmation and confirmation of a life already lived in relationship with Christ. This does not preclude a need for a confession of sin at the time that sin becomes known to the child. Dallas Willard, a professor at the University of Southern California, a Southern Baptist minister, and one of today's leading Christian thinkers, reminds the church that the goal is not to get people forgiven and into heaven, but to lead others to "put [their] confidence in Jesus and,

---

[15] W. Brueggemann, *Biblical Perspectives on Evangelism: Living in a Three-Storied Universe* (Nashville, TN: Abingdon, 1993), 94.
[16] Smith, *Beginning Well*, 211.
[17] Ibid., 208–11.

out of that confidence, live with him as his disciple now in the present kingdom of the heavens."[18] This view raises questions about the need for a specific conversion moment and allows for a gradual growth in a personal relationship with God that includes many significant moments of confession, commitment, and consecration to God. Children have the capacity to enter into this personal relationship, and in the case of second-generation Christians, the process may be less formal than is often mandated.

Cognition and Conversion

If a child is not capable of a cognitive understanding of the need for repentance and for recognition of Christ's sacrifice on the cross for their sin, does this mean that the child is incapable of an acquaintance with Christ? What exactly did Christ mean when He said, "Let the little children come to me"? Was it a polite way to include the children in the conversation? Was Jesus just being nice? Or was he demonstrating that even though the children were limited in their understanding of all that was taking place, they had the ability to enter into an acquaintance with Him? Could it be that many children that grow up in strong Christian homes, where Christ is the focus of the life of the family, have the ability to enter into an acquaintance with Christ long before they understand their need for forgiveness and salvation? Could it be that as these children become cognitively aware of their sin and need for forgiveness, and they repent of their sin, that this act is the next step in their acquaintance with Christ?

Take, for instance, Sarah. Sarah begins loving Jesus at an early age. She prays to Jesus, plays with Jesus, and includes Jesus as a part of her everyday life. When she plays with her toys she often includes Jesus by name. At the age of seven, Sarah attends a children's revival service where she becomes more aware of her personal sin and need for forgiveness. Following an invitation to receive Christ as her Savior, she asks her mom, "Have I ever done that?" Her mom replies, "No, honey, not to my knowledge." Sarah's response is clear, direct, and somewhat expected: "Then I need to do that." Sarah went to the altar and prayed to ask Jesus to forgive her of her sins and be her Savior. Was this the moment in which she was saved? Or, should it focus more on the acquaintance she had with Christ? Was this a significant moment? Absolutely, but was this the moment she became a Christian for the first time, or was this act of obedience an affirmation and confirmation of a relationship that perhaps previously existed? Perhaps this is the next significant step in an already established lifelong journey with Jesus. Perhaps this child's journey with

[18] D. Willard, "Teaching for Transformation," Lecture at North American Professors of Christian Education Conference (Orlando, FL: October 21–23, 2004).

God does not look exactly like that of an adult, but it is essential that children be allowed to develop at a rate that is consistent with their cognitive abilities. The role of the parents and the church community is to affirm the children's decisions as the journey is walked together.

The most important moment in a child's spiritual life is the moment that he or she makes a decision to accept Jesus Christ as Savior. It is important that regular opportunities be provided for children to make decisions to follow Christ. The parent and church leader must recognize that first-generation Christians are likely to become Christians in a more traditional way, and the plan of salvation needs to be clearly stated on a regular basis. It is also important that the plan of salvation be presented in a way that is understandable to the child without compromising or watering down the process. The parent and church leader must also recognize that second-generation Christians have grown up in the faith and their experience may be more of loving Jesus from early days in their lives, and the cognitive decision to accept Jesus Christ as Savior is a significant moment in a life already lived for God. Adults must be careful to recognize that the love for God many second-generation Christians have before their confession of faith is real and should be honored.

Baptism

> Therefore go and make disciples of all nations, baptizing them in the name of the Father and of the Son and of the Holy Spirit." (Matt 28:19 NIV)

Baptism is another key moment in the spiritual growth journey of children. As an outward sign of an inward grace, the ordinance of baptism should be a part of the child's life following conversion. It is important that the child understand the significance of the act of baptism based on the cognitive ability of the child. Baptism functions as a milestone because it serves as a reminder of a commitment made to Christ.

Whereas believer baptism is an act that has roots that go back to the early church and occurs subsequent to a commitment to Christ, the act of baptism in the church takes on different roles and purposes depending on the tradition of the particular congregation. In many churches the age of the child being baptized is insignificant as long as the child has made a profession of faith. In other churches children must reach a particular age and cognitive level of understanding before they are permitted to be baptized. This may involve the inclusion of class requirements or completion of baptismal curriculum. In many churches believers baptism is considered an ordinance, whereas in other churches it is considered a sacrament. In many churches children are baptized as infants in recognition of God's prevenient grace at work in their lives. As these baptized children grow in their knowledge of God, they are given further training and eventual opportunity to participate in confirmation where they confirm their infant baptism. In other churches children are dedicated to the Lord as parents and congregation express their intention to raise the child in the training and admonition of the Lord in the hope that they will choose to follow God at a later time in their lives and then be baptized.

Whatever the tradition regarding baptism, one thing is clear—the milestone of being baptized or confirming one's baptism is a significant moment in the life of a child. This scrapbook picture serves as a constant reminder of a moment when the child chose, in a willful and intentional way, to acknowledge the saving work that God has done by this public confession. This moment should be a time of celebration. This is a date to remember and to be celebrated in years to come. Many churches issue certificates or present new Bibles to the participants as a way of commemorating this significant moment. These items should be included in this scrapbook to serve as a reminder of this event.

For these reasons the educational ministry in the child's life must be intentional. Because baptism functions as a serious moment that will continue to affect the child into adulthood, it is necessary that the child be educated in the beliefs of the church and at a level that is understood but without a "watering down" of the truth. When a child is baptized or confirms her baptism, she should know what Christ has done for her and that this moment serves as a public profession of what Christ has already done in her life.

Two types of Christian education should take place in the child's life. He should be exposed to general Christian education that teaches the stories of God and helps him hear the truth of the text while learning how to apply it to his life. This is the more traditional approach to education with children. The important difference from what is often taught is that the focus is on the truth of the text, rather than a nice moral lesson, and application to life.

The child also should be involved in doctrinal education that addresses the specific beliefs of the church. In these sessions topics such as baptism should be discussed in detail at a level the child understands so when he is ready to be baptized he knows what baptism means and represents. Some churches create baptismal packets that walk the child through the meaning of baptism at a level that he understands. For a thorough look at doctrinal statements of belief, some churches choose to use the Apostle's Creed as an outline to address these topics. As with all teaching opportunities with children, these two educational approaches should always respect the cognitive abilities of the children while challenging them to stretch to a deeper level of understanding.

Communion (Lord's Supper)

> And he took bread, gave thanks and broke it, and gave it to them, saying, "This is my body given for you; do this in remembrance of me." (Luke 22:19 NIV)

Participation in the Lord's Supper is another significant opportunity not only for children to experience God's grace but also to be trained in the rituals of the church community. A clear explanation of the meaning of each element and its spiritual application is a meaningful moment for children as they navigate the spiritual journey and mature in their understanding of this key celebration of the church. This event serves as an opportunity for children to add another snapshot to their spiritual scrapbook.

The symbolism found in the partaking of Communion is central in helping children discover the spiritual truth found in the Lord's Supper. The simplest and most effective way to teach children about Communion is to bring it back to its original context—the Passover. It was not a mistake that the middle of the three matzos that were wrapped in linen plays a central role in the Passover celebration. At the appointed time the middle matzo was removed and broken, and half of it was wrapped in linen and hidden away for a later time in the celebration. This *afikomen* was later found by the children in the home and unwrapped by the paternal leader in the family. It was this bread, according to the tradition of the ceremony, that Jesus unwrapped, gave thanks, broke, and gave to his disciples, saying, "Take and eat; this is my body" (Matt 26:26b NIV). The symbolism is unmistakable. Jesus' body was broken, wrapped in linen, and hidden away for three days. After three days He resurrected from the dead and lives today.

It also is not a mistake that the third cup used in the Passover celebration, the cup of redemption, is the same cup Jesus used when he said to the disciples, "This is my blood of the covenant, which is poured out for many for the forgiveness of sins" (Matt 26:28 NIV). What was a symbol of freedom from slavery through the blood of the lamb that was placed on the doorposts in the Hebrew's homes in Egypt is, in this text, given a new meaning. Jesus, the perfect Lamb of God, has shed His blood to provide freedom from slavery to sin.

When Communion is placed in its original context of Passover, new life is brought to a rite of the church that for many has become bland and routine. Once an understanding of the celebration Jesus was honoring and the new meaning He gave to these ancient symbols occurs, the act of eating the bread and drinking the juice takes on a deeper and more profound meaning. Children are not only capable of understanding the tradition of Passover; they are often engrossed in the details of the story. Once the details of the story are understood, a new respect and honor often accompany the partaking.

Recognizing that Communion does not stand alone but is imbedded in the celebration of Passover provides an opportunity to make the act of "do[ing] this in remembrance of me" truly effective. It is necessary to help children understand the context behind Communion. This ancient Old Testament celebration that began in the exodus from slavery in Egypt has deep Messianic undertones that are seen clearly in the life of Jesus. No longer is Communion just another tradition of the church that occurs every so often in worship, but the celebration takes on the meaning of the event—remembering what Christ did for us. Now when the significance of the celebration is explained to children and they are asked not to lick the inside of the cup or crack the cup when they finish the juice, they have a context that helps them understand why. When it is explained that out of reverence we are usually quiet when we receive the elements, they now understand why. Participating in the celebration of Communion together as a family is a time to teach our children about our story while remembering what Jesus has done for us. What more important spiritual snapshot should be included with the snapshots of their conversion and baptism?

Evangelism

> Therefore go and make disciples of all nations.
> (Matt 28:19a NIV)

The Great Commission is God's call to the church to share His love with the world. Children play an important role in this call not only as those who need to hear the message of redemption but also as those who deliver it. Children in the church are to be evangelized, but they are also to evangelize others. Children are not only capable of a real, intimate relationship with God; they are also called and capable of sharing their love for God with others. Parents and the church are responsible not only to lead children into a personal relationship with God but also to challenge children to share that love with their friends.

One sure sign that children are growing in their journey with God is to observe their desire and passion to share God's love with others. Children have a level of boldness about their faith that is often absent in adults. Children overlook the hesitancies that many adults have when sharing their faith. In these moments of inhibition biblical passages such as "Truly I tell you, unless you change and become like children, you will never enter the kingdom of heaven" (Matt 18:3) begin to make sense. Children are capable and expected to share their faith with their friends and family, and they serve as models of boldness and fearlessness for the church family.

Children share their faith in a variety of ways. Those who have been taught that their actions speak as loud, or louder, then their words can often be seen showing compassion to others. Whether treating their teacher with respect, sitting with the new kid at lunch, or sharing a pencil with a friend, children participate in sharing the love of Jesus with others by the way they live their lives. Children also share their faith in verbal ways. Children have the ability to share the plan of salvation with a friend on their porch, comfort a friend who is going through a difficult time, or invite a friend to attend church with them. Although these are all ways children evangelize the world they live in, perhaps the most common form of evangelism in children is inviting their friends to church. Children recognize that church provides an enjoyable environment that allows for friends to learn about Jesus. Children know this is a place where they are loved and their friends will be accepted. Parents and the church should never underestimate the impact a child who loves God can have on the life of another.

Involvement in evangelism is a sign that spiritual growth is taking place in the lives of children. Children should be taught the importance of sharing their faith with their friends. The act of sharing one's faith can be accomplished by children in a variety of ways. Some children who are a bit more spiritually mature will personally share their faith, whereas others will attempt to live as an example before their friends. Whatever the case may be, children are capable of sharing their faith with others, and parents and the church should teach them how to share their faith.

Service

> Teaching them to obey everything I have commanded you.
> (Matt 28:20a NIV)

The church generally understands the concept of serving children, but many do not recognize the importance of teaching children to serve others. It is unhealthy for children to be served without helping them understand the importance of serving others. Perhaps one of the reasons many Christian adults expect others to serve them is because they were never taught to serve others when they were young. Learning to serve helps them be more productive adults, and more important, it helps them to grow in their relationship with God. The final milestone to be discussed in this chapter is children serving others. This may occur in the church or outside the church.

Children love to serve. Anytime an opportunity arises when children can help at church, they are first with their hands up or in line to begin assisting. It is important for parents and church leaders to provide intentional opportunities for children to serve inside and outside the church walls. Giving children an opportunity to move from being hearers to doers is an important transition for them. It is important to take their love to serve and develop it into skills to be used to serve God. Although it is important that young children be teamed with an adult or older child so ministry can be modeled, once trained, older children can take on certain ministry responsibilities by themselves. An intentional service program should be developed that allows children to sign up for areas of interest, and training should be a part of the program.

Many churches have recognized the importance of helping children serve others by providing intentional opportunities to serve. These opportunities of service include training and mentoring. Children are allowed to select from a list of ministry options such as ushering, greeting, leading worship music, helping with younger children, and reading Scripture. Once children are trained, they are teamed up with a mentor, and they often serve together until the child is capable of serving independently. In addition, opportunities are given to assist in community service such as raking leaves in the fall, singing at a local retirement home, or stacking cans at the local food pantry. These opportunities provide children with skills, allow them to learn the importance of serving others, help them be less selfish, and assist them in their journey with Christ. By participating in serving others, they will begin living out the call of Gen 12:3—blessed to be a blessing.

Conclusion

These five biblical and spiritual milestones are significant moments in the life of a child who is growing in relationship with God. Parents and church leaders must be intentional in providing opportunities for all children to experience these milestones. A response from each child to these milestones is completely their decision, but every effort should be made to provide many opportunities for these decisions to be made. To paraphrase Bushnell, we must immerse them in the faith so they grow to know nothing other than loving and serving God.

These biblical milestones serve as snapshots in the spiritual scrapbook of children. As children grow in their relationship with God, these photos serve as reminders of God's faithfulness and the significant moments that shaped their journey. These snapshots also serve as measuring devices that assist parents and the church in determining if they are being effective in nurturing their children's faith. No longer will success be measured by the ability of children to repeat information that has been taught in class or to answer correctly the true/false and multiple-choice questions. Success will be determined by participation in the biblical milestones that serve as snapshots of life-changing moments in their journey with God.

8 A Theology of Grandparenting and Generational Faith

Gordon R. Coulter
James W. Thompson
Haggard School of Theology

The Challenge Ahead

In 1997 I began one of the most challenging fights of my life with the diagnosis of non-Hodgkin's lymphoma. Given only a 50 percent chance of survival, the protocols of chemotherapy and radiation were initiated. Our family was overjoyed with the seeming success of my treatments. Alas, after experiencing several months of health and healing, in 1998 the cancer returned. In October 1998 I went through my first bone marrow transplantation at the City of Hope hospital in southern California.

At the time our daughter, Kim, had been married to her husband, Bobby, for slightly more than a year. Enjoying one of the special privileges of clergy, I had officiated at their wedding on July 13, 1996. Unbeknownst to me, Kim and Bobby decided to have a child earlier than planned, aware that my remaining days could be few and knowing how much it would mean to me to become a grandfather. On November 1, 1999 Kim gave birth to a delightful little girl named Madison.

It would be no exaggeration to say that the birth of Madison was a life-transforming experience for me. It gave me the opportunity to be a part of her life in all of her stages of growth and development—spiritually, physically, and emotionally. Certainly, I wanted to live for my wife and our daughter, but there is something different about being a *grandfather.* To experience that joy fully, I desperately wanted to live.

Through this arduous experience I developed an appreciation for the privilege and responsibilities of being a grandparent and saw from a new perspective the invaluable role grandparents can play in the life of their grandchildren. Even though I had read, taught, and preached the

Scriptures throughout my life, I now discovered a new way to read the biblical narratives about family and multigenerational relationships.

Mandate for Intergenerational Caregivers

This chapter will describe the ever-evolving roles of grandparents and other support systems for children in today's changing world. The reader is challenged to see the role of grandparents, extended family members, and other caregivers from a biblical and theological perspective. Anthony states, "Theology seeks to study and express the key tenets or beliefs of Christianity."[1] The role that a family plays in the growth, development, and education of children is highly influenced by one's theology, whether intentional or not. For many, their theology is embedded from childhood and only rarely revisited. An assumption of this chapter is that the role of a Christian grandparent and others in a position to influence children should be intentionally formed and shaped by biblical theology. It is especially important for Christian caregivers who find it necessary to fill the roles of absentee parents to have a theological awareness of their important role.

A Biblical Theology of Grandparents: Family, Clan, and Tribe

Hellerman's book *When the Church Was a Family* is subtitled *Recapturing Jesus' Vision for Authentic Christian Community.* Scripture's perspective of the people of God is that a community should be gathered together for worship, nurture, spiritual formation, and acts of service to the world. This authentic community is evident when faith is lived out in the intergenerational "family, clan, and tribe," as it is referred to in Scripture. The importance of the community of faith as a place of spiritual formation is one element of the *Shema,* found in Deut 6:4–8 (NASB).

> Hear, O Israel! The Lord is our God, the Lord is one! You shall love the Lord your God with all your heart and with all your soul and with all your might. These words, which I am commanding you today, shall be on your heart. You shall teach them diligently to your sons and shall talk of them when you sit in your house and when you walk by the way and when you lie down and when you rise up. You shall bind them as a sign on your hand and they shall be as frontals on your forehead.

---

[1] M. J. Anthony, "The Nature of Theology and Education" in *A Theology of Christian Education,* ed. J. R. Estep Jr., M. J. Anthony, G. R. Allison (Nashville, TN: B&H, 2008), 7.

The importance of the precepts of the *Shema* is also reflected in the words of Jesus. "You shall love your God with all your heart, and with all your soul, and with all your mind. This is the great and first commandment. And a second is like it. You shall love your neighbor as yourself" (Matt 22:37–39 NASB). In commenting on the *Shema,* Lawson writes, "Time and again God declares the great value he places on the nurture of children. Often he commands both parents and the entire faith community to teach children so they will come to know God and follow him."[2]

This intergenerational family is reflected in the Hebrew phrase *betab* and the Greek term *oikos.* According to Wolff, a chief responsibility of the father is "above all to offer a certain refuge in which [the generations] can find everything that they need for a secure life."[3] In Hebrew, "the family is called the father's house, *betab.*"[4] Wolff also demonstrates the common practice of a woman joining her husband's family and clan upon marriage. "As a rule man and wife find their place in the grouping of the family (*betab*) to which four generations generally belong."[5] According to the *Theological Dictionary of the Old Testament,* the word *bayith* is used as a "designation for Family, Clan, or Tribe."[6] This term is used to describe "[t]he household of Abraham [as] composed of Abraham, his wife, Sarah, his concubine Hagar, his sons Isaac and Ishmael, his dependent relative Lot and his family, [and] his servants."[7] In the *New International Dictionary of Old Testament Theology and Exegesis, bayit* is defined as "familial relationships, such as immediate family or the extended clan/tribe."[8] These familial communities would have been large, intergenerational families consisting of an extended network of grandparents, parents, children, brothers, sisters, aunts, uncles, cousins, and servants and their families.

Likewise, the Greek word *oikos* as defined in Kittel, *Theological Dictionary of the New Testament, Volume V,* refers to the community of Israel as the "house of God." Although this is often understood as a "spiritual house," the word also refers to the actual community of people gathered together in the household including the extended family of relatives and others within the community. "When an Israelite spoke of his house, he did not refer only to the four walls of his dwelling, but rather to his children and grandchildren, to his family. The house of God is His community, His people, the host of those who are bound to Him and whom He has

---

[2] K. E. Lawson, "Restoring Children: Serving Boys and Girls for Christ—Both Near and Far," in *Introduction to Christian Education and Formation,* ed. R. T. Habermas (Grand Rapids, MI: Zondervan, 2008), 151.
[3] H. W. Wolff, *Anthropology of the Old Testament* (Mifflintown, PA: Sigler, 1996), 182.
[4] Ibid.
[5] Ibid.
[6] G. J. Botterweck, H. Ringgren, eds., *Theological Dictionary of the Old Testament* (Grand Rapids, MI: Eerdmans, 1975), 113.
[7] Ibid.
[8] W. A. VanGemeren, *New International Dictionary of Old Testament Theology and Exegesis, Vol. 1* (Grand Rapids, MI: Zondervan, 1997), 656.

called to be His possession."[9] New Testament usage shows *oikos* referring to the extended community as illustrated in 2 Tim 1:16, "May the Lord grant mercy to the household of Onesiphorus." In Acts 10:1–2, *oikos* refers to the household of Cornelius. "At Caesarea there was a man named Cornelius, a centurion of what was known as the Italian Cohort, a devout man who feared God with his entire household." The Greek *oikos* and the Hebrew *betab* both illustrate the nature of the community of faith as a large, intergenerational family sharing the responsibility for the spiritual formation of the people of God. The norm for the Hebrew household usually consisted of at least four generations, including men, married women, unmarried daughters, slaves and servants of both sexes, and other members of the clan or tribe.

The New Testament often shows that the conversion of an individual would lead to the whole family becoming part of the Faith Community—". . . this would include children, servants and relatives living in the house."[10] The story of the Philippian jailer in Acts 16:30–31 illustrates this usage of *oikos*. After discovering that Paul and the other prisoners were still present following an earthquake that shook open all the jail cell doors, the jailer asks, "[W]hat must I do to be saved?" Paul responds by declaring, "[B]elieve in the Lord Jesus, and you will be saved, you and your household."

How different this is from the typical, Western nuclear family. Kornhaber and Woodward comment,

> "We do not regard the modern nuclear family as a natural or sufficient environment for raising children, especially when both parents are working outside the home. Viewed historically, the 'nuclear family' familiar to the contemporary western world is an aberration. For the past 4000 years of humankind, children have been typically raised by tribes, clans, and variously extended networks of kin."[11]

Or, as in the Hebrew tradition, the "house of the father."[12]

A Biblical Theology of Grandparents

Naomi and Ruth. An interesting text that illustrates the importance of family, clan, and tribe is revealed in the book of Ruth and the lineage of Jesus through King David. The story of Ruth begins with the family of Elimelech from Bethlehem in Judea fleeing the famine

---

[9] G. Kittel, G. Friedrich, trans. by G. Bromiley. *Theological Dictionary of the New Testament, Vol. V.* (Grand Rapids, MI: Eerdmans, 1967), 126, fn 29.

[10] Ibid., 130.

[11] A. Kornhaber and K. L. Woodward, *Grandparents/Grandchildren: The Vital Connection* (New Brunswick: Transaction Books, 1985), xi–xii.

[12] Ibid.

afflicting Bethlehem. After a short while in Moab, Elimelech died, leaving his wife, Naomi, a widow. Her two sons, Mahlon and Chilion, each married Moabite women, Orpah and Ruth. Tragically, her two sons also died, leaving Naomi and her two Moabite daughters-in-law widowed. Naomi seeks to return to Bethlehem and the house of her fathers but insists that Orpah and Naomi remain in Moab in order for them to find husbands. Orpah returns to her Moabite home, but Ruth insists on staying with her mother-in-law, declaring, "[W]here you go I will go, and where you lodge I will lodge; your people shall be my people, and your God my God" (Ruth 1:16b NASB).

As the story continues to unfold, Ruth is enabled to marry Boaz, a kinsmen of Elimelech, and bear to him a son named Obed. Obed is considered the son of Naomi, not of Ruth, a reflection of the tradition of levirate marriage. Upon the birth of this child, the women of the village rejoice, proclaiming, "A son has been born to Naomi." Wolff identifies the responsibilities and importance of levirate marriage. "The Levirate marriage . . . [m]akes it a duty for the brothers of a man who has died without male issue to continue the marriage to his widow."[13] The urgency of maintaining the family, tribe, and clan is illustrated by the practice of levirate marriage. Towns, in his new book *Grandparents of the Bible,* states, "Naomi is given more importance in the Bible than Ruth. The child is identified with this grandmother (not father or grandfather)."[14] In the case of Naomi and Ruth, levirate marriage enables the all-important lineage of Jesus, the Christ of David lineage.

As we read the closing verses of Ruth, we discover the importance of this text for the overall biblical narrative: ". . . Boaz [was the father of] Obed, Obed of Jesse, and Jesse of David" (Ruth 4:17 NASB). This lineage is reflected in the opening verses of Matthew's Gospel, where one reads, ". . . and Boaz [was] the father of Obed by Ruth, and Obed the father of Jesse, and Jesse the father of David the king (Matt 1:5–6 NASB). Twenty-eight generations pass when we once again focus upon the city of Bethlehem and the birth of Jesus Christ, the son of David (Matt 1:1 NASB). As Winner writes in *Girl Meets God,* "The Book of Ruth . . . makes Jesus' birth biologically possible: Obed is Jesus' ancestor, his grandfather some thirty generations back. Had Ruth not slipped onto the threshing-room floor, we would have no Obed, no Jesse, no David, no Joseph, and no Messiah."[15] The beloved story of Naomi, Ruth, and the child Obed conceived by fulfillment of levirate marriage demonstrates the importance to the Old Testament world of "family, clan and, tribe."

---

[13] Wolff, *Anthropology of the Old Testament*, 168–69.
[14] E. Towns, *Grandparents of the Bible* (currently under development by Zondervan).
[15] L. F. Winner, *Girl Meets God* (New York: Random House, 2008), 247.

Samuel and Eli. Both Old Testament and New Testament principles can be appealed to in order to strengthen today's families, especially those families facing the challenges described in this story. We will now turn our attention to two different biblical narratives that illustrate the importance of grandparents, or those serving as surrogate grandparents, for the journey toward the spiritual maturity and discipleship of the minors in their care. The first, an example of a "surrogate grandparent," is found in the story of Samuel and Eli. The second narrative illustrates the ongoing influence of a godly grandmother upon her daughter, who in turn is a spiritual influence for her son, who would become the disciple Timothy.

Found in 1 Samuel 1 the story of Samuel begins with Elkanah's barren wife, Hannah, who as tradition understood it was believed to have had her womb closed by the Lord. As a result of her inability to conceive and give her husband a son, year after year Hannah suffered the derision of Elkanah's other wife, Peninnah. Each year Elkanah would travel to the temple at Shiloh with his wives to offer prayers and sacrifices. On one such occasion her heart filled with anguish, and just as her eyes were filled with tears, Hannah remained at the door of the temple after the others had left and begged the Lord to remove from her the shame she had borne for so many years. The priest Eli, on seeing the woman whose mouth was moving while making no sounds, assumed she was drunk and soundly rebuked her. Hannah responded by telling the priest her sad tale and explaining to him the countless entreaties she had raised to the Lord. In response Eli bestowed his blessing upon her, saying, "Go in peace and the God of Israel grant your petition which you have made to him" (1 Sam 1:17). At long last came conception and the birth of Hannah's firstborn son. "In due time Hannah conceived and bore a son, and she called his name Samuel, for she said, 'I have asked him of the Lord'"(1 Sam 1:20). As soon as her baby was weaned, as she had promised, she gave him over to the care of Eli, the priest.

As we read 1 Samuel, it appears that Eli did not have good fortune raising his own two sons, Hophni and Phinehas. "Now the sons of Eli were worthless men, they did not know the Lord" (1 Sam 2:12 NASB). Later in the same chapter we find, ". . . the sin of the young men was very great before the Lord; for the men despised the offering of the Lord with contempt"(1 Sam 2:17). One can only wonder how these two "preacher's kids" came to be so worthless. Was their father so focused on ministry that he had little time for his children? One cannot help but wonder what kind of a father Eli had been to his two sons or, for that matter, what kind of a husband he had been to their mother. On these subjects, alas, the Scriptures remain silent. This is beside the point because his role as the surrogate grandparent in the nurturing and training of Samuel is the primary concern of these Scriptures.

These chapters of 1 Samuel truly are a study in contrasts. Quite differently from Hophni and Phinehas, the Scripture shows a *positive* influence on the part of Eli toward his young protégé, Samuel. Unlike Eli's own two sons, one reads of Samuel, "Now the boy Samuel continued to grow, both in stature and in favor with the Lord and with men" (1 Sam 2:26). We hear almost identical words referring to another young boy at the end of the second chapter of the Gospel of Luke where we read of Jesus, "And Jesus increased in wisdom and in stature, and in favor with God and men" (Luke 2:52). It should not be lost on the reader that behind the hand and wisdom of Eli was the hand and wisdom of God in preparing Samuel for the important role he would fill as his ministry developed throughout the Old Testament.

The "parenting" role is of the greatest importance if one is to raise up adults who can be responsible disciples of the Lord. Spiritual instruction should begin at an early age. It should also be encouraging to realize that this role of spiritual leadership can and should be accompanied by the divine guidance and leadership of the Holy Spirit. In this task Eli failed the first time around. But, having been given a second chance, the Scriptures reveal the wisdom with which Eli raised and mentored Samuel.

One striking example of Eli's wisdom is found in the dramatic conversation that Samuel has with God as recorded in 1 Samuel 3. During the night Samuel hears a voice calling to him, which he naturally assumes is the voice of Eli, but he is incorrect. The young boy goes to Eli, only to be told that the priest had not called him. This happens three times. After the third time Eli wisely comes to the conclusion that it may well be the voice of God that Samuel is hearing. Eli then gives Samuel this advice, "Go, lie down; and if he calls you, you shall say, 'Speak, Lord, for thy servant hears'" (1 Sam 3:9). Though the voice of God had been absent from Israel for many long years, Eli, the priest of Shiloh, recognizes that it is God's voice that Samuel is hearing. His role as Samuel's surrogate "grandparent" enabled Eli to have the privilege of training a disciple of the Lord who would be the last of the judges and the first to anoint a king for Israel. God had a special role assigned to Samuel from before the creation of the world. And God's role for Eli was to nurture and mentor Samuel to prepare him for the crucial ministry he would fulfill. He did not do well with Hophni and Phinehas, but he fully accomplished God's purpose for him with Samuel.

How many people like Eli are sitting in the pews of our churches? How many older adults whose children are grown or who have moved away could be spiritual mentors, providing a positive spiritual influence in the lives of children at the church who do not have a close relationship to a grandparent? How many children in the neighborhood around the church or near their homes could grow and mature as a result of having a special connection with an older, mature adult? Thousands of young people need the advantage of surrogate grandparents. Many children have never been around older people; they know nothing of the generations. They live as "cut flowers" and have few if any roots. They desperately need contact with caring, Christian grandparents.[16]

Eli was a powerful teacher and spiritual mentor to Samuel. In many different ways our older church members can be a powerful influence in the lives of the children today.

Lois and Eunice. Another significant text that reveals the important role of grandparents as spiritual mentors can be found in the New Testament in the life of the disciple Timothy; Timothy's grandmother, Lois; and his mother, Eunice. Readers of the New Testament are most likely to meet the young Timothy first in 1 Cor 4:17. Here we find the apostle Paul describing his young protégé in the warmest and most endearing terms: "Therefore I am sending to you Timothy, my beloved and faithful child in the Lord, to remind you of my ways in Christ, as I teach them everywhere in every church" (1 Cor 4:17 NASB) Paul often refers to Timothy in such warm terms. The first letter to Timothy opens with Paul describing him as "my true child in the faith" (1 Tim 1:2). He refers to his young student as "my beloved child" in the prologue to 2 Timothy. It is with such *fatherly* terms that he describes Timothy to the Philippians, "But Timothy's worth you know, how as a son with a father he has served me in the Gospel" (Phil 2:22).

What also makes Timothy's story so compelling is his background. Timothy was born the son of a Jewish mother, Lois, but of an unnamed Greek father. This fact in and of itself was unusual. It is usually the other way around, with the father being identified by name and the mother left unnamed. As Haenchen points out, "[I]n the eyes of Israel this would not have been considered a legal marriage. At best, the marriage of a Jewish woman with a pagan and the uncircumcision of the son reveal not a devout but rather a lax Judaism."[17] One can speculate that Timothy's lack of circumcision was the result of his father's refusal to allow his son to be considered a Jew rather than a Greek.

Rather than having been raised with a "lax Judaism," the faith of Timothy's mother and grandmother is described in the most glowing of terms. In 2 Tim 1:4, Paul recognizes Timothy is a young man of genuine and sincere faith, and this is the result of the care and nurture he received from a deeply devout mother and grandmother, who are described as women of mature and sincere faith. As Paul writes to Timothy, "I am reminded of your sincere faith, a faith that dwelt first in your grandmother Lois and your mother Eunice and now, I am sure, dwells in you"

---

[16] J. Kessler, *Grandparenting: The Agony and the Ecstasy* (Ann Arbor, MI: Servant Publications, 1993), 161.

[17] E. Haenchen, *The Acts of the Apostles: A Commentary* (Oxford, England: Western Printing Services, 1971), 478, fn 3.

(2 Tim 1:4–5 ESV). Paul chooses a marvelous word to describe Timothy's faith—*anupokritos*. It is a word that means unfeigned, real, sincere, or genuine. There was depth and maturity to the faith of Timothy. This was the result of the depth of his mother's faith and of the faith passed down from his grandmother. This depth of faith so evident to Paul was Timothy's inheritance from his mother and his grandmother.

It is not unusual for children to be at odds with a parent when it comes to matters of faith. This seems to have been the case for Timothy and his father. There is no mention of his grandfather. One cannot help but ponder how Timothy's grandfather may have felt when the child born to his wife was female. In the context of the culture of the first century, especially if there were only one child born to the family, it is likely that Timothy's grandfather was sorely disappointed. If other children were born to Lois, the New Testament does not speak of them. As is so often seen throughout the Old and the New Testament, what the world considers a disappointment, God sees as an opportunity. The sincere faith of his mother, as she had learned it from *her* mother, prepared Timothy for his future role as the protégé of the great apostle Paul. The sincere faith of Lois, and her daughter Eunice, prepared the soil from which would be born the sincere faith of Timothy, the future, disciple-making-disciple of Jesus Christ. Lois and Eunice would have had no idea of how their influence in the life of Timothy would eventually affect the world, beginning with his ministry alongside Paul in the churches of Galatia.

Among his early assignments, the apostle Paul dispatched the young Timothy to the church at Corinth. Paul conveys to the Corinthians that Timothy is the messenger he considers best suited to deliver to them his wishes for the church at Corinth. Paul, however, is also aware that the Corinthians can be a stubborn and troublesome group of people, so he specifically asks them to be kind to his young disciple. "When Timothy comes, see that you put him at ease among you, for he is doing the work of the Lord, as I am. So let no one despise him" (1 Cor 16:10–11 ESV).

As time passes, Timothy's reputation as the protégé of Paul grows. Timothy was a man of sincere faith and a devoted disciple of Jesus Christ, and word of his ministry spread to the other churches throughout the region. Regarding Timothy, F. F. Bruce makes the observation, "Timothy had probably become a Christian when Barnabas and Paul visited Lystra, and now older Christians from Iconium as well as Lystra spoke enthusiastically of his spiritual development and promise."[18] In Timothy, the spiritual legacy of Lois and Eunice continued to grow.

The Prodigal Son. The *Parable of the Prodigal Son*, or as Helmut Thielicke describes it, the *Parable of the Waiting Father*, may be one of the most

---

[18] F. F. Bruce, *Paul: Apostle of the Heart Set Free* (Grand Rapids, MI: Eerdmans, 1977), 214.

preached texts from the Gospels. Typically this passage suggests that a child who has left home in disgrace can return and will find that the father has been prayerfully and anxiously awaiting his child's return. And the son does return, but the son does not return to an empty house. Some have interpreted the point of the parable arguably to mean that Jesus is waiting to welcome back those who have broken fellowship with him and the community of faith.

The *Parable of the Prodigal Son* is set in a traditional Jewish family. Although there is no mention of grandparents, it is appropriate to assume, based on what we know about the Hebrew and Canaanite family, that if they were still living, the grandparents would be an integral part of the prodigal's compound where this joyful reunion would have taken place. The story of the prodigal son is the story of a young man who returns to the family home and is accepted, welcomed, forgiven, and celebrated.

The Current State of Grandparenting in America: Changing Demographics

According to the 2000 U.S. Census (the latest available at the time of this writing), 5.8 million grandparents live with their grandchildren age 18 years or younger. Of those, 2.4 million grandparents are the primary caregivers responsible for raising their grandchildren. Kearney's research showed that in 1995 grandparents were raising 6 percent of all children in the United States.[19]

The phenomenon of grandchildren living with or being raised by their grandparents is not unique to the United States but is found worldwide. Internationally, it is difficult to comprehend the growing number of families torn apart by divorce, HIV/AIDS, war, death, incarceration, teenage pregnancy, and many other causes that have contributed to this growing phenomenon. According to a report produced by the U.S. Census Bureau, *Grandparents Living with Grandchildren: 2000,* the 2000 census was the first time the government asked questions specific to the role of grandparents as caregivers.[20] The importance of these statistics becomes clear when one realizes the increasing number of grandparents who have become responsible for the primary needs of their grandchildren. In California alone, nearly 32 percent provide the primary care of food, clothing, and housing for their grandchildren. California has had an almost 50 percent increase,

---

[19] Ibid., 3.

[20] U.S. Bureau of the Census. *Grandparents Living with Grandchildren: 2000: Census Brief.* Prepared by T. Simmons and J. Lawler Dye, the U.S. Department of Commerce: Economics and Statistics Administration, U.S. Bureau of the Census. Washington, D.C: Government Printing Office, issued October 2003.

with 625,934 children younger than age 18 now living in grandparent-headed households."[21]

As reported in the online newsletter *Grandparents as Parents*, "More than six million children—approximately 1 in 12—are living in households headed by grandparents (4.5 million children) or other relatives (1.5 million children). In many of these homes, grandparents (approximately 2.4 million) and other relatives are taking on primary responsibility for the children's needs. Often they assume this responsibility without either of the child's parents present in the home."[22] This has resulted in an almost 30 percent increase in the number of children younger than age 18 living in grandparent-headed households nationally since the 1990 census.

Wimberly rightly points out that the traditional image of the grandparent is "providing the Sunday dinner has been replaced by restaurants, fast-food outlets, and junk food."[23] She also makes note of the role "caretaker as now being associated with television, movies, video-games, and the internet."[24] The weekly visit to grandma's house for Sunday dinner is a thing of the past.

The church can and should be a source of information, encouragement, and support for these intergenerational caregivers whose challenges are more than just providing food, housing, and clothing. In the past the church often participated in filling this role in a variety of ways based on the continuity of multigenerational families growing up in the same communities and congregations. However, in our contemporary social context the church is being called on to do more. As Wimberly argues, "[T]here is more for the faith communities to do than simply see and marvel at the contribution of grandparents raising grandchildren to communal life. There is the need for concrete expressions of appreciation to these members of our communities as well as care and support for them and their grandchildren."[25] Grandparents and intergenerational caregivers need encouragement and support. They need to know they are not the only ones facing the challenges of raising children. In many of our urban settings, where the increase of grandparents becoming the primary caregiver of the child(ren) is nothing short of alarming, the needs are even more acute. Coupled with economic, relational, spiritual, and legal stresses, these families also have the complexity of ethnic distinctions to consider.

---

[21] *Grandparents as Parents.* Statistic, http:// www.grandparentsasparents.org/aboutGAP/statistics.php 2008, (accessed June 30, 2009).

[22] "State Fact Sheets for Grandparents and Other Relatives Raising Children" (October 2007), http://www.grandfactsheets.org/state_fact_sheets.cfm.

[23] A. E. Streaty Wimberly, "From Intercessory Hope to Mutual Intercession: Grandparenting Raising Grandchildren and the Church's Response," *Family Ministry*, 14:3 (Fall 2000), 21.

[24] Ibid.

[25] Ibid., 30.

Diversity Considerations

The distinctive features of various ethnic communities throughout the United States should also be factored into the contemporary role of grandparenting. A report compiled by the Child Trends Data Bank in 2006, based on the *Child Trends Calculations of the U.S. Census Bureau Current Population Survey,* showed that only 35 percent of African-American children younger than age 18 were living with two parents in the home, and 51 percent of African-American children live with only the mother.

This contrasts with the white, Hispanic, and Asian populations, in which 74 percent, 66 percent, and 84 percent of the children are living with both parents, respectively. By contrast, 18 percent of whites, 25 percent of Hispanics, and 10 percent of Asian children live with only the mother present in the home (see chart).

	Living with Both Parents	Living with One Parent
African-American children	35%	51%
Hispanic children	66%	25%
Caucasian children	74%	18%
Asian children	84%	10%

The data referring to children living with grandparents are equally significant. "In 2006, 9% of all black children did not live with either parent, compared with 5% of Hispanic children, 3% of White children, and 3 percent of Asian children."[26] Amy J. Kearney's doctoral research from 2001 showed that in 1995, "12% of African-American children, 6% of Hispanic children, and 4% of White children [were] under the primary care of their grandparents."[27] The numbers show that in many places throughout our country, the "traditional" family of the past is being replaced by a wide diversity of changing family systems.

---

[26] See http://www.childtrendsdatabank.org/pdf/53_PDF.pdf.

[27] A. J. Kearney. "The Phenomenology of Coping Among Grandparents Raising Their Grandchildren," PhD diss. (Azusa Pacific University, 2001), 24.

	Not Living with Either Parent	Primary Care of Grandparent
African-American children	9%	12%
Hispanic children	5%	6%
Caucasian children	3%	4%
Asian children	3%	N/A

Regarding grandparents, Martins says, "Generally they [grandparents] establish a close relationship with their grandchildren and upon listening to the stories of their parents' infancy, the grandchildren fill the void between past and present, they build their values, and their family history."[28]

The Church's Response: Developing a Theology of Grandparenting

Current data show an increase in nontraditional family systems and the need for alternatives that will give children the spiritual, social, and emotional stability critical for their holistic development. Scripture reveals many principles that can serve as guidelines for the modern family. After examining the scriptural record, Estep observes that throughout the history of Israel, "educational responsibility was placed primarily on the family."[29] As was noted in chapter 4, extended family members played a significant part in the Hebrew household. The older adults offered the younger family members the ability to understand their lived history and to learn the meaning of the traditions on which their households were established. Estep goes on to say, "Christian education has always included the passing down of the history and traditions of the faith community, so our faith becomes an intergenerational affair."[30] To the children, observes Kenneth Woodward, "grandparents were far more important than nannies, babysitters or temporary day care providers."[31]

---

[28] M. S. Martin, *Revista Argentina para el Desarrollo de la Inteligencia*, Publicación del CELADI, Centro Latinoamericano para el Desarrollo de la Inteligencia. Año lll No 2 [Ismari Villa: "Grandparenting in the Hispanic Community," November 18, 2009, 3–4. Unpublished Masters paper.]

[29] J. R. Estep Jr., "Biblical Principles for a Theology for Christian Education," in *A Theology of Christian Education*, ed. J. R. Estep Jr., M. J. Anthony, G. R. Allison (Nashville, TN: B&H, 2008), 51.

[30] Ibid., 52.

[31] K. L. Woodward, "The Grandparent's Role," *Newsweek*, March 1, 1997.

The role of grandparenting is a social norm that always had built into it certain expectations. These *traditional* expectations are undergoing tremendous transformation. Where the "traditional" role of grandparents was secondary to that of parents, today, in increasing numbers, the grandparent or grandparents have become the *primary* caregiver to their grandchildren. In this primary role grandparents are becoming those responsible for the emotional, physical, and spiritual well-being of these children. In addition, whereas grandparents normally have lived in their own homes, not in the home of their children or grandchildren, in growing numbers, grandchildren are now living full-time with their grandparents. Whereas the grandparents' role once was perceived as that of indulging their grandchildren, as shall be seen, many grandparents are now becoming those solely responsible for providing these children with food, clothing, shelter, transportation, discipline, and spiritual instruction.

This transition from secondary to primary care provider often comes to grandparents unexpectedly and, too often, reluctantly. Wimberly states that, although it "is largely assumed that the grandparental role is voluntary and flexible,"[32] in many cases the role of the primary caretaker to their children's children is a role imposed upon them unexpectedly and often suddenly. Gail Gallagher describes this painful reality when she writes, ". . . [G]randparents have literally been taken by surprise when their grandchildren were dropped off on their doorstep and were told, 'the kids are yours.' They are stunned and perhaps even disoriented, but through their grief, they know one thing: they love their grandchildren and they will take care of them."[33] Kearney reported, "Most of the grandparents reported they had little choice in the decision to raise their grandchildren on a permanent basis."[34]

How prepared are these grandparents for the new tasks suddenly thrust upon them? The truth is, a great number of these older adults are not at all prepared for the challenges and responsibilities of assuming the primary care of their children's children. For many, the emotional, financial, physical, and relational adjustments can be severe. In addition, they may be dealing with their own grief if their children have suddenly been taken through illness or death. Wimberly identifies many of these experiences in her essay "From Intercessory Hope to Mutual Intercession: Grandparents Raising Grandchildren and the Church's Response." She writes:

---

[32] Wimberly, "From Intercessory Hope to Mutual Intercession: Grandparents Raising Grandchildren and the Church's Response," 20.

[33] G. Gallagher, "Grandparents Raising Grandchildren Parenting Again," http://www.crosswalk.com/parentint/11605357/print (accessed, September 7, 2009).

[34] Kearney, "The Phenomenology of Coping Among Grandparents Raising Their Grandchildren," 24.

> Grandparents experience grief over the inability of the grandchildren's parents to parent, over the parents turning out differently than the grandparent had hoped, or over the death of the grandchild's parent and of whom the grandchild stands as a reminder. Grandparents experience anger for being thrust in the situation, anger at the grandchildren's parents for causing the situation, guilt for what they, the grandparents, might have done but didn't do to prevent the situation and fear that their own life changes, health, or death will cut short the care they offer.[35]

Grandparents and Surrogate Grandparents as Spiritual Mentors

In 2001 I published an article in the *Evangelical Dictionary of Christian Education* on the subject of mentoring in the family. In this article I pointed out the difference between *parenting* and *mentoring* and suggested that the "Father Figure" in Luke 15 "moved from parent to mentor in letting go and allowing for the son's voluntary selection of the father's values."[36] As has been stated already, grandparents often become surrogate parents who end up providing long-term care for their grandchildren.[37] In this capacity these grandparents become significant *mentors* to their grandchildren. Boucher strongly affirms the important role of grandparents when she writes:

> Each of us can make a valuable contribution to our grand-children's lives through [the] gift of companionship. People of different ages need each other. The child rekindles in us a sense of play, adventure, and surprise. The grandparents can add a sense of appreciation, a stepping back, a reflection on life that deepens the child. Timelessness can be shared.[38]

In the past, if a member of a family went off to war, or for other reasons left the household, the family was held together often with the aid of both sets of grandparents or other extended family members who would automatically assume the responsibility of caring for and mentoring the children and the grandchildren. In many non-Western societies today, families continue to live in close proximity to one another. What a dramatic contrast to America, where 95 percent of the children have limited or no contact with their grandparents at all, as discovered by the Kornhaber and Woodward study.

---

[35] Wimberley, "From Intercessory Hope to Mutual Intercession: Grandparents Raising Grand-children and the Church's Response," 27.

[36] G. Coulter, "Mentoring in the Family" in *Evangelical Dictionary of Christian Education*. ed. M. Anthony (Grand Rapids, MI: Baker Book House, 2001), 460.

[37] Kearney, "The Phenomenology of Coping Among Grandparents Raising Their Grandchildren," 4.

[38] Boucher, 21.

The Church as an Intergenerational Community of Faith

As has been the case in the past, in today's world the church can and should become the *betab*, the intergenerational community of faith where wisdom, care, mentoring, and parenting occur as they do in the birth family. There are often many "grandfather and grandmother" figures in our local churches who can become available to the lives of these young people. This idea is supported by Hellerman in *When the Church Was a Family.*

> Spiritual Formation occurs primarily in the context of community. People who remain connected with their brothers and sisters in the local church almost invariably grow in self-understanding, and they mature in their ability to relate in healthy ways to God and to their fellow human beings. This is especially the case for those courageous Christians who stick it out through the often-messy process of interpersonal discord and conflict resolution. Long-term interpersonal relationships are the crucible of genuine progress in the Christian life. People who stay also grow.[39]

A key element of this chapter is the need to give greater attention to the influences that grandparents and substitute grandparents or caregivers can bring to bear upon the task of raising and nurturing young children and adolescents. A number of informative examples of just how the people of God have filled these in children's lives in the past can be found in the Scriptures of both the Old and the New Testaments. In 1 John 2:12–14 we find these family and generationally oriented words of the apostle John, "I write to you, my children, because your sins are forgiven for the sake of Christ. I write to you, fathers, because you know him who has existed from the beginning. I write to you, young men, because you have defeated the Evil One" (1 John 2:12–14 TEV). In commenting on this text Kesler points out the intergenerational influences *assumed* by the apostle. "[This] passage contains the essential characteristics of each generation. This scriptural passage is gender neutral—it speaks of both men and women, the people of God's concern. In reference to biblical culture, this passage speaks of children, parents, and grandparents."[40] Kesler identifies the different characteristics of each generation. According to Kesler, children "are obsessed with *getting* from God. Young adults are obsessed with *doing* for God. . . . Grandparents, however, are noted for being—for knowing God."[41]

---

[39] J. H. Hellerman, *When the Church Was a Family* (Nashville, TN: B&H Academic, 2009), 1.
[40] J. Kessler, *Grandparenting: The Agony and the Ectasy* (Ann Arbor, MI: Servant Publications, 1993), 85.
[41] Ibid.

Today's children are certainly concerned with getting "stuff," such as the latest brand of court shoe, the coolest skateboard, the newest iteration of a cell phone. Unquestionably, today's adults are constantly under pressure to meet the family's financial obligations and provide for their children's material needs. Too often these responsibilities alone consume much of their time, leaving parents physically and emotionally drained, with little energy left for the nurturance of their children. This reality is even more challenging for the single parent, who is solely responsible for the care and provision of their children. This raises a pertinent question: "Is there time to provide for these children's spiritual or emotional needs? This question can be even more pertinent when one speaks of fractured or broken families. As already observed, the biblical culture assumes that grandparents are in the home as part of a family's intergenerational community of faith. Or as Kesler observed, grandparents can effectively model for their grandchildren the essential importance of coming to *know* God. In today's context this ancient biblical tradition can provide a critical antidote to the effects of working, exhausted parents, and broken homes.

We now turn our attention to the grandparenting and mentoring role that can appropriately be filled by the local congregation. In the era of the church of the first century, the family compound filled the important cross-generational responsibility of caring for and nurturing its children. This, however, is not a model unique to the biblical narrative and the world of the Ancient Near East. In a 1997 *Newsweek* article, the editor commented on contemporary family structures in Africa by making reference to Hilary Clinton's book *It Takes a Village.* He writes:

> In her best-selling book, Hillary Rodham Clinton misconstrues the old African proverb "It takes a village"—her title "to raise a single child." Those African villages were not at all like small-town America in the 1950s. They were tribal clans, extended-family networks of grandparents and aunts and uncles with strong spiritual, emotional and biological ties. A more apt proverb for today's truncated nuclear family would be 'It takes a whole village to replace a single grandparent." Indeed, in terms of nurture and emotional commitment, grandparents are infinitely more precious to grandchildren than a whole villageful of babysitters, child-development specialists, day-care centers and after-school programs. And when it comes to support for working single mothers, close grandparents can be indispensable.[42]

[42] K. L. Woodward, "The Grandparents' Role," *Newsweek*, March 1, 1997.

If the secular world recognizes the significance of "community" for the nurturance of a child, how much more significant should be the role of the church? The church should become the ultimate God-created community of faith for the care and nurture of the many children identified by Kornhaber and Woodward who have only limited or no contact at all with their grandparents.

There is another side of this grandparent/grandchild coin, which is the emotional and spiritual needs of our elderly members. Kearney found in her study that some grandparents "felt they received a second chance to do right by their grandchildren and make up for missed time with their own children."[43] The Old Testament account of the prophet Eli provides an example of a father who was given a "second chance" with Samuel after he had failed to raise his own children properly.

The church should be aware of the needs of its senior members who are also home alone. These are older members of our churches who themselves have survived a divorce in their earlier years or who may be survivors of broken or fractured homes. These may be seniors who are alone because of the death of a spouse, or they could be alone because their children have relocated to another community. How valuable would it be if the church were able to connect these older disciples, with their life experiences, historical roots, and spiritual giftedness, with the young people who do not have grandparents or parents available to be a positive influence in their lives? Boucher asked 30 people what they liked best about being grandparents. What she discovered was that "[a] majority of grandparents liked watching children, appreciating their freedom, imagination, liveliness, and personalities. They were aware of growth and celebrated life through their grandchildren's activities."[44] Too many of our older members are missing such opportunities when the church fails to bring the generations together.

Such experiences as these need not be restricted solely to one's biological grandchildren or grandparents. Just as the "grandparent-grandchild relationship is nurtured by sharing experiences and spending time with each other,"[45] so also these special relationships can be developed and nurtured between our congregation's elderly citizens and its younger members. When an older member of a church takes the opportunity to develop a relationship with a young person, the benefits could be limitless for both. The youngsters would have somebody who shows an interest in them and their life. They would experience the joy of being in a relationship with an older adult that has the time and concern to watch them

---

[43] Kearney, "The Phenomenology of Coping Among Grandparents," 4–5.

[44] T. M. Boucher, *Spiritual Grandparenting: Bringing Our Grandchildren to God* (New York: The Crossroad Publishing Co., 1977), 18.

[45] D. Evans, *Ready or Not, You're a Grandparent* (Colorado Springs, CO: ChariotVictor, 1997), 112.

grow and to appreciate their youthful liveliness. These young people could face the possibilities of a life-transforming relationship that comes from receiving the gift of their surrogate grandparent's grace-filled love. And the senior citizen could enjoy the wonder and privilege of serving as spiritual mentors to these children. What Boucher says of grandparents can also be said of the substitute or surrogate grandparent.

> Grandparenting means building bridges across three generations. . . . We can delight in the bridge work involved in relating to our grandchildren. A bridge is firmly anchored on two shores. It holds fast and so do we. . . . A successful bridge also spans an open area with a great deal of flexibility. In the same way grandparents can guard important breathing and growing space between the generations. A bridge relies on the natural tension of its building materials. We must accept mid-life and family tensions as part of our experience, relying on the power of God's love. Finally, the goal of a bridge is the communication it allows. We can enjoy the same goal as we reach out across the generations.[46]

Conclusion

So much can be learned from grandparents or surrogate grandparents. When these mature, older believers give of their lives to another generation, who knows what fruit will be harvested? When these mature believers step into the lives of these children, often rootless and troubled, they can become a truly profound source for spiritual transformation and the renewal of these young lives. They can lead them into the Scriptures. They can teach them about Jesus. They can show them how to pray. They can model for them real lives of faith that are built on a lifetime of experiences with Jesus.

In addition, building relationships, experiencing mutual love, and sharing lives and histories with one another are activities whose benefits could be experienced by both the young person and the senior citizen in our congregations. Influencing the growth and development of the spiritual and emotional life of a child can be a reward in and of itself. Discovering and using the spiritual gifts bestowed upon them by God would be a great privilege for the senior citizen, as would being valued and respected by someone from a younger generation. The seniors' lives can be greatly enhanced as they overcome the possible feelings of loneliness and uselessness that often afflict the elderly in our churches.

Learning about the realities of life from one who has lived life; discovering the importance of their place within God's community of faith;

---

[46] Boucher, *Spiritual Grandparenting: Bringing Our Grandchildren to God,* 46–47.

and learning in a new and fresh way the meaning of God's precious love, acceptance, forgiveness, and grace could become vehicles for powerful and genuine spiritual transformation in the lives of the young persons in and around our churches. For this reason, a biblical theology of grand-parenting and other care providers should provide us with the perspective we need to turn our resolve into action. Grandparents or surrogate grandparents can and should be equipped by the church to make a difference in the lives of young people because in so doing they are helping to pass on the baton of faith to the next generation.

9 Family Ministry Models

Timothy Paul Jones
Randy Stinson
The Southern Baptist Theological Seminary

How does family ministry look in the context of the local church? And how can church leaders guide a congregation toward healthy models for family ministry?

Well, that depends on the church and on how you define "family ministry."

In one church "family ministry" may simply refer to a counseling program for troubled families. Another congregation's family ministry might require a churchwide emphasis on parental involvement in their children's Christian formation. Some communities of faith perceive family ministry as a program that provides a full roster of intergenerational events.

No wonder, then, that whenever a church leader asks us how to implement family ministry, our first response is, "What do *you* mean by 'family ministry'?" What we find is that, for some ministers, implementing a family ministry means they want a program to help fractured families. For others *family ministry* simply describes the way their preschool, children's, and youth ministries work together. Still others understand family ministry as a way to eliminate their youth and children's ministries. A few have no clue what they mean by "family ministry," but they have heard the term so often they are certain that—whatever it is—their church must need one.

Why this disparity in definitions? Youth ministry professor Chap Clark put it this way: "Unlike other areas of ministry focus, family ministry emerged without any sort of across-the-board consensus of what it is. Because of this lack of a common perception of family ministry, people responsible for family ministry in churches are often confused and frustrated."[1]

---

[1] C. Clark, *The Youth Worker's Handbook to Family Ministry* (Grand Rapids, MI: Zondervan, 1997), 13.

Conceptualizing Family Ministry

In addition to the challenge associated with defining family ministry, developing and implementing family ministry models for local church's application becomes even more difficult. One family ministry specialist provided this whimsical progression after being asked how to implement a particular model for family ministry: "Try something. Fail. Try something else. Fail again. Try something else. Stumble on one thing that works. Repeat what works. Try something else . . . you get the idea."[2] Although we appreciate his honesty and good humor, we also know that church leaders desperately need a more accurate understanding of family ministry. Good stewardship requires better intentionality than this trial and error approach of ministry programming.

A well-articulated model for family ministry can provide us with practical handles for what family ministry might look like in the local church. As such, the first item on our agenda will be to determine what a biblical model for family ministry might look like. Next we will consider a brief overview of selected family ministry models from across church history. Finally, we will examine three specific, contemporary models for the future of family ministry.

Biblical Foundations for a Family Ministry Model

In other fields of study, a "model" must meet three criteria: A model is based on an original object or idea *(Abbildung)*; the model must include only relevant properties from the original *(Verkürzung)*; and the model must be transferable to other contexts *(Pragmatismus)*.[3] When it comes to models for church ministry, what this means is that the models must have been implemented in some other congregation (if they have not been implemented anywhere, they are merely ideas, not models); they must include specific properties or patterns that are applicable in other congregations; and these patterns must be transferable into other contexts.

In one sense, no one in the biblical world or throughout most of church history was talking about "models for family ministry." Then again, no one was talking about models for adult ministry, student ministry, or any other ministry either. Thinking in terms of this type of model is not necessarily incorrect, but it is certainly a product of

---

[2] M. DeVries, "Focusing Youth Ministry Through the Family," in *Starting Right: Thinking Theologically About Youth Ministry,* ed. K. C. Dean et al. (Grand Rapids, MI: Zondervan, 2001), 152.

[3] H. Stachowiak, *Allgemeine Modelltheorie* (New York: Springer, 1973), 20–24, 254–64, 320–31. A model must exhibit *Abbildung* (derivation from an original or illustration), *Verkürzung* (capacity to be reduced), and *Pragmatismus* (practicality in another context). See also W. Dangelmaier, *Fertigungsplanung* (New York: Springer-Verlag, 2001), 11–13; A. Karer, *Optimale Prozessorganisation im IT-management* (Berlin: Springer, 2007), 21; B. Reinhoffer, *Heimatkunde und Sachunterricht im Anfangsunterricht* (Bad Heilbrunn, Germany: Klinkhardt, 2000), 50.

modern, Western ways of thinking. At the same time, specific practices and expectations *did* characterize these congregations, and many practices and expectations *are* transferable even to congregations today. Furthermore, although first-century churches may not have explicitly discussed family ministry models, it *is* possible to identify clear expectations in Scripture that relate to the role of the family in Christian formation. Chief among these expectations was the assumption that the Christian formation of children was not a responsibility for the church alone. It was the result of a partnership in which parents took the primary role. Central to first-century Christians' "family ministry model" was the expectation that parents would engage actively in the discipleship of their households.

The apostle Paul specifically commanded Christian fathers to nurture their offspring "in the discipline [*paideia*] and instruction [*nouthesia*] that comes from the Lord" without frustrating or discouraging them (Eph 6:4; Col 3:21). *Paideia* ("discipline") suggests more than using correctives and consequences to prevent a child from engaging in inappropriate behaviors—although that is certainly implied in the term. It also includes intentional and deliberate patterns of training and educating the child in the ways of God—what we might refer to as "discipleship." *Nouthesia* ("instruction") implies calling to mind what is right, good, and true in the day-by-day experiences of life. If a model for family ministry is to be biblical, one essential characteristic of the model must be a prioritized capacity to equip parents, particularly fathers, to engage actively and personally in the discipleship of their children in both planned and spontaneous ways. Given that Paul provided similar instructions in two separate contexts, it would seem that this characteristic is not only practicable but also reducible and transferable.

These expectations were not unique to Paul. When Paul wrote these words, he was drawing from a legacy that had shaped the Jewish people for centuries—a legacy of songs, statutes, and ceremonies that explicitly recognized the primacy of parents in the formation of children's faith. The primary pathway to passing on the truth that "the LORD is one" was by parents engraving this truth in their children's hearts (Deut 6:4–7). One purpose of the ancient Passover was to retell the story of Israel's redemption to the children (Exod 13:14–22). Even the psalmists of Israel called fathers to train their children in the stories and statutes of Israel's God (Ps 44:1; 78:1–8). As such, even though Scripture may not present a distinct model for family ministry in the modern sense, a clear biblical model does exist: Parents are called to personal engagement as primary faith trainers in their children's lives. This occurred both in the daily events of life and through intentional training in the contexts of family festivals and rituals. See chapters 4 and 5 for more detailed teachings on the family in the Old and New Testaments.

Perspectives on the Family in the Early Church

This model for family ministry not only began before Paul's generation but also persisted far beyond the lifetimes of the first followers of Jesus. *Didache* and *Letter of Barnabas* provide summaries of Christian practices that date to the first and second centuries AD. Both of these writings include an identical command for parents—a command that was evidently well known and oft repeated in early churches, which was, "You shall train [your son and your daughter] in the fear of God from their youth up."[4] In a letter to Christians in Philippi, the second-century church leader Polycarp specifically held husbands responsible to partner with their wives "to train their children in the fear of God."[5] Another early Christian leader, Clement of Rome, urged parents to pursue the privilege of sharing with their children "the instruction that is in Christ."[6] Church father Chrysostom described how children should become "athletes for Christ."[7] How, according to Chrysostom, were children to be coached toward such athleticism?

> To each of you fathers and mothers, I speak: Just as we see artists fashioning their paintings and statues with great precision, so we must care for these wondrous statues of ours. . . . Like the creators of statues, give all your leisure time to fashioning these wondrous statues of God. As you remove what is unhelpful and add what is lacking, inspect them day by day, to see with which good qualities nature has supplied them so that you can increase these qualities, and to see which faults so that you can eradicate them.[8]

Throughout the earliest centuries of Christianity, households remained central to Christian practices,[9] and parents were expected to play

---

[4] Unless otherwise indicated, all Greek and Latin texts are rendered by the author from primary source materials. *Didache,* in *The Apostolic Fathers, I,* ed. B. D. Ehrman (Cambridge, MA: Harvard University, 2003), 4:9; *Epistle of Barnabas,* in *The Apostolic Fathers, II,* ed. B. D. Ehrman (Cambridge, MA: Harvard University, 2003), 19:5

[5] Polycarp of Smyrna, *Pros Philippesious Epistole,* 4:2, http://www.ccel.org/l/lake/fathers/polycarp-philippians.htm.

[6] Clement of Rome, *First Epistle,* in *The Apostolic Fathers, I,* ed. B. D. Ehrman (Cambridge, MA: Harvard University Press, 2003), 21:6-8.

[7] J. Chrysostom, *De Inani Gloria,* ed. A. M. Malingrey (Paris: Editions du Cerf, 1972), §19; 39; 63; 90.

[8] J. Chrysostom, *De Inani Gloria,* ed. A. M. Malingrey (Paris: Editions du Cerf, 1972), § 22.

[9] J.G. Davies, *Daily Life in the Early Church* (London: Lutterworth, 1952) 25, 130-34; J. McRay, *Paul* (Grand Rapids, MI: Baker, 2003), 391–92; Wayne Meeks, *The First Urban Christians* 2nd ed. (New Haven, CT: Yale University Press, 2003), 75–81. For sociological reflections, see R. Wuthnow, *Producing the Sacred* (Champaign, IL: University of Illinois Press: 1994), 40. The earliest believers did meet in public areas around the Jerusalem temple (Acts 2:46; 5:42). In some cases congregations may have gathered in the *tabernae* (single-room shops with barrel-vaulted roofs) of Christian merchants (P. Lampe, *Die stadtrömischen Christen in den ersten beiden Jahrhunderten* [Tübingen: Mohr, 1987], 156–62). The earliest known structure dedicated for Christian worship was a house, converted in the mid-third century for usage as a meeting place (L. M. White, *Building God's House in the Roman World* [Baltimore: Johns Hopkins University Press, 1990], 15–21). Nevertheless, prior to the fourth century, assembling in homes remained the dominant Christian practice.

a primary and personal role in the formation of their children's faith. This primary parental role did not, however, require every event of spiritual formation to occur in nuclear or even extended family units.[10] In churches of the third century AD—perhaps even earlier—all the generations worshipped together, but men, women, and young people sat separately.[11] Furthermore, this perspective on the discipleship of children did not diminish the responsibility of Christians to care for children who had no parents. The church in general and elders in particular were held responsible for the care of abandoned children and orphans.[12]

Family Ministry Models in the Middle Ages and Reformation

With the dawning of imperial favor in the early fourth century and the crumbling of the Roman Empire in the fifth, the primary locus of Christian practice drifted from homes to dedicated institutional structures. Especially in the early Middle Ages, there appears to have been a loss of the ancient model for discipleship in families. Generations grew less literate, and training in Christian traditions increasingly became the domain of professional clergy in ecclesiastical institutions.

In the latter centuries of the medieval era, church leaders called anew on clergy and fathers and mothers to embrace more active roles in the Christian training of children; this training consisted primarily of memorizing prayers, creeds, and the Commandments.[13] Prayer primers and catechetical books became available to assist parents.[14] However, feudal responsibilities frequently removed fathers from their families for long

---

[10] Earlier generations did, of course, have a concept of nuclear family (Pierre Guichard, J. P. Cuvillier, "Barbarian Europe," in *A History of the Family*, vol. 1 [Cambridge: Polity, 1996], 318–78); however, the concept of the nuclear family as primary, disembedded from a larger clan and community, was inconceivable. F. and J. Gies contend that, prior to the eighteenth century, no European language even possessed any distinct word to describe a father–mother–children unit (*Marriage and the Family in the Middle Ages* [New York: Harper and Row, 1987], 4).

[11] "Let the men sit in another part of the house, toward the east. . . . If anyone be found sitting out of his place, let the deacon who is within reprove him and make him to rise up and sit in a place that is appropriate for him. . . . Let the children stand on one side, or let their fathers and mothers take them to them; and let them stand up. Let the young girls also sit apart; but if there be no room, let them stand up behind the women. Let the young women who are married and have children stand apart, and the aged women and widows sit apart. ... Let the deacon also see that no one whispers, or falls asleep, or laughs, or makes gestures. For so it should be, that with decency and decorum they watch in the Church, with ears attentive to the word of the Lord" (*Didascalia Apostolorum* 12). For text of *Didascalia Apostolorum*, see J. V. Bartlet, "*Fragments of the Didascalia Apostolorum* in Greek," in *Journal of Theological Studies* 18 (1917); R. H. Connolly, *Didascalia Apostolorum* (Oxford: Clarendon Press, 1929).

[12] *Didascalia Apostolorum*, 17.

[13] N. Orme, *Medieval Children* (New Haven, CT: Yale University Press: 2001), 200.

[14] R. Pecock's *The Donet* (ed. E. V. Hitchcock [London: Oxford University Press, 1921], 264) provided a summary of Christian doctrine presented as a dialogue between a father and son. By the fourteenth century, a laypeople's catechism was available for parents to teach children what they learned from priests (John of Thoresby, *The Lay-Folks' Catechism*, ed. H. Nolloth, T. Simmons, http://www.bibliobazaar.com).

periods, especially in noble households.[15] Even when children *did* learn commandments, creeds, catechisms, and prayers in their homes, the instructors were often mothers or perhaps godparents rather than fathers.

Recognizing this movement away from previous practices, sixteenth-century reformers called fathers to recommence their role as primary faith trainers in their children's lives. According to Martin Luther:

> If we would re-instate Christianity in its former glory, we must improve and elevate the children, as it was done in the days of old. . . . It is the chief duty of the father of a family, to bestow more, greater, more constant care upon the soul of his child than upon his body—for this is his own flesh, but the child's soul is a precious jewel, which God has entrusted to his keeping.

Because the father is responsible to instruct his children in godliness, he is responsible to serve, Luther claimed, as "bishop and priest in his house."[16]

Such a model for family ministry did not, however, exclude the possibility of age-organized classes for the discipleship of children, at least among the English Reformers. The 1549 *Book of Common Prayer* required pastors to spend one half hour on Sunday afternoons, at least once every six weeks, instructing children in the Apostles' Creed, the Lord's Prayer, and the Ten Commandments. By 1552 this had become a weekly pastoral responsibility.[17]

The Puritan Model for Family Discipleship

In many ways even the most contemporary models of family ministry can be traced clearly back to the Puritans. Among these heirs of the Reformation, there was a clear model for family discipleship that could be learned and transferred from one context to another. Brief, daily times of family worship were central to this model; in fact, family worship and order were perceived as a primary means for the prospering of true religion in all of life. "You are not likely to see any general reformation," Baxter noted in 1656, "till you procure family reformation. Some little religion there may be, here and there; but while it is confined to single persons, and is not promoted in families, it will not prosper, nor promise

---

[15] B. A. Hanawalt, *Growing Up in Medieval London: The Experience of Childhood in History* (Oxford: Oxford University Press, 1995), 45; B. A. Hanawalt, *The Ties That Bound* (Oxford: Oxford University Press, 1986), 246; L. E. Mitchell, *Family Life in the Middle Ages* (Westport, CT: Greenwood Press, 2007), 152, 179.

[16] M. Luther, "Lectures on Genesis: Chapters 21–25," in *Luther's Works*, 55 vols., trans. G. Schick (Saint Louis: Concordia, 1964), 4:384; cf. Lebrun: P. Aries, "The Two Reformations," in *A History of Private Life: III: Passions of the Renaissance* (Cambridge, MA: Belknap Press of Harvard University Press, 1993).

[17] N. Orme, *Medieval Children* (New Haven, CT: Yale University Press, 2001), 201, n 8.

much future increase."[18] In Scotland the church leadership instructed ministers to discipline any "Head of the Family" who neglected family worship[19] and to discern in their pastoral visits "Whether God be worshipped in the family, by prayers, praises, and reading of the Scriptures? Concerning the behavior of servants towards God and towards man; if they attend family and public worship? If there be catechizing in the family?"[20] In New England officers known as "tithingmen" maintained family order by publicly reporting fathers who failed to manage their households well.[21] In 1750 Jonathan Edwards admonished a congregation that had forcibly terminated him with these words:

> Let me now therefore, once more, before I finally cease to speak to this congregation, repeat, and earnestly press the counsel which I have often urged on the heads of families, while I was their pastor, to great painfulness in teaching, warning, and directing their children; bringing them up in the training and admonition of the Lord; beginning early, where there is yet opportunity, and maintaining constant diligence in all labors of this kind. . . . Every Christian family ought to be as it were a little church, consecrated to Christ, and wholly influenced and governed by His rules. And family education and order are some of the chief means of grace. If these fail, all other means are likely to prove ineffectual.[22]

This model for family ministry did not, however, prevent church leaders from gathering age-organized groups for the purpose of teaching biblical truths. In 1674 a resident of Roxbury, Massachusetts, recalled the restoration of his church's "primitive practice" of "training up . . . male youth" by gathering them on Sundays to "examine their remembrance" of the sermon and to hear them recite portions of the catechism. Female youth gathered for a similar meeting on Mondays. Church records from Norwich, Connecticut, in 1675 and from Plymouth in 1694 suggest that such practices were widespread in New England.[23]

---

[18] R. Baxter, *The Reformed Pastor,* 93, http://books.google.com.

[19] *Confessions of Faith, Catechisms, Directories, Form of Church Government, Discipline, & c. of Publick Authority in the Church of Scotland* (Glasgow: John Bryce, 1764), 252.

[20] Act of Assembly 1596, ratified 1638, recorded in *Overtures of the General Assembly, A.D. 1705, Concerning the Method of Proceeding in Kirk-Sessions and Presbyteries. The Confessions of Faith and the Books of Discipline to the Church of Scotland of the Anterior to the Westminster Confession* (London: Ellerton and Henderson, 1831), 154

[21] S. Coontz, *The Social Origins of Private Life: A History of American Families, 1600–1900* (London: Verso, 1988), 79.

[22] J. Edwards, "A Farewell Sermon," http://www.sermonaudio.com/sermoninfo.asp?SID=370611425.

[23] *Publications of the Colonial Society of Massachusetts, Volume 21* (Boston, MA: The Colonial Society of Massachusetts, 1920), 259–65. Young people also gathered as early as 1717 in "singing schools" (Francis Otis Erb, *The Development of the Young People's Movement* [Chicago: University of Chicago, 1917], 16–17).

Christians of this era may not have discussed models for family ministry per se. They did, however, pursue a clear, practicable, and transferable model for the Christian formation of families. Fundamental to their expectations was the notion that parents bore first responsibility for the Christian formation of their children. Each Christian family should function, in the words of Edwards, "as it were a little church." The primacy of family discipleship did not, however, exclude or negate the necessary role of the larger faith community. Neither did the primacy of the parents' role preclude regular, age-organized gatherings of children and youth for the purpose of instruction in Scripture and theology.

Family Ministry after the Industrial Revolution

The Enlightenment, the Industrial Revolution, and the conquest of the American frontier reshaped Western culture in the eighteenth and nineteenth centuries. In the shadow of these social shifts, many long-standing expectations—including the ideal of parental responsibility for children's spiritual formation—began to shift. Especially in the lands most affected by the Enlightenment, the concept of family moved from a clan, embedded in a community and united by a common covenant, to a nuclear unit commenced by the mutual consent of two individuals.[24]

Prior to the eighteenth century nuclear and extended families had worked together on farms and then in cottage industries centered in homes.[25] As the Industrial Revolution reshaped economic structures, family members in urban areas found themselves separated from one another, with each one working at different tasks in factories or mills.[26] The Puritan model that had prized family education and worship began

---

[24] J. Q. Wilson, *The Marriage Problem: How Our Culture Has Weakened Families* (New York: HarperCollins, 2003). The transition to nuclear family had been under way since the ninth century or earlier (J. A. Brundage, *Law, Sex, and Christian Society in Medieval Europe* [Chicago: The University of Chicago, 1987]), but the unique development in this era was the shift to a nuclear family initiated by individual choice based on attraction rather than a covenant embedded in clan and community (G. R. Quale, *A History of Marriage Systems: Issue 13 of Contributions in Family Studies* [Santa Barbara, CA: Greenwood Press, 1988]).

[25] D. M. Scott, B. W. Wishy, *America's Families: A Documentary History* (New York: Harper and Row, 1982), 219.

[26] S. J. Keillor, *This Rebellious House: American History and the Truth of Christianity* (Downers Grove, IL: InterVarsity Press, 1996), 118; N. Smelser, *Social Change in the Industrial Revolution: An Application of the Theory to the British Cotton Industry* (London: Routledge Taylor & Francis Group, 1959), 185–200. "The invention of steam-driven machinery led directly to the rise of the factory system with its beneficent and maleficent effects. The old system of home manufacture, in which personal skill was so large a factor, in which the master and his family were on friendliest terms with journeyman and apprentice, in which the children of the household early made their contribution of labor under the parental eye, and so learned the family trade, was swept away. In its place came largely increased production and the crowding of people about the factories" (F. O. Erb, *The Development of the Young People's Movement* [Chicago: University of Chicago Press, 1917], 2). All family members might be employed by the same factory (D. M. Scott, B. W. Wishy, *America's Families: A Documentary History* [New York: Harper & Row, 1982], 219), but the nature of factory work prevented familial interaction.

to falter. In the early and mid-1700s, father-led family worship had been a daily fixture in many homes.[27] By the waning years of the eighteenth century, paternal involvement in children's spiritual formation seems to have grown increasingly rare.[28] "Attendance at church was greatly neglected and particularly by men," one examiner noted in 1793. "Evenings were frequently loose and riotous; particularly owing to bands of apprentice boys. . . . Family worship was almost disused."[29]

Employed by factories but disconnected from multigenerational communities, "large numbers of young men and women were left virtually without moral oversight."[30] Children who worked in factories or whose parents worked in factories could not attend school during the week. Sunday schools arose to provide education, in addition to moral and religious instruction, for these children.[31] Although well-intended and effective in many ways, Sunday school also helped to transfer religious instruction out of the home.

Faced with increasing family fragmentation, a new social epitome began to take shape: In an ideal family, the father—once the coordinator of labor and production within the household—would become a breadwinner whose sphere of labor was outside the household while wife and children remained in the home.[32] And thus, "in the rise of the factory system," Henry Frederick Cope observed, "to a large extent the family lost the father."[33]

On the American frontier, post-Enlightenment fragmentation took a somewhat different form, but the results were no less radical. In the earliest American colonies, churches and communities constrained family clans. As cheap land became readily available on the frontier, fathers moved their families west to rule as sovereigns over their own

---

[27] The ideal was twice each day. See, e.g., W. Hurd, *A New Universal History of the Religious Rites, Ceremonies, and Customs of the World* (Blackburn: J. Hemingway, 1799), 681; I. Backus, *A History of New England with Particular Reference to the Denomination of Christians Known as Baptists*, vol. 1 (Boston: Edward Draper, 1777), 100.

[28] For other references to the decline in family worship, see, e.g., J. Newton, "Letter IV," in *The Works of the Reverend John Newton*, vol. 1 (Weybridge, Surrey: S. Hamilton, 1808), 128.

[29] J. Sinclair, *The Statistical Account of Scotland* (Edinburgh: William Creech, 1793), 609.

[30] F. O. Erb, *The Development of the Young People's Movement* (Chicago: University of Chicago Press, 1917), 2. In 1819 Parliament limited factory work to children nine years and older; given that mothers and fathers both worked in factories, this still had the effect of separating children from parents in their labors (F. O. Erb, *The Development of the Young People's Movement* [1917], 6).

[31] Early Sunday schools educated children from six years old until they were 14. The focus of Sunday schools quickly extended to adults and youth, with classes that remained separated. In 1798 in Nottingham, W. Singleton and S. Fox established a Sunday school for working women. By 1817 the Sunday and Adult School Union had been formed in Philadelphia. These schools formed the foundations for "senior" classes for youth aged 14 and older and adult Sunday schools (Erb, *The Development of the Young People's Movement*, 13–15).

[32] For a clear statement of this ideal, see "Matrimony, Our Most Neglected Profession," in *McClure's Magazine* 38 (1912): 626.

[33] H. F. Cope, *Religious Education in the Family* (Chicago: University of Chicago Press, 1915), 20.

forests and fields.[34] Unconstrained by larger clans and faith communities, frontiersmen tended to disengage from their families spiritually and relationally. In some cases, women oversaw both the farms and the formation of their children, while husbands were absent for months—even years—on "long hunts."[35] For men, religious responsibilities, both in their homes and in communities, became constraints to be avoided rather than vital expressions of shared faith.[36]

Not only in the industrialized cities but also on the American frontier, cultural and social revolutions resulted in widespread disengagement of fathers from their children's Christian formation. Earlier ideal models for family ministry had centered on a father who guided his family spiritually through family worship and discipline. This expectation persisted—at least as a theoretical ideal—in the eighteenth and nineteenth centuries. When one individual in rural Kentucky moved toward faith in Christ, one of his first acts was to restore the lapsed practice of family worship "right away the same evening after my return."[37] Working from a theologically liberal perspective, Horace Bushnell's 1847 *Christian Nurture* downplayed "family prayers" but still called fathers to active involvement in their children's religious training, proclaiming that a child "is to grow up a Christian, and never know himself as being otherwise."[38] An 1856 guide for young men entitled *How to Be a Man* flatly declared, "All well-regulated Christian families are assembled, morning and evening, to worship God."[39] It is unclear, however, whether most families—even in the churches—fell into such "well-regulated" models.[40] Admittedly,

---

[34] S. J. Keillor, *This Rebellious House: American History and the Truth of Christianity* (Downers Grove, IL: InterVarsity, 1996); see also D. M. Scott, B. W. Wishy, *America's Families: A Documentary History* (New York: Harper & Row, 1982), 181; A. Skolnick, "Changes of Heart," in *Family Self and Society: Toward a New Agenda in Family Research,* ed. P. A. Cowan (Mahwah, NJ: Lawrence Erlbaum Associates, 1993), 43–68.

[35] Keillor, *This Rebellious House*, 103–9.

[36] Skolnick, "Changes of Heart," 43–68. These remarks from an early nineteenth-century settler represent a typical frontier male response to religion: "I quit Virginia to be out of the way of [preachers]; . . . in my settlement in Georgia I thought I should be beyond their reach. There they were, and they got my wife and daughter into their church. Then I . . . find a good piece of land, feel sure that I shall have some peace from the preachers, and here is one before I've unloaded my wagon! ("Editor's Drawer," *Harper's New Monthly Magazine* 39 [1869]: 935).

[37] "Thomas Cleland," in *The Biblical Repertory and Princeton Review, Index Volume from 1825 to 1868, Part 2, Index to Authors* (Philadelphia: Peter Walker, 1870), 132.

[38] H. Bushnell, *Christian Nurture* (repr. New York: Charles Scribner's, 1903), 10, 333–35.

[39] H. Newcomb, *How to Be a Man* (Boston: Gould and Lincoln, 1856), 56.

[40] By the midpoint of the nineteenth century a flood of books and articles was deploring the fragmented state of modern families (J. Demos, *Past, Present and Personal: the Family and the Life Course in American History* [Oxford: Oxford University Press, 1986], 30). Cope suggested in the early twentieth century that family worship had never been widespread: "Daily family worship was observed in practically all the Puritan homes of New England; but there is no evidence for it as a uniform custom, either in other parts of this country or in other parts of the world, save perhaps in sections of Scotland" (H. F. Cope, *Religious Education in the Family* [Chicago: The University Chicago Press, 1915], 126).

family worship is only a single aspect of a larger ideal, but it is a helpful aspect to trace when it comes to the history of family ministry simply because descriptions and discussions have been preserved. Of note, from the mid-eighteenth to the early twentieth century, the emphases in descriptions of family worship tend to shift from *descriptions of how family worship should occur* to *discussions of how family worship had declined* coupled with *calls for recovery of the practice.*[41]

Antecedents of Twentieth-Century Family Ministry

In this context the foundations for modern and contemporary family ministry models took shape. As early as the seventeenth century, "friendly societies" had linked laborers together to provide mutual aid in times of illness or loss of income.[42] In the late eighteenth and early nineteenth centuries, new forms of these earlier voluntary associations surfaced to provide supports that communities and clans had once supplied. Among laborers, these mutual improvement societies expanded to provide technical training and even instruction in religion.[43]

Other associations emerged alongside mutual improvement societies to address specific societal issues.[44] With each new association there arose a new cause to rally like-minded people and a deluge of books and periodicals to support the society's aims. Sunday school societies sought and trained teachers to educate impoverished children; temperance societies arose to promote abstinence from alcoholic beverages; and mission societies raised funds to convert "the heathen." Most significant for the present discussion, *family improvement societies* and *young people's societies* began to develop.

---

[41] For examples of typical laments about the decline of family worship in popular literature, see, e.g., J. W. Alexander, *Thoughts on Family-Worship* (Philadelphia: Presbyterian Board of Publication, 1847), 2; K. Moody-Stuart, *Brownlow North: The Story of His Life and Work* (London: Hodder and Stoughton, 1879), 226; J. G. Pike, *A Guide for Young Disciples of the Holy Saviour in Their Way to Immortality*, 3rd ed. (London: Richard Baynes, 1831), 233. There are exceptions to these sentiments, however: "In some Presbyteries family worship is nearly universal; other Presbyteries sadly record the too frequent neglect of this ordinance" (W. Caven, "The General Assembly of the Presbyterian Church in Canada," in *The Presbyterian and Reformed Review* [1899]: 657).

[42] D. Burlingame, ed., *Philanthropy in America*, vol. 3 (Santa Barbara, CA: ABC-CLIO, 2004), 324; J. Paisana, "Tipplers, Drunkards, and Backsliders" (PhD diss., Universidade de Minho), 16.

[43] *The Nineteenth Century*, vol. 24 (London: Kegan Paul, 1888), 494; J. Kett, *The Pursuit of Knowledge Under Difficulties*, xii; *Development of the Young People's Movement* (1824), 13. D. Naismith founded the first "Young Men's Societies for Religious Improvement." In 1839, he gave up on them and predicted their speedy demise because of ineffective organization. Many eventually became YMCAs.

[44] With these societies came literature for "self-improvement," which became a consistent theme in this era. See, e.g., G. W. Light, ed., *The Young American's Magazine for Self-Improvement*, vol. 1 (Boston: Rand, 1847), 3–4.

Training the Family: Societies for Family Improvement

Family Improvement Society. One of the first family improvement societies began gathering around 1815 in Portland, Maine, for the purpose of enhancing child-rearing practices. Soon afterward, "maternal associations" organized in other areas.[45] Publishers were quick to provide publications to support family educational efforts. In virtually every instance, the improvement of parenting practices was closely tied to some semblance of Christian faith. A plethora of nineteenth-century books and periodicals provided parents with resources to develop habits of prayer, singing, and Scripture reading in their households.[46] In what may have been an implicit acceptance of paternal disengagement, the bulk of societies and resources seem to have focused on equipping mothers.

Young People's Associations. Influenced by the Sunday school movement and earlier societies for youth,[47] young people's associations also emerged in the 1800s. The first Young Men's Christian Association (YMCA) was organized in 1844 to improve "the spiritual condition of young men engaged in the drapery and other trades."[48] Evangelism of young men was central to the YMCA's mission.[49]

Sixteen years after the founding of the YMCA, the pastor of Lafayette Avenue Presbyterian Church in Brooklyn launched the first "Young People's Association." Although inspired by the YMCA, the Young People's Association was connected to a local church and built on previous practices of youth prayer meetings.[50] The purpose of the Young People's

---

[45] M. Lewis-Rowley, R. E. Brasher, J. J. Moss, S. F. Duncan, and R. J. Stiles, "The Evolution of Education for Family Life," in *Handbook of Family Life Education,* vol. 1: *Foundations of Family Life Education,* ed. M. E. Arcus, J. D. Schvaneveldt, J. J. Moss. (Newbury Park, CA: Sage, 1993).

[46] *Mother's Assistant* and *The Mother's Magazine* became the earliest known periodicals for parents. Even in these periodicals, practices of family worship were recommended repeatedly, with laments that fathers had disengaged from guidance of the household. See, e.g., *The Mother's Assistant and the Young Lady's Friend,* vol. 18–20, 101; F. E. Willard, *Glimpses of Fifty Years* (Chicago: Women's Temperance Publication Association, 1889), 494; "The Family Altar and Its Influences," in *The Mother's Magazine* 18 (1850): 121–23

[47] The teachers in many early Sunday schools first became instructors around 16 years of age; in some areas, these young men and women met on Fridays or Saturdays to prepare their lessons (S. H. Tyng, *Forty Years' Experience in Sunday Schools* [Boston: Gould and Lincoln, 1860], 22–23, 41). This pattern of teacher's meetings was a significant precursor for the later young people's societies. Additionally, by 1861 some Sunday school unions were sponsoring gatherings for youth "of a social and recreative character" (Groser, *Hundred Years' Work for the Children,* 65).

[48] Erb, *The Development of the Young People's Movement,* 29.

[49] C. Brainerd, "Association First Principles," in *The Jubilee of Work for Young Men in North America* (New York: YMCA, 1901), 79.

[50] A. A. Plant, "Young People's Association," in *Lafayette Avenue Church, Its History and Commemorative Services, 1860–1885,* ed. T. Cuyler (New York: Robert Carter, 1885), 256. One of the motivations was the boredom and exclusion of youth participation in the adult prayer-meeting; the association provided places of responsibility and service—but sadly no place for these for young men and women in intergenerational settings (Erb, 38, 53–54).

Association included evangelism ("conversion of souls") and Christian growth and service ("development of Christian character and the training of new converts in religious work").[51] "A small minority" urged that the association gather in church lecture rooms, but the youth chose to meet in a church member's home each week for an hour of singing, Scripture reading, and prayer, followed by "thirty minutes for social intercourse."[52] Although the youth met in homes and the pastor typically made an appearance, the meetings operated independent of church or parental involvement. "The young people," one church member observed, "want this meeting to themselves, they organize it for themselves, and so long as it continues in private houses they will have it to themselves . . . to look after the interests of the young as they come into the church."[53]

"Stimulated and guided" by an article about these Young People's Associations, Clark launched the Society for Christian Endeavor in 1881.[54] The growth of Christian Endeavor societies was nothing short of phenomenal. Within a decade the number of Christian Endeavor societies in local churches had grown from 1 to 16,274 with nearly one million youth enrolled.[55] Denominations that desired more sectarian societies developed distinctive associations that repackaged Christian Endeavor for their youth.[56] Yet, even at these societies' height of popularity, it was "greatly feared that [youth societies] would divide the church on the basis of age, and supplant the church in the affection of the young."[57]

Comprehensive and Programmatic Models for Family Ministry

By the turn of the twentieth century, a single church might have Sunday schools for each age group, mission societies, temperance leagues, young people's prayer meetings, literary societies, and a Young People's

---

[51] L. A. Weigle, *American Idealism* (New Haven, CT: Yale University, 1928), 204.

[52] A. A. Plant, "Young People's Association," in *Lafayette Avenue Church, Its History and Commemorative Services, 1860–1885,* ed. T. Cuyler (New York: Robert Carter, 1885), 257–62. Clearly the implication of "intercourse" in 1885 was different from today.

[53] Ibid., 259. By this point young people were increasingly separated from parents either in labor in factories or in schools. Compulsory elementary schools are widespread, and high schools are growing. H. Mann, "Report for 1848: The Capacity of the Common-School System to Improve the Pecuniary Condition, and Elevate the Intellectual, Moral, and Religious Character, of the Commonwealth," in *Annual Reports on Education* (Boston: Horace Fuller, 1868), 669. W. Reese, *The Origins of the American High School* (New Haven, CT: Yale University Press, 1999), 78; but cf. B. Burrell and R. Eckelberry, "The High School Question Before the Courts in the Post-Civil War Period," *The School Review* 42 (April 1934): 255–65.

[54] Erb, *The Development of the Young People's Movement,* 53.

[55] L. Bacon, C. Northrop, *Young People's Societies* (New York: Lentilhon, 1900), 30. Christian Endeavor worked to remain rooted in the local church (Francis Otis Erb, *The Development of the Young People's Movement* [Chicago: University of Chicago, 1917], 62; L. Bacon, C. Northrop, *Young People's Societies* [New York: Lentilhon, 1900], 33).

[56] L. Bacon, C. Northrop, 33–44.

[57] F. O. Erb, *The Development of the Young People's Movement* (Chicago: University of Chicago, 1917), 59.

Association—all in addition to a Christian Endeavor society for youth and perhaps one or more Endeavor societies for children and even adults. Each program ran parallel to other programs, but the goals and curricula of each group remained unrelated.[58] Furthermore, Sunday school and Christian Endeavor, although connected to the local church, functioned as institutions "outside the church, self-appointed as 'nursery,' and 'feeder,' and 'agency.'"[59]

The ideal of regular religious practices in Christian homes remained strong,[60] yet such customs were still perceived as fading.[61] Herman Horne reported in 1909, "Family worship is almost an extinct custom."[62] In a 1915 survey of congregational churches, 54.9 percent of church leaders reported "worship and religious training in the home" as "Poor" or "Hopeless" among their congregants. Nine percent of churches did nothing at all to encourage family religious training, whereas 26.6 percent did "Nothing Specific."[63] The Presbyterian Church pursued a similar research project and dubbed the results "nothing short of tragic."[64] There was a rising suspicion that daily family worship might never have been as widespread as people had previously perceived.[65] Yet it was lamented that parents—and particularly fathers—had released "the discipline of faults and the moral and religious education of children . . . to the school, the state and the church."[66] Theologically liberal and conservative leaders alike called for the restoration of religious training in the home.

Partly in response to this pattern of parental abdication, the first modern family ministry models began to emerge. The *term* "family ministry" did not enter the common vocabulary of churches until the last half of the twentieth century, but three clear and identifiable family ministry models began to materialize in the first half of the twentieth century. Rooted

---

[58] Bacon and Northrop, *Young People's Societies*, 181; Erb, *The Development of the Young People's Movement*, 60, 113.

[59] Blackall, *The Sunday School Situation* (1913), 3. It appears that, despite the common perception, the "one-eared Mickey Mouse" preceded 1950s by several decades.

[60] See, e.g., S. W. Adriance, "The Child at Family Altar," in *The American Magazine, Supplement* 6 (1887): 241–42; *The Constitution of the Presbyterian Church in the United States of America* (Philadelphia: Presbyterian Board of Publication and Sabbath-School Work, 1901), 441–42; W. S. Harris, *Sermons by the Devil* (Atlanta: Hudgons, 1904), 110–16. Additionally, publications of manuals for family worship and denominational calls for publication of family worship manuals (*Annual of the Northern Baptist Convention*, 146).

[61] T. Cuyler admitted in 1899, "I fear . . . household religion is at a lower ebb than formerly, and family worship is too much neglected." T. Cuyler, quoted in "Is the Armor of God Wearing Out?" in *The Literary Digest* (November 25, 1899): 648–49; "Family Worship," in *The Lutheran Witness* 34 (October 5, 1915): 307; Cope, *Religious Education in the Family*, 126.

[62] H. Horne, *Psychological Principles of Education* (New York: MacMillan, 1909), 367–73.

[63] *The National Council of the Congregational Churches of the United States, Sixteenth Regular Meeting* (Boston: Office of the National Council, 1915), 431–32.

[64] *Minutes of the General Assembly of the Presbyterian Church in the United States of America,* " Appendix" (1909): 126.

[65] Cope, *Religious Education in the Family*, 126.

[66] W. B. Forbush, *The Boy Problem*, 4th ed. (Boston: Pilgrim, 1902), 52.

in the earlier system of separate "societies" for each ministry, none of these approaches to family ministry focused on bringing families together in the context of the church. Each one did, however, attempt to strengthen healthy families and to reconstruct ruptured family relationships.

1. A Comprehensive-Coordinative Model for Family Ministry. Samuel W. Dike, a pastor in Vermont, launched one of the first modern attempts at *coordinating* learning at church with parent-led discipleship in homes. In the 1880s Dike had pointed out how churches were

> enriching [their own programs] of centralized activities at the expense of the home's chance to cultivate family religion. Sunday-school sessions, missionary societies, temperance and other reformatory meetings, young people's meetings, brotherhoods and guilds—each as it came in seized on some Sunday or week-day hour and appropriated it for the use of its own church-centered activity. The churches, in fact, have done for religious training what the factories had done for industrial training. They have taken it out of the home.[67]

Dike did not deny that the church societies were doing some good. He simply contended that these societies had usurped habits of religious training that should occur first and foremost in the Christian home.

Dike dubbed his solution "the Home Department." The Home Department plan was simple: Leaders visited homes of church members to equip the families with recommendations and resources so that parents could engage in discipleship practices with their children. Home Department leaders were urged to "beware of methods that aim to substitute the influence of the teacher or any other school institution in place of that of the parents."[68] The goal was to recognize Christian families as primary units of religious training. It was declared in 1904 that the Home Department was "the only invention of any importance that has been made in the last hundred years in the interests of the home as a religious force."[69] By 1906 approximately 12,000 churches had established Home Departments.

With this growth came considerable confusion of purpose, partly because Dike did not publish a clear statement of his plan until 1904. By the time Dike clarified his intentions, Home Departments in many churches were understood to be Sunday school classes that gathered underprivileged children in teachers' homes.[70] In still other churches,

---

[67] E. M. Fergusson, *Church-School Administration* (New York: Revell, 1922), 124–25.
[68] Ibid., 126, 133.
[69] A. W. Calhoun, *A Social History of the American Family,* vol. 3 (Cleveland, OH: Clark, 1919), 314–15.
[70] "Review of *The Beginnings of the Home Department of the Sunday School,*" in *Hartford Seminary Record* 14 (1903): 78.

Home Departments were established with the primary purpose of providing Bible lessons for "such adults as for various reasons are not regular attendants at Sunday-school."[71]

In 1920 one religious educator declared that the "*first* . . . big thing" needed in Sunday schools was to reinstitute Home Departments with their original function:

> *Rejuvenate the Home Department* until it becomes something more than simply an instrument of carrying . . . Sunday School lessons to invalids, shut-ins, and the aged and infirm. . . . What is the Home Department doing to give parents a vision of the home as the finest educational institution on earth and themselves as the child's natural and best educators?[72]

In the end Dike's vision for the Home Department was not rejuvenated. The Home Department dwindled to a literature distribution ministry to shut-ins and, in the end, expired completely. The results of other attempts to promote household discipleship were equally dismal: As early as 1901, Christian Endeavor called members to join the "Home Circle" and to promote "Family Religion."[73] In 1909 the Federal Council of Churches founded "the Family Altar League" with a similar goal. Although each effort initially enlisted many households, any lasting effect seems to have been slight.

2. A Segmented-Programmatic Model for Family Ministry. In a clear majority of twentieth-century congregations, ministry to families took the form of separate, age-organized programs. In keeping with the ideals of the efficiency movement, ministries were centralized in church buildings, segmented by age, and—if possible—staffed by professionals. In many churches, ministry to youth already operated as a separate component. The economic boom after World War II enabled increasing numbers of churches to hire professional youth ministers whose primary purpose was to engage adolescents.[74]

The segmented-programmatic model was so popular that, by the 1970s and 1980s, it served as the predominant paradigm not only for youth

---

[71] This shift in purpose had occurred at least as early as 1897. See, e.g., W. Gladden, *The Christian Pastor and the Working Church* (New York: Charles Scribner's, 1898), 238; *Saint John Reformed Church of Riegelsville, Pennsylvania* (Riegelsville, PA: B. F. Fackenthal, 1911), 73; G. W. Mead, *Modern Methods in Church Work* (Cambridge, MA: John Wilson, 1897), 238.

[72] F. L. Brownlee, "Church School and Public Opinion," in *Religious Education* 15 (1920): 140.

[73] F. E. Clark, *The Christian Endeavor Manual*, rev. ed. (Boston: United Society for Christian Endeavor, 1912), 195–99.

[74] M. Senter III rightly notes that some churches began to call youth ministers in the mid-1950s. However, this phenomenon did not become widespread until the 1960s and 1970s. Cf. M. Senter III, *The Coming Revolution in Youth Ministry* (Wheaton, IL: Victor, 1992), 142; D. Robbins, *This Way to Youth Ministry* (Grand Rapids, MI: Zondervan, 2004), 440–41.

ministry, but also for preschool, children's, singles, seniors, and other ministries. Ministry to families meant a segmented and professionalized ministry for each member of the family. At their best such ministries trained family members separately in ways that unified them in other contexts.

Whether the segmented-programmatic approach should be called "family ministry" is debatable, but the dominance of this perspective is beyond argument. The segmented-programmatic perspective so thoroughly dominated twentieth-century ministry to families that many churches refer to it as the "traditional" approach—despite the fact that it has yet even to celebrate its sesquicentennial birthday. One result of this disintegrated approach has been that parents have increasingly perceived professionals at church as the persons primarily responsible to engage personally in their children's spiritual formation.[75]

3. An Educational-Programmatic Model for Family Ministry. In the late nineteenth and early twentieth centuries, family improvement societies and maternal associations gave way to formal training programs for "Family Life Education."[76] By the mid-twentieth century, universities, states, and counties had Family Life Education departments in place. Family Life Educators provided training events and programs—typically in the context of a community—to strengthen and enrich family well-being.[77]

A broad range of churches were quick to board the Family Life Education bandwagon. Denominations and congregations established Family Life Education programs, called Family Life Ministers, and even renamed their gymnasiums "Family Life Centers." In this model family ministry was primarily expressed through specific programs that strengthened family relationships. One advantage of this educational-programmatic approach was that it could be easily added to the existing array of programs in a segmented-programmatic church.

At their best these Family Life Education programs looked closely at families in their communities and worked to equip them for healthier relationships. Whereas some family ministry efforts might involve whole families, the family activities and events functioned separately from other church ministries. Most Family Life Education ministries included both *ambulance programs* (families in crisis) and *guardrail programs* (preventing future problems). Family Life Educators also focused on the formation of family-like relationships in churches.

Family Life Education was the perspective promoted in some of the most popular twentieth-century textbooks for church-based family

---

[75] Barna Research Group, "Parents Accept Responsibility for Their Child's Spiritual Development but Struggle with Effectiveness," http://www.barna.org/FlexPage.aspx?Page=BarnaUpdate&BarnaUpdateID=138.

[76] S. Wallace, H. W. Goddard, *Family Life Education* (Thousand Oaks, CA: SAGE, 2005), 3.

[77] For discussion of nature and function of Family Life Education, see M. E. Arcus et al., "The Nature of Family Life Education," in *Handbook of Family Life Education*, ed. M. E. Arcus et al. (Newbury Park, CA: SAGE, 1993).

ministry. In 1957 Oscar Feucht edited a text entitled *Helping Families Through the Church: A Symposium on Family Life Education.*[78] Feucht's approach provided practical helps for developing programs to educate families for healthier relationships and to equip parents to train their children. In the 1960s and 1970s many churches expanded their Family Life Education programs to provide counseling and support groups for troubled family members. Textbooks from Charles Sell and Diana Garland provided foundations for educational-programmatic family ministry that incorporated therapeutic components.[79] Even in the opening years of the twenty-first century, dozens of Christian colleges and seminaries still maintain thriving Family Life Education programs.

Twentieth-Century Models for Family Ministry

Comprehensive-Coordinative	Segmented-Programmatic	Educational-Programmatic
The comprehensive-coordinative model for family ministry equipped parents to function as primary disciple-makers in their children's lives by providing resources and training in their homes. Promoted by Samuel W. Dike in the late 1800s and early 1900s, the "Home Department of the Sunday School" faded, primarily as a result of confusion of purpose and the popularity of the efficiency movement.	In the segmented-programmatic model, ministry to families means a separate and specific program for each member of the family. Driven by a variety of factors—including the earlier society system, the efficiency movement, and (influenced by Young Life and Youth for Christ) the rise of professional youth ministers—the segmented-programmatic model became a dominant approach in the last half of the twentieth century.	The educational-programmatic or Family Life Education model for family ministry establishes *ambulance programs* to assist families in crisis and *guardrail programs* to strengthen healthy families. Family Life Education continues in many congregations, typically as a distinct program for family education and counseling.

78 O. Feucht, ed., *Helping Families Through the Church: A Symposium on Family Life Education* (St. Louis: Concordia, 1957).

79 D. Garland, *Family Ministry* (Downers Grove, IL: InterVarsity, 1999); C. Sell, *Family Ministry*, 2nd ed. (Grand Rapids, MI: Zondervan, 1995).

Contemporary Models of Family Ministry

Unlike the previously discussed segmented-programmatic and educational-programmatic models, more contemporary family ministry models require far more than the addition of one more new program to the church's current roster of activities. These newer contemporary models require the reorientation of every ministry in the church. In essence, a new wineskin is needed. Proponents of these models recognize that the church is in a state of crisis because parents have disengaged from the personal processes of Christian formation with their children.[80] Foundational to this disengagement seems to be that ministry leaders have neither acknowledged nor equipped parents as primary disciplers of their children.

Three contemporary models for family ministry have emerged to meet this challenge: *family based, family integrated,* and *family equipping*. All three rising models represent a break from the segmented-programmatic approaches that dominated twentieth-century churches. In all three of these models, *family ministry* could be defined as "the process of intentionally and persistently realigning a congregation's proclamation and practices so that parents are acknowledged, trained, and held accountable as persons primarily responsible for the discipleship of their children."

Such perspectives do not absolve the church of its responsibility to partner with persons from every age grouping and social background in the task of discipleship—including divorced persons, never-married singles, children from single-parent households, and children with unbelieving parents.[81] What all three of these models recognize is that, because God designed families to serve as the foremost framework for a child's Christian formation, churches must equip parents to function as vital partners in this process. The family is the normative context for the discipleship of children. Every Christian parent is, therefore, responsible to engage personally in the formation of his or her child's faith.

Contemporary Model 1: The Family-Based Model

In the Family-Based Model, no radical changes occur in the dominant segmented-programmatic structure. The congregation still maintains children's ministry, youth ministry, singles ministry, and so on. To train members to perceive parents as crucial partners in children's Christian formation, family-based churches sponsor consistent intergenerational

---

[80] See, e.g., T. P. Jones, ed., *Perspectives on Family Ministry* (Nashville, TN: B&H Academic, 2009), 22–34.

[81] Among early Christians, the church in general and elders in particular were responsible to include orphans in the life of the congregation: "If any child among the Christians is an orphan, it is well that if any brother has no children, he should adopt the orphan in place of children. . . . And you who are overseers: Watch carefully over the orphan's upbringing that they lack nothing! When a virgin girl is of age, give her in marriage to a brother. As a boy is brought up, let him learn a craft so that, when he becomes a man, he will earn a worthy wage" (*Didascalia Apostolorum*, 17).

classes, activities, and events. Students are still likely to experience worship and small groups in peer groups, separated from other generations. Yet each ministry is responsible for planning and pursuing intentional learning experiences that are designed to draw generations together. Mark DeVries pioneered this approach and first presented its implications in his book *Family-Based Youth Ministry.*

In the Family-Based Model, "the job of the church is to keep the priority of family at the forefront of our mission, to give families the understanding and tools they need to raise their children to continue to grow their legacy of faith,"[82] DeVries has noted.

> Most people confuse the starting of a family-based youth ministry with a radical change in programming. . . . But family-based youth ministry is not about what the programming looks like. It's about what you use the programming for. We try to point as much of our programming as possible in the direction of giving kids and adults excuses to interact together.[83]

One way to envision the Family-Based Model is to think of a sunflower: Each petal remains separate, yet all the petals come together at the central disk. In the same way each ministry in a Family-Based Model remains separate; central to the congregation's mission, however, is the expectation that every ministry will consistently plan events and learning experiences that draw families and generations together.

Contemporary Model 2: The Family-Integrated Model

The Family-Integrated Model represents a complete break from the segmented-programmatic approach. Family-integration is by far the most radical model for family ministry. In a family-integrated church, all or nearly all age-graded classes and events are eliminated. That's right: *No* youth group, *no* children's church, *no* age-segmented Sunday school classes. Generations learn and worship together, and parents bear primary responsibility for the spiritual formation of their children. Here's how the National Center for Family-Integrated Churches has described the structure and values of a family-integrated congregation:

> The biblical family is a scripturally-ordered household of parents, children, and sometimes others (such as singles, widows, divorcees, or grandparents), forming the God-ordained building blocks of the church (2 Tim. 4:19). We . . . reject the church's implementation of modern individualism by fragmenting the family through

[82] J. Burns, M. DeVries, *Partnering with Parents in Youth Ministry* (Ventura, CA: Regal, 2003), 16.
[83] M. DeVries et al., "Youth Ministry Architects," http://www.ymarchitects.com/resources.html.

> age-graded, peer-oriented, and special-interest classes, thus preventing rather than promoting family unity.[84]

Proponents of the Family-Integrated Model describe the church "as a family of families."[85] In this they are *not*, however, redefining the essential nature of the church. When it comes to the nature of the church, family-integrated churches stand with other models of church ministry, affirming the orthodox confessions of faith. "Family of families" is a functional description of how family-integrated churches structure their processes of evangelism and discipleship.

Families participating in the Family-Integrated Model view their households as primary contexts for mutual discipleship and evangelism of unbelievers. As a result, they are likely to invite unbelievers into their homes for meals on a regular basis. Through intentional hospitality, unbelieving families observe the dynamics of a Christ-centered family, providing opportunities for the believing family to share the gospel. Small-group Bible studies typically bring entire families together—including singles, single-parent households, and children of nonbelieving parents who have been enfolded into believing families. Many family-integrated churches also gather men for monthly meetings to equip them to disciple their families. Family-integrated congregations do not target homeschooling families. However, because of their emphasis on the need for Christian education in every aspect of life, many family-integrated communities of faith tend to develop and attract home educators.

Contemporary Model 3: The Family-Equipping Model

In the Family-Equipping Model, many semblances of age-organized ministry remain intact. In some cases the family-equipping church might even retain a youth minister or a children's minister. Yet none of these ministries continues in the segmented-programmatic modes of past generations. Every practice at every level of ministry is reworked completely to champion the place of parents as primary disciple-makers in their children's lives.

Whereas churches using the Family-Based Model develop intergenerational activities within existing segmented-programmatic structures, churches using the Family-Equipping Model redevelop their entire structure to call parents to disciple their children. Because parents are the primary disciple-makers of their children in the Family-Equipping Model, every activity for children or youth resources, trains, or involves parents.[86] Children whose parents are unbelievers are connected

---

[84] See http://www.visionforumministries.org/projects/ncfic/a_biblical_confession_for_unit.aspx.

[85] For this quotation and a fuller description of family-integrated ministry, see V. Baucham, *Family Driven Faith* (Wheaton, IL: Crossway, 2007), 191–95.

[86] For the "resource, train, involve" principle, see S. Wright with C. Graves, *reThink: Is Student Ministry Working?* (Raleigh, NC: InQuest, 2007).

with mature believers in the types of relationships Paul described in Titus 2:1–8. Every level of the congregation's life is consciously reworked to "co-champion" the church's ministry *and* the parent's responsibility.[87]

To envision the Family-Equipping Model in action, imagine a river with large stones jutting through the surface of the water. The river represents children's growth and development. One riverbank signifies the church, and the other riverbank connotes the family. Both banks are necessary for the river to flow forward with focus and power. Unless both riverbanks support the child's development, you are likely to end up with the destructive power of a deluge instead of the constructive possibilities of a river. The stones that guide and redirect the river currents represent milestones or rites of passage that mark the passing of key thresholds in the child's life points of development that the church and families celebrate together.

Relating the Models to One Another

None of these ministry models is absolutely exclusive of the others. Each one is likely to overlap with one or two other models. For example, congregational worship celebration in a Family-Integrated Model could look a lot like the intergenerational worship services practiced in churches using the Family-Equipping Model. Much of the programming for a congregation in a Family-Based Model will likely look similar to the programmatic models of previous decades, although Family-Based Model churches will involve parents in as many events as possible.[88] And there could be similarities between parent-training programs in

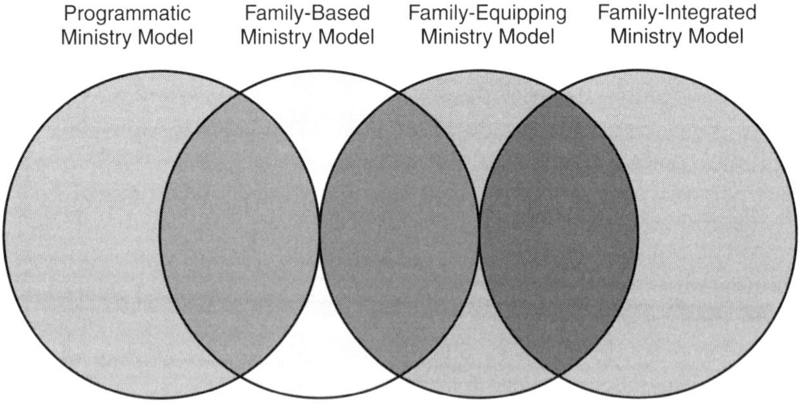

Envisioning the Relationship Between the Models of Ministry

[87] S. Wright with C. Graves, *reThink: Is Student Ministry Working?*
[88] M. DeVries et al., "Youth Ministry Architects."

Family-Equipping and Family-Based congregations. Still, each model of family ministry represents a distinct and identifiable approach to the challenge of drawing the home and the church into a life-transforming partnership.

Conclusion

The family ministry models presented in this chapter are far from the final word. Each of these models has been and is a temporary tool, constructed by well-meaning but imperfect people. Yet there are some perennial truths to be found in these models. As we examine the Scriptures and the approaches to family ministry throughout church history, we find three axioms that ought to characterize present and future family ministry models.

Axiom 1: God has called parents to take personal responsibility for the Christian formation of their children. In the shadow of Mount Sinai, God "established a testimony, . . . which He commanded our fathers to teach to their children, that the next generation might know them" (Ps 78:5–6 ESV). The apostle Paul commanded fathers to train their children "in the education and correction that comes from the Lord" (Eph 6:4, author's translation). These imperatives for spiritual formation have not changed in time. Although professionals may partner with parents in the task of training children in God's ways, such a vast and serious undertaking as a child's discipleship is too important to be relinquished to professionals. The primary formation of a child's faith is not a job for specialists. It is a job for parents.[89]

Axiom 2: The generations need one another. Alongside the drift toward surrendering discipleship to professional ministers, another trend has developed too: Church programs have tended to become so radically age segmented that, in many congregations, persons from different generations rarely if ever interact with one another in the context of the faith community. Barbara Hirsch acknowledged in a study of adolescent culture, "They need the telling of stories, the close ongoing contact so they can learn and be accepted. If nobody is there to talk to, it is difficult to get the lessons of your own life so that you are adequately prepared to do the next thing."[90]

The biblical authors assumed the presence of generational connections that equipped children and youth to gain wisdom from older generations. In the divine law God declared to His people, "You shall stand in honor of the gray head and respect the face of the older people." Then,

---

[89] G. Barna, *Revolutionary Parenting* (Carol Stream, IL: Tyndale House, 2007), 12.
[90] P. Hersch, *A Tribe Apart: A Journey into the Heart of American Adolescence* (New York: Fawcett, 1989), 364.

he linked this respect to his own sacred identity: "You shall fear your God; I am the LORD" (Lev 19:32, author's translation). Titus 2:1–8 clearly suggests that Paul expected intergenerational relationships to develop in the Cretan church.

Axiom 3: Family ministry models must be missional. One of the earliest usages of the term *family ministry* in a religious context is in an obscure book from 1867 titled *The Home Life, in Light of Its Divine Idea.* What the author meant by "family ministry" in this book was not, however, a church program. Neither was his intended meaning a process of discipleship within the home—although he certainly emphasized that calling in other portions of the book. What this author meant by "family ministry" was *the family's ministry to the world.* "Family ministry" described how families demonstrated the love of Jesus Christ to the poor, the fatherless, and the widow. Family ministry, as presented in this text, focused not merely on the internal dynamics of the family but also on the needs of those beyond the family.

Families are not the goal or the center of family ministry. A biblical model for family ministry must mobilize families to be on mission together. The gospel of Jesus Christ must stand as the center and the goal, even of family ministry models.

Comparative Chart of Contemporary Family Ministry Models

	Programmatic Ministry Model	Family-Based Ministry Model	Family-Equipping Ministry Model	Family-Integrated Ministry Model
What does this model look like in the local church?	Ministries are organized in separate "silos," with little consistent intergenerational interaction. "Family ministry," when it exists, is one more program. The program may provide training, intervention, or activities for families. In scheduling programs, churches may deliberately seek to be sensitive to family's needs and schedules.	Church's programmatic structure remains unchanged, but each separate ministry plans and programs in ways that intentionally draw generations together and encourage parents to take part in the discipleship of their children and youth.	Although age-organized programs and events still exist, the church is completely restructured to draw the generations together, equipping parents, championing their role as primary disciple-makers, and holding them accountable to fulfill this role.	The church eliminates age-segregated programs and events. All or nearly all programs and events are multi-generational, with a strong focus on parents' responsibility to evangelize and to disciple their own children.

Continued

Comparative Chart of Contemporary Family Ministry Models—Cont'd

	Programmatic Ministry Model	Family-Based Ministry Model	Family-Equipping Ministry Model	Family-Integrated Ministry Model
What other approaches might be included in this ministry model?	Therapeutic-Counseling Family Ministry (Chap Clark)[91] Church-Centered/ Home-Supported Ministry (Ben Freudenburg)[92] Family-Sensitive Ministry (Michelle Anthony)[93]	Family-Friendly Youth Ministry; Family-Focused Youth Ministry (Dave Rahn)[94] Family-Based Youth Ministry (Mark DeVries)[95] Family-Friendly Ministry (Michelle Anthony)[96]	Youth-Focused Family Ministry; Youth-Friendly Family Ministry (Dave Rahn)[97] Home-Centered/ Church-Supported Ministry (Ben Freudenburg)[98] Co-Champion Model (Steve Wright)[99] Family-Empowered Ministry (Michelle Anthony)[100]	Family Discipleship Model (Alliance for Church and Family Reformation)[101] Family-Centered Ministry (Michelle Anthony)[102] Inclusive-Congregational Ministry (Malan Nel)[103]

---

91 C. Clark, *The Youth Worker's Handbook to Family Ministry* (Grand Rapids, MI: Zondervan, 1997).
92 B. Freudenberg, *The Family-Friendly Church* (Loveland, CO: Group, 1998).
93 M. Anthony, "New Models of Family Ministry," North American Professors of Christian Education, 2008.
94 D. Rahn, "Parafamily Youth Ministry," in *Group* (May/June 1996), http://archive.youthministry.com/details.asp?ID51701.
95 M. DeVries with E. Palmer, *Family-Based Youth Ministry*, rev. ed. (Downers Grove, IL: InterVarsity, 2004).
96 M. Anthony, "New Models of Family Ministry," North American Professors of Christian Education, 2008.
97 D. Rahn, "Parafamily Youth Ministry" in *Group* (May/June 1996), http://archive.youthministry.com/details.asp?ID51701.
98 B. Freudenberg, *The Family-Friendly Church* (Loveland, Colorado: Group, 1998).
99 S. Wright with C. Graves, *reThink: Is Student Ministry Working?* (Raleigh, NC: InQuest, 2007).
100 M. Anthony, "New Models of Family Ministry," North American Professors of Christian Education, 2008.
101 http://www.gracefamilybaptist.net/GFBC_/Alliance.html.
102 M. Anthony, "New Models of Family Ministry," North American Professors of Christian Education, 2008.

Unit 3

Family Ministries in the Local Church

10 Equipping Parents to Be the Spiritual Leaders in the Home[1]

Michelle D. Anthony
***ROCK**HARBOR Church*

I have spent my entire adult life serving in children's and family ministry. Other than being a wife and a mother, I have had no greater passion than to invest in the next generation. Yet despite this dedication to see young people grow spiritually, there were many years that I professionally neglected the most vital setting in which children develop a compelling and lasting faith . . . the home. Certainly God awakens His people and the church in each generation for the mission He desires, and with the dawn of a new century came a universal awakening in children's ministry leaders to partner with parents.

The twenty-first century brought new paradigms for children and family ministries and has influenced the way the church establishes ministry programs, hires staff, and assesses curriculum. However, one of the most profound impacts this fresh approach to ministry has brought is that it has challenged parents to assume their biblical role in spiritually nurturing their children. Such attention to training, equipping, and mobilizing parents to take the primary lead in spiritual development is inspiring, yet ministry workers must be prepared to evaluate carefully current ministries in order to determine which practices will encourage growth in families and which ones need to be eliminated or restructured.

In generations past the church often allowed parents to abdicate this role to her by creating structures that enabled mothers and fathers to outsource religious and spiritual training to the "professionals." Yet the church was designed by God to be a place of community and

---

[1] The content of this chapter is a condensed version of the book *Spiritual Parenting: Awakening Faith in Today's Families*, written by Dr. M. D. Anthony (Colorado Springs, CO: David C Cook, 2010).

worship and an environment where gifts would be used to equip the saints for the work of the Lord (Eph 4). Because Scripture makes it clear that God intends the family to be the primary place where faith is nurtured in children, it is fitting that the role of the church becomes one of equipping parents for this responsibility.

Faith Through the Family

In Ps 78:2–7 we find a blueprint of God's grand method for faith replication throughout all generations. He chose to use the *family* as the primary place to nurture faith. The psalmist, Asaph, unveils God's plan:

> I will open my mouth in parables, I will utter hidden things, things from of old—what we have heard and known, what our fathers have told us. We will not hide them from their children; we will tell the next generation the praiseworthy deeds of the LORD, his power, and the wonders he has done.
>
> He decreed statutes for Jacob and established the law in Israel, which he commanded our forefathers to teach their children, so the next generation would know them, even the children yet to be born, and they in turn would tell their children. Then they would put their trust in God and would not forget his deeds but would keep his commands. (NIV)

This beautiful psalm shares God's intent for the family and for each generation to pass their faith on to the next. God set up an infrastructure that He envisioned would be best for faith replication: *the family.*

Moses addresses this concept of faith formation in the family in Deut 6:4–9 in what is known in Hebrew as the *Shema*. This is the first prayer a child learns in a Jewish home and the words they hear every night at bedtime. God reveals through Moses that faith teaching occurs best in the *natural daily flow of life*—from the living examples of parents who are modeling it. In the *Shema*, Moses says:

> Hear, O Israel: The LORD our God, the LORD is one. Love the LORD your God with all your heart and with all your soul and with all your strength. These commandments that I give you today are to be upon your hearts. Impress them on your children. Talk about them when you sit at home and when you walk along the road, when you lie down and when you get up. Tie them as symbols on your hands and bind them on your foreheads. Write them on the doorframes of your houses and on your gates. (NIV)

Moses commissions the parents *first* to be lovers of God with everything that is within them, and *then* to pass this compelling faith down to their children in the everyday occurrences of life. This is the natural flow of our lives. The *Shema* teaches us that learning to know God happens in real-life situations, and what better place to have "real life" than in the home? In addition, Stonehouse observes that only people of faith can pass on faith to another; therefore any conviction to help children grow spiritually must also attend to the needs of the adults who are parenting them.[2]

Although there is a place for parents to formalize teaching and training, the natural flow of their lives offers the most fertile soil for knowing God personally. Every single opportunity, every single hour that we are given in a day is an opportunity for our children to discover who God is, and Scripture commissions us to be wise with the time we have been entrusted.

Redeeming Faith Moments in the Home

In Eph 5:15–17, Paul instructs the new believers in Ephesus to look at the culture in which they were living—one that was evil—and to take assessment of how they were using their time and their opportunities. He simply instructed them to "Be wise!" This is a great charge for parents today as well. To parent children spiritually in the twenty-first century, in a world where sexuality, greed, pride, and evil run rampant, Paul's exhortation has lasting relevance. He says that the way to be wise in such an environment is to make the most of every opportunity—by *making the most of the time.* The original Greek word that is translated in verse 16 as "making the most of" or "redeeming" is *exagorazō.* It is a grand concept. *Exagorazō* is the word used to describe something that you would buy or purchase in *totality.* This word is interesting because it is only used four times in the New Testament, twice to refer to our redemption from sin and twice in regard to time.

This word for *redeem* means to "completely buy out." It is *everything.* In Ephesians, *exagorazō* has to do with *time.* So then the questions become: How does one completely buy out time, and how does this affect spiritual parenting? First, we must understand what kind of time God is referring to. The time referred to in this passage is not time marked by calendars or watches; this kind of time would be the word *chronos,* from which we derive the English word chronological. Paul, however, uses the Greek word *kairos,* which describes an "opportune or ripe season."

Kairos is a specific, opportune time. Parents must be guided to recognize that there is no greater *kairos* moment than childhood for faith development. They are wise when they seize this *kairos*—this opportune, ripe season in their child's life—to participate as the Holy Spirit propels them toward faith, the right kind of faith. This is the kind of faith that puts conduct into action based on what they say they believe.

---

[2] C. Stonehouse, *Joining Children on the Spiritual Journey* (Grand Rapids, MI: Baker Books, 1998), 25.

To "buy out" the totality of "opportune time" that parents have with their children for the purpose of faith formation, the church must ensure training and support so that the homes in our ministries are filled with environments that nurture faith. Make no mistake: The *kairos* moment that parents have been given is short. It is tempting to be deceived into believing that we have more time than we do in the faith-formation years. Studies have shown that moral and faith development are shaped in the early years of childhood. Some research shows that the moral compass of a child's life is determined as early as age seven[3] and that what one believes about God and eternity at the age of 13, he or she will most likely die believing.[4]

Researchers are finding that many children raised in Christian homes are walking away from their faith as early as middle school and in even larger numbers after they finish high school.[5] The church and parents are partnering together to do something significant to address this lack of fidelity. We are choosing to behave wisely now in order to pass on a genuine kind of faith that will breed longevity for future generations.

What Is a Transforming Faith?

Leading parents to understand this vital role can be one of the most defining moments in their lives because, although many parents agree that the spiritual mantle has been given to them by God, they often do not feel prepared or equipped to pass on their faith to their children. This is a compelling call—to pass on a vibrant and transforming faith, the kind of faith that Paul seems to be describing in Phil 2:13 when he states, "For it is God who works in you to will and to act according to his good purpose" (NIV). It is the kind of faith that transcends good behavior and at its heart lives in the confidence that God is transforming the inner man day by day. The church is positioned to equip parents with the resources that will bring them confidence to build faith in their homes. This kind of faith envisions a future where:

- Children would *know* and *hear* God's voice, discerning it from all others.
- *Desire* to obey Him when they heard His voice.
- And *obey* Him not in their own power, but in the power of the Holy Spirit.

---

[3] Barna Research Group, "A Year in Review Perspective," 2009, http://www.barna.org/barna-update/article/12-faithspirituality/325-barna-studies-the-research-offers-a-year-in-review-perspective.

[4] G. Barna, *Transforming Children into Spiritual Champions* (Ventura, CA: Regal, 2003), 47.

[5] Barana Research Group, "Americans Are Most Worried About Children's Future," 2009, http://www.barna.org/barna-update/article/15-familykids/97-americans-are-most-worried-about-childrens-future.

This is a future worth dedicating our lives to if we believe that the most significant part of one's life—and that of their child's life—is spiritual vitality. Researcher Barna once stated that every dimension of a person's life experience hinges on his or her moral and spiritual condition.[6] Think about it: What you believe and where you aim your heart determines the direction and outcome of your entire life. When it comes to the church training parents to spiritually guide their children, eternity is at stake.

Jesus said that my purpose, as a child of God, is to love Him with my whole life and to love others generously (Luke 10:27). The purpose of spiritual parenting fulfills the groundwork for this commission. Spiritual parents teach their children about the awe-inspiring wonder of who God is, how to have a relationship with Him, and to model the difficult beauty of living a life surrendered to Him for the sake of others. Miller once said, "Too much of our time is spent trying to chart God on a grid, and too little is spent allowing our hearts to feel awe. By reducing Christian spirituality to formula, we deprive our hearts of wonder."[7]

As parents who want our faith to endure for all generations, we must become increasingly confident and focused about the *kind of faith* we are trying to pass on. Deep down I think most parents realize that there is a critical part of faith that requires us to *act* or *respond* if we are really going to be transformed.

When Jesus spoke of His imminent return in Luke 18:8 (NIV), He said, "When the Son of Man comes, will he find faith on the earth?" Reflecting on this, Westerhoff asks if our children will have faith, citing that the God of this universe, the holy God, is telling us the *one thing* that He will be looking for upon His return.[8] He could have chosen one of a myriad of things, but He chose *faith*.

Faith is supernatural. Parents are not capable of creating it in their children. It takes a supernatural transformation. Just as belief and trust that produce faith in a person's life are a supernatural transaction, the behavior and action that align with faith need to flow supernaturally. When we try to manufacture this or impose it on others, they become resistant or even rebellious.

This can produce a sense of freedom for parents who are skeptical about their qualifications to be the spirituality nurturers of their children. As parents put their children in proximity to God, to fall in love with Jesus, the Holy Spirit is the one who makes their actions congruent with their belief. He is the one who causes the process of their hearts to become more and more like Jesus.[9] This is true transformation. As their

---

[6] G. Barna, *Transforming Children into Spiritual Champions* (Ventura, CA: Regal Publishing, 2003), 12.
[7] D. Miller, *Blue like Jazz* (Nashville, TN: Thomas Nelson Publishing, 2003), 205.
[8] J. Westerhoff, *Will Our Children Have Faith?* (Toronto: Morehouse, 2000), 32.
[9] V. Schorr, *Compass: A Guide for Character and Spiritual Formation in Children* (Erie, CO: Vernie Schorr, 2008),140.

faith is vibrant, their actions become vibrant. So often the temptation for parents is to spend all of their time and energy striving to fix their child's behavior—a process that is not their responsibility.

Consider this description of faith: "We can conclude, that faith, as an affair of the heart and a commitment of the mind that results in service and spiritual behavior, is a very close personal relationship with God."[10] The joy of parenting can be spent on cultivating environments (which will be addressed later in this chapter) for faith to grow, teaching their children how to cultivate a love relationship with Jesus as they cultivate their own, living authentic lives in front of them so that they become eyewitnesses to their parents' transformation.

For parents to pass on their faith to the next generation and to be equipped by the church to do so, we need to understand what biblical faith is and how it is connected to action. James alerts us that our faith without works is dead (Jas 2:14–26). He says that this concept would be as lifeless as a body without the spirit inside it. It is dead. So faith must have this expression of obedience for it to be alive.

The Greek word for faith is *pistos.* Within it are three constructs. The first is that there is a *firm conviction* about something or someone. Next, there has to be a *personal surrender* to this thing or person. Finally, the *corresponding behavior of action* defines my life. This definition of faith supports that when one possesses a firm conviction and a personal surrender, then the corresponding behavior, inspired by the prior two, will follow. *This* is where behavior comes in.

Behavior is not something parents simply manage; otherwise Christianity is nothing more than what Dallas Willard refers to as "sin management."[11] Too often parents merely focus on the "corresponding behavior" part, missing the point that behavior is a by-product. This by-product is first the outcome of a *firm conviction,* but it is also from a posture of *personal surrender.* The aspect of surrender is something that we as parents do not always do an adequate job of acknowledging in our own lives, let alone teaching it to our children.

Faith is based on a strong belief from a heart of self-surrender. When parents begin to see behavior as a by-product of genuine faith, they begin to understand what it means to pursue a spiritual life and spiritual parenting.

Faith in Action

There are several accounts in the Gospels where Jesus experienced faith in others and was even described as being *amazed* by it. He stopped and applauded it when he witnessed it. There are even times when

---

[10] M. Strommen, D. Hardel, *Passing on the Faith* (Winona, MN: St. Mary's Press, 2000), 59.
[11] D. Willard, *The Divine Conspiracy* (San Francisco: Harper Collins, 1997), 57.

He observed faith in action and He was surprised. He encountered a Roman centurion's faith on display and said, "I have not found anyone in Israel with such great faith" (Matt 8:10 NIV). He always acknowledged it, always responded to it, and always blessed it. Likewise, when Jesus expected to see it and did not, He would chastise, "O you of little faith!" Faith is imperative to our God, and He has given parents the commission to pass it on to their children.

However, James cautions us against adopting a solely intellectual belief system of biblical knowledge and the things that we *say* we believe. James writes:

> What good is it, my brothers, if a man claims to have faith but has no deeds? Can such faith save him? Suppose a brother or sister is without clothes and daily food. If one of you says to him, "Go, I wish you well; keep warm and well fed," but does nothing about his physical needs, what good is it? In the same way, faith by itself, if it is not accompanied by action, is dead. But someone will say, "You have faith; I have deeds."
>
> Show me your faith without deeds, and I will show you my faith by what I do. You believe that there is one God. Good! Even the demons believe that—and shudder. You foolish man, do you want evidence that faith without deeds is useless? . . . As the body without the spirit is dead, so faith without deeds is dead. (Jas 2:14–20,26 NIV).

At the same time, however, we note other places in Scripture where we see Jesus condemning people (the Pharisees among others) for simply *doing things* in the flesh but not actually being led by the Spirit or by His power to do those things. It is not about just "doing good stuff." It is tempting for parents to reduce the holy call to ensuring that their kids are "being good."

Furthermore, faith is not a mere intellectual assent. It is a blend of intellectual conviction and the works that flow from it. The parable recorded in Matthew 7 describes a wise man who built his house on a rock, and when the rain and storms came, his house stood firm. There was also a foolish man who built his house on the foundation of sand, and when the rain and storms came upon this house, it was utterly destroyed. Jesus was making a distinction between the two foundations.

If this story depicts such dramatic implications, it raises the question, "What is the rock?" It is vital to the story that we know what the rock is because Jesus is giving us a metaphor to instruct us to build our house upon it. Take a moment and think about it: What do you understand the rock foundation to be according to this story? It is tempting to think that the rock is *Jesus.* There are places in Scripture where Jesus is referred to as the rock, but in this parable He is not. Reading the passage, in context, will determine what the rock is:

> Therefore, everyone who hears these words of mine and puts them into practice is like a wise man who built his house on the rock. The rain came down, the streams rose, and the winds blew and beat against that house; yet it did not fall, because it had its foundation on the rock. But everyone who hears these words of mine and does not put them into practice is like a foolish man who built his house on sand. The rain came down, the streams rose, and the winds blew and beat against that house, and it fell with a great crash. (Matt 7:24–27 NIV)

Jesus says that everyone who *hears these words* and *puts them into practice* is like a wise man who built his house on the rock. Therefore, the rock becomes one of obedience. The foundations refer to the response of someone who hears the truth. The individual either chooses to put that truth into practice (obedience) or chooses not to put it into practice (disobedience).

Obedience can be problematic to model, in that a child can see the action without seeing the heart or intent of that action. God is concerned with my heart in obedience. Jesus even told the crowds who were following Him, "Unless your righteousness surpasses that of the Pharisees and the teachers of the law, you will certainly not enter the kingdom of heaven" (Matt 5:20 NIV). The Pharisees were not lacking in obedience by any measure. No one in Jewish society followed the letter of the law more than they did. I suspect that Jesus was referring to the righteousness of His followers not being something *quantitatively* more than that of the Pharisees, but rather being something *qualitatively* more. He wanted obedience of a different kind.

When children are little, parents need them to obey their words without question. Commands such as "Don't touch the stove," "Stay out of the street," or "Don't talk to strangers" are imperatives that must be obeyed without question. But as children mature, parents need to transition from blind obedience to obedience out of wisdom and relationship—trusting that their parents know what is best.

Creating Environments for God's Spirit to Be at Work

If parents believe that the Holy Spirit is God's chosen teacher in children's hearts and that He is the one who causes spiritual growth when and as He chooses, then they must be willing to cultivate environments in their home that will allow their children not only to hear God's words but also to have an opportunity to put them into practice.

It is important for parents not to create environments for their children that look religious on the outside or to create environments to manipulate their child's behavior. Instead, parents should create environments in their homes and in their children's lives for the purpose of allowing the work of the Holy Spirit. The responsibility of spiritual parenting is to place each child in the path where God is already at work. Parents get to come alongside where He is already moving. The remainder of this chapter will focus directly on ten environments that parents can actively pursue and create in their homes to allow the Spirit of God to move freely among their children.

1. The Environment of Storytelling. With self-absorption raging in the hearts and minds of children, how can parents help them understand that there is a storyline much bigger than their own? How can they parent in such a way that tells the Big God Story (the biblical redemptive narrative between God and humanity), explains how their own story has been grafted in by grace, and describes how each child has the opportunity to be a part of that narrative? Each of these is essential for faith development to occur. Westerhoff once said, "At the heart of our faith is a story. . . . Unless the story is known, understood, owned, and lived out, we and our children will not have Christian faith."[12]

Understanding the Big God Story can help us to see that we can never play the role of the main character. But when we understand why we cannot, we rest in the knowledge that we were never created to do so. When this happens, we are able to worship God and not ourselves. We are free to be who we were created to be: true worshippers in every aspect of our lives.

The apostle Paul refers to this in Rom 12:1–2 (MSG):

> So here's what I want you to do, God helping you: Take your everyday, ordinary life—your sleeping, eating, going-to-work, and walking-around life—and place it before God as an offering. Embracing what God does for you is the best thing you can do for him. Don't become so well-adjusted to your culture that you fit into it without even thinking. Instead, fix your attention on God. You'll be changed from the inside out. Readily recognize what he wants from you, and quickly respond to it. Unlike the culture around you, always dragging you down to its level of immaturity, God brings the best out of you, develops well-formed maturity in you.

It is inspiring to know that God has given each of us a part in His story, but we must first know His story before we can truly understand our role in it. With this in mind, the environment of storytelling encourages us to share the Bible's content in the context of its original storyline. Often in the church

[12] J. Westerhoff, *Will Our Children Have Faith?* (Harrisburg, Morehouse, 2000), 32.

and the home, we tell fragmented stories of God, Jesus, or other characters in the Bible, and we do so in ways that are not linear. Even most children who know the stories of the Bible cannot tell you whether Abraham was born before David, or if baby Jesus was alive when baby Moses was.

Our stories are told in isolation and do not tell the bigger storyline where God is central. Instead, baby Moses is the key figure one day, Noah is the key figure a different day, and Jesus is merely the key figure on another occasion. But by putting each story in context with the main story, we can begin to elevate Jesus, the Redeemer, to His rightful place as the primary focus of the storyline.

Applebee, in his studies regarding effective storytelling, observed that the processes of *centering* and *chaining* function as basic structuring principles in children's conception of story. His idea of *full narrative* showed that children learn best when the elements are linked to one another (chaining) and linked to the core (centering).[13] Telling God's story within an integrated and linear approach aligns with what Applebee found to be most transforming.

For parents to grasp the entirety of the biblical narrative, the church will need to equip parents to understand this reality themselves. Many parents do not know the grand narrative of how sin entered the human race and therefore broke the perfect union between God and man. From this point forward, biblical history sets the stage for God to set apart a holy people from which His redeemer, the Christ, would be born. Throughout Scripture this Messiah is promised, prophesied, preserved, and then presented at the appointed time. During the life of Christ on earth, Jesus told us how a reconciled relationship would occur—through His death and resurrection—and He demonstrated how to live in this relationship with the Father. Then the early church set out on the mission to make this good news of the gospel known until the day that Jesus Himself returns to bring final judgment and reward for those who received this gift.

This overall storyline can get lost in the multitude of characters and details, yet this is the spiritually forming story for parents to pass down to their children. Parents can create an environment where their kids feel the awe of being part of something much bigger than themselves. When my children were young, I often told them before they left for school, "I wonder how God will use you in His story today. I don't know how He's going to do it, but He will. Watch for it! Today *you* will be a part of the greatest story ever told."

2. The Environment of Identity. Gire describes our identity as Christians like this: "In J. R. R. Tolkien's *The Hobbit,* the magician Gandalf told the reluctant and unlikely hero Bilbo Baggins, 'There is more

---

[13] A. N. Applebee, *The Child's Concept of Story* (Chicago: University of Chicago Press, 1978), 58.

to you than you know.' He said this knowing that within the hobbit's veins coursed blood not only from the sedentary Baggins side of the family but also from the swashbuckling Took side. We have a similar mingling of blood within us from a lineage that is both human and divine. . . . Most of the time, though, we are burrowed away in our hobbit holes and don't give a thought to our heritage."[14]

It is evident that as we endeavor to live within these two realities of flesh and spirit that we wrestle with our true identity. Questions such as "*Who am I* that I should get to be a part of the greatest story ever told?" or "*Who am I* in that storyline?" shape the environment of identity. The fact that you and I are even invited to be a part of God's grand narrative of life, love, and redemption is true only because of Christ. This is why we affirm that our identity with God is found in Christ.

As parents live their lives in a posture of true identity, seeking to live out the life they were created to live in Christ, then they can genuinely ask the next question: "Who did God create my *child* to be?" This is the Father's heart for identity in spiritual parenting.

Each of us was created in God's image. We bear His fingerprint—and no two are alike. At the end of our season of parenting, don't we ultimately want children who look like Christ? Ephesians 1 describes in beautiful imagery what is true about our identity in Christ when we have received Jesus as Savior:

> Praise be to the God and Father of our Lord Jesus Christ, who has *blessed us* in the heavenly realms with every spiritual blessing in Christ. For he *chose us* in him before the creation of the world to be *holy and blameless* in his sight. In love he predestined us to be *adopted as his sons* through Jesus Christ, in accordance with his pleasure and will—to the praise of his glorious grace, which he has freely given us in the One he loves. In him *we have redemption* through his blood, the *forgiveness of sins*, in accordance with the riches of God's grace that he *lavished on us* with all wisdom and understanding. . . . In him we were also *chosen*, having been predestined according to the plan of him who works out everything in conformity with the purpose of his will, in order that we, who were the first to hope in Christ, might be *for the praise of His glory*. And you also were included in Christ when you heard the word of truth, the gospel of your salvation. Having believed, you were *marked in him with a seal*, the promised Holy Spirit, who is a deposit guaranteeing *our inheritance*. (vv. 3–8,11–14 NIV, emphasis author's)

[14] K. Gire, *Windows of the Soul* (Grand Rapids, MI: Zondervan, 1996), 48.

Nancy Pearcey reminds us that "[t]he Bible does not begin with the Fall but with Creation: Our value and dignity are rooted in the fact that we are created in the image of God, with the high calling of being His representatives on earth. In fact, it is only *because* humans have such high value that sin is so tragic. . . . In redemption, He restores us to the high dignity originally endowed at Creation recovering our true identity and renewing the image of God in us."[15] What if the children in this generation were to grasp this identity that is available in Christ? What if this truth were to sink down deep into the bedrock of who they are? This would be life changing.

The Enemy will seduce our children. He will offer them a multitude of counterfeit identities. He will lie to them, deceive them, and rob them of their true identity if he can. He wants nothing more than to destroy them. First Peter 5:8 (NIV) says, "Your enemy the devil prowls around like a roaring lion looking for someone to devour." As a parent, I want to protect my child at all cost, but I lose sight of *this* enemy at times. I lose sight that the real enemy of my children's heart and soul is a powerful evil that preys on them. With trickery and distortion, he promises everything and gives nothing but pain, regret, and bondage.

The Bible tells us that our enemy, the Devil, began his treachery against mankind in the garden by deceiving Eve and that his final act in this world will be when he is unleashed to deceive the nations. His favorite tool is *deception*. When deception seduces our children, they can encounter a moment or season of "identity lost." Spiritual parents guide their children from the guilt that naturally ensues to a place of restoration and redemption found in Christ.

Max Lucado once said, "Satan sows seeds of shame. If he can't seduce you with your sin, he'll let you sink in your guilt. Nothing pleases him more than for you to cower in the corner, embarrassed that you're still dealing with the same old habit. 'God's tired of your struggles', he whispers. 'Your father is weary of your petitions for forgiveness,' he lies . . . but your temptation isn't late-breaking news in heaven. Your sin doesn't surprise God."[16]

Our children are tempted by counter-identities every day. The question is not whether they will choose one, but *which one* they will choose. Spiritual parents take the environment of identity seriously because they understand how much is at stake. If we do not offer them the identity of knowing Christ and being transformed by His Spirit, make no mistake about it: The world will offer them a wide array of alternative choices.

3. The Environment of a Faith Community. We were not created to live in isolation. Without being involved in a vibrant faith community, we can begin to live secluded lives of faith. When this happens, we literally

---

[15] N. Pearcey, *Total Truth* (Wheaton, IL: Crossway Books, 2004), 87, 89.
[16] M. Lucado, *In the Grip of Grace* (Dallas: Word Publishing, 1996), 144–45.

start to forget who we are. As the battle rages against our identity, a faith community brings us strength. God designed the faith community to build up each believer for this battle that we face when we leave the security of "family." This faith community offers a support system among people who are like-minded, who believe the same truths, and who ultimately want the same things out of this life. These shared beliefs and values provide a powerful foundation for children, especially during their developmental years.

Christian educators Strommen and Hardel illustrate this point in their book, *Passing on the Faith,* where they state, "We live in a time when many families are disintegrating. There will continue to be hurting people, more psychologically scarred youth, more fragmented families in the future of every congregation. Fewer youth will know close family life and the security of being loved and cared for. For them a congregation of faith can provide the experience of being part of a close family."[17]

It is tempting for parents to have the perspective that life has become too busy and cluttered, and therefore having Sundays off is the only time to simply rest. They may have good intentions, but often getting to church can become just one more thing in a busy family schedule. Many churches across the United States consider a regular attendee someone who goes to church once a month.[18] Yet Catherine Stonehouse notes, "The faith of children is most likely to grow when they have the opportunity to associate with adults who are growing persons who know and love God. The child's faith is inspired when he or she belongs to an inclusive community that seeks to live out God's love."[19]

God also designed us to live within the faith community in order to experience Him in ways that can only happen in close proximity to one another. The faith community creates an environment to equip and disciple parents and children, to celebrate God's faithfulness, and to bring a richness of worship through tradition and rituals. All of these things ultimately offer children a strong sense of identity, security, and belonging.

In ancient Jewish culture, children participated in seven festivals every year where they were able enjoy the faith community in all of its richness. They ate delicious food, learned and joined in on cultural dances, and shared a common experience with people they had not seen in perhaps months—cousins, friends, and family members from all over the region. They would come together to celebrate for somewhere between seven and ten days. Those days together in the faith community were rich marker points of faith development. It would have been a spiritually

---

[17] M. P. Strommen, R. A. Hardel, *Passing on the Faith* (Winona, MN: St. Mary's Press, 2000), 157.
[18] Barna Research Group. "New Statistics on Church Attendance and Avoidance," 2008, http://www.barna.org/barna-update/article/18-congregations/45-new-statistics-on-church-attendance-and-avoidance.
[19] Stonehouse, *Joining Children on the Spiritual Journey*, 37.

shaping experience for children to live in that type of communal expression of worship. Today we need to be diligent to ensure that we are creating an environment that offers this kind of community for our children.

Remember Shadrach, Meshach, and Abednego? They were three young Hebrew men living as aliens in the evil empire of Babylon, yet they were unwilling to compromise their faith and worship a golden idol at the king's whim. God provided courage and salvation to these young men in the midst of difficulty (Dan 3). One thought that strikes me in this biblical narrative is that the young men *had one another.* I wonder if knowing that there were others who felt the same conviction somehow gave them the courage to stand firm—*together.*

The world acts as a leech on our children's hearts and souls, and none are unscathed by it. In the faith community they gain strength. We must be wise to understand that our children will bear the marks of the world's harsh conditions and therefore make provisions for a different kind of community—a community of refuge.

4. The Environment of Serving. God's story, our identity in Him, the community of those who love Him—all of these feed our children's hungry souls. But if their lives are all about intake, they will grow up to be flabby Christians. That is why even small children need to discover that part of responding to God's love for us is serving Him.

We all had chores growing up, right? Every good home has some form of them. Let's face it—chores are a way to get things done and to help out, but ultimately they are also a way for kids to learn to serve the other members in our family, at least in theory. Then why, I wonder, have we for so many decades called this act of service a chore? Think about the word *chore.* It is not compelling.

So when I became a parent, I had visions of children who would scurry about in joy, much like Cinderella's mice, knowing that the work just needed to be done. I envisioned them wanting to help out of the abundant gratitude in their hearts for all that we had provided for them. Well, it did not take long for that dream to be squelched. Innate in each of us is a bent toward selfishness. Instinctively we know how to serve ourselves and eliminate all else from distracting us in this pursuit. We are not born servants.

Most of us (if not all of us) just naturally come into this world saying, "Serve me." We do not naturally seek to serve others. We are self-centered. We are completely immersed with our needs from infancy. Training a child's heart toward service is counterintuitive to who they are as human beings. Willard describes the importance of this discipline like this, "Service is more than a simple act of love and kindness; it is a way in which we train ourselves away from the worldly constraints of arrogance, possessiveness, envy, resentment and covetousness . . . and put God as our center."[20]

[20] D. Willard, *The Spirit of the Disciplines* (New York: Harper Collins, 1988), 41.

Parents who create the environment of service for their children from the earliest days help them ask an important question that is critical for their faith development. The critical question that service asks is, "What needs to be done?" This is one of the best questions that parents can teach their children to ask. To have them walk into any room, situation, or relationship and ask this will change the way they see their world. It is simple. It is profound. Yet this is a posture that will *not* naturally be cultivated in children unless parents set out on an intentional course, making it a priority.

Foster identifies service as one of the main spiritual disciplines of our life because, of them all, "service is the most conducive to the growth of humility. When we set out on a consciencely chosen course of action that accents the good of others, and is for the most part, a hidden work, a deep change occurs in our spirits."[21]

The early church could not even imagine worship outside of this concept of service. The Greek word for worship is *latreia.* This happens to be the same word for service. *Latreia* is service. *Latreia* is worship. So the New International Version renders Romans 12:1 like this: "Therefore, I urge you, brothers, in view of God's mercy, to offer your bodies as living sacrifices, holy and pleasing to God—this is your spiritual act of *worship.*" The original Greek text can also be translated, "this is your spiritual act of *service.*" The two are inseparable. It is the same word. For children to be worshippers with their lives, they must learn to be servants also. Each of us must enter into every situation and ask the question, "What needs to be done?"

5. The Environment of Out of the Comfort Zone. I have a friend named Josh who faithfully prays over his three-year-old son. He often prays for his son to be made into a strong and courageous man. He asks God to make him mighty and use him for the sake of Christ. One night while he was holding his son and praying these words, he felt as if God said, "If you're serious about this prayer, then I'm going to have to hurt him." Now these are not words that you expect to hear from God, so instinctively Josh pulled his son in tighter as if to say no. With that, he felt that God responded, "So you're going to try to protect him from *Me?*"

What a strong realization that must have been for a young father. To realize that in order for his son to become the mighty man he desired, God would have to let his son suffer and at the same time to realize that God is our protector and the perfect parent because He is willing to do this when we are not.

This story frames the environment of the comfort zone. This young father innately desired to protect, love, and offer comfort to his son. Parents are not taught this; normally they simply react and respond from

---

[21] R. Foster, *Celebration of Disciplines* (San Francisco, Harper, 1978), 130.

the first time their infant cries. They are wired to bring resolution to their child's pain in any way they can. However, this environment exposes children to circumstances and experiences that take them away from their ultimate places of comfort. In this, children discover that they can no longer rely on their own strength and securities in order to learn what it means to depend on God for His strength.

Francis Chan observes, "Life is comfortable when you separate yourself from people who are different from you. But God doesn't call us to be comfortable. He calls us to trust Him so completely that we are unafraid to put ourselves in situations where we will be in trouble if He doesn't come through."[22] Likewise, the apostle Paul shared these words with the church in Corinth, "That is why, for Christ's sake, I delight in weaknesses, in insults, in hardships, in persecutions, in difficulties. *For when I am weak, then I am strong*" (2 Cor 12:10 NIV, author's emphasis). Here Paul is describing how God uses uncomfortable situations and trials to accomplish the work He wants to do in us. Paul recognized that God was not trying to be mean-spirited toward him but rather that He was using these trials to help him grow in righteousness. And righteousness is true strength, not the strength that the world promises through our comfort.

Children need the skills and faith muscles to be able to walk through the trial and be strengthened, not victimized, by it. This is an essential life lesson for them because life will not be fair. The best gift parents can give their children in this is the confidence to believe that everything is filtered through God's hands. Parents can release their control of life's circumstances knowing that God is at work to *refine lives*—and then walk with their children, prayerfully, modeling for them how they should respond in grace under trial.

6. The Environment of Responsibility. Let's be honest—responsibility is a word that can often make us feel burdened. The mere word seems to conjure up feelings about those things that we *have* to do—not those things that we *get* to do. But to be responsible for someone or something simply makes us accountable. If I live in an environment where I am not responsible for anything or anyone, I become self-centered, selfish, and myopic in my perspective. This is why Paul said to the young church in Philippi, "Each of you should look not to your own interests, but also to the interests of others" (Phil 2:4 NIV). He knew that they, like us, would be tempted to live in a way that looked out for "number one" and in doing so would miss out on the adventure to which God was calling them.

In God's kingdom, when He calls us to responsibility, He *entrusts* His plans to us. Each of us has been entrusted with accomplishing what God

---

[22] F. Chan, *Crazy Love* (Colorado Springs, CO: David C. Cook, 2008), 124.

desires. As He has entrusted His will to us, we are responsible to act. Miller notes, "But the trouble with deep belief is that it costs something. And there is something inside me, some selfish beast of a subtle thing that does not like the truth at all because it carries responsibility, and if I actually believe these things I have to do something about them."[23]

Ultimately, the concept of creating an environment of responsibility in our homes is a charge from God that encompasses a variety of areas. First, it captures the ability to take ownership before God for one's life, gifts, and resources. Second, it challenges us to take responsibility for those in our family and our spiritual family in Christ, for their well-being. Last, it calls us to seek out in love those who are hurting, poor, and spiritually lost, recognizing our responsibility to those who do not yet know Jesus and His forgiveness.

The early church described in the book of Acts took these three things seriously. As they were awakened to their new life in Christ through the Holy Spirit, they lived radically different lives. With great sacrifice, they generously gave of their time, talents, money, homes, and meals to anyone who was part of their new family in God. In addition, these same people sought to take care of the poor, the outcast, the lost, and the homeless in their towns. They lived what they believed, and it was compelling to those who were watching. In this environment where each person took responsibility for himself and for those around him, the church grew like wildfire. It was unstoppable.

One foundational aspect of responsibility is sowing and reaping. Many families do not live in an agrarian culture where children are familiar with farming techniques. But for those who do, farming is one of the most powerful means to help children understand the law of sowing and reaping. In sowing and reaping, what you plant is what you get. Farmers learn how much the environment has to do with what they plant. And what they plant in the ground and what comes up out of it correspond to each other. You cannot plant corn seeds and harvest from a peach tree. Paul made this point clear to the Galatians:

> Do not be deceived: God cannot be mocked. A man reaps what he sows. The one who sows to please his sinful nature, from that nature will reap destruction; the one who sows to please the Spirit, from the Spirit will reap eternal life. Let us not become weary in doing good, for at the proper time we will reap a harvest if we do not give up. Therefore, *as we have opportunity, let us do good to all people,* especially to those who belong to the family of believers. (Gal 6:7–10 NIV, author's emphasis)

---

[23] D. Miller, *Blue like Jazz,* 107.

Parents who learn to cultivate an environment of responsibility will reap a harvest well beyond their years of child-rearing.

7. The Environment of Course Correction. The environment of course correction describes biblical discipline. For parents the discipline of their children is probably one of the most time and energy-intensive aspects of daily life. Furthermore, how does discipline fundamentally reflect who God is? Nouwen once said, "This is how God has chosen to reveal to us the divine love: by bringing us back into an embrace of compassion, and convince us that anger has been melted away in endless mercy."[24] Parenting will always require mercy and forgiveness in the midst of course correction.

The author of Hebrews explains how course correction works:

> No discipline seems pleasant at the time, but painful. Later on, however, it produces a harvest of righteousness and peace for those who have been trained by it. Therefore, strengthen your feeble arms and weak knees. "Make level paths for your feet," so that the lame may not be disabled, but rather healed. (Heb 12:11–13 NIV)

As we seek God in this passage for His design of discipline, it is imperative that we do not stop at verse 11. Although we might agree that "no discipline seems pleasant at the time, but painful," we might be led to believe that discipline is merely a painful and negative experience if we simply stop there. That kind of discipline deserves a different name: *punishment.* Where punishment prevails, we most always find several other things: hiding, blame, guilt, and shame. Yet the goal of biblical discipline is altogether different—it is far more redemptive.

If only pain and punishment follow my wrong actions, then the root issue remains unchanged. It is not given the opportunity to come into the light and receive restoration. As children grow into adults, they become more and more aware of their depravity, and sin management can become a full-time job. Because the root is merely managed and never dealt with, shame and guilt prevail—and these things make them want to hide from God.

What then is the goal of course correction? If punishment's goal is God's wrath, then according to the previously mentioned verses, what is the goal of course correction or biblical discipline? It is found in the last word of verse 13: *healing.* The end goal for parents is to conduct God's discipline in their children's lives in such a way that they experience healing from their sin. Spiritual parenting digs deeper to penetrate the heart and give children a glimpse of their soul and their motivation toward sin. This is a tool parents can give their children so that when they are older

---

[24] H. Nouwen, *Finding My Way Home* (New York: Crossroad Publishing, 2001), 33.

and mom and dad are not around, they can say with conviction, "Search me and know me, God. Search my heart, and let me know if there's any wicked way within me" (Ps 139:23–24, author's translation).

Hebrews 12 outlines a three-step process for course correction. Verse 11 says, "No discipline seems pleasant at the time, but painful." The first step is *pain*—true healing starts with pain. The second stage comes from verse 12: "Strengthen your feeble arms and weak knees." Think about this for a minute. This is a word picture of arms and knees that have broken down. The parts of the body that allow us to move forward productively have gone limp.

That first step of pain has broken down the child's will, bringing them to a place of submission. This step is necessary, but it is destructive if the child stays in a broken state. Therefore, step two is strengthening what you broke down. So in course correction, immediately after we bring the pain we also bring restitution to that child in love, in reassurance, and in encouragement. It is important to note that the one who brings the pain must be the one who brings the love and encouragement.

The third step in God's plan for course correction is stated in Hebrews 12:13: "'Make level paths for your feet,' so that the lame may not be disabled, but rather healed" (NIV). Making a level path for our children's feet is simply plotting out the new course for them. Here we teach them what it means to change and acknowledge that they will need God's help to do this. Making a level path is telling them you have an idea of how they can navigate differently should the experience arise again and then walking through those steps. This is where God can use our wisdom gained from having lived and made our own mistakes. We share ourselves with our children candidly.

The final piece of this discipline journey is that later on, this corrective path produces a *harvest of righteousness and peace.* We live in a world where people live in tremendous turmoil and where righteousness is the oddity instead of the norm, even among Christ followers. Wise parents create an environment where God can work in their children's lives on this path of course correction.

8. The Environment of Love and Respect. Ken Gire confesses, "I want to live in such a way that I don't lose sight of what's important or lose a sense of the sacredness of others. I want to live in a way so that I can see windows of the soul."[25] In observing the soul of another, especially in children, love is primary, and respect is also of enormous importance because it is critical to the *way* we love. Probably one of the more subtle things that we inadvertently do as parents is use guilt and shame to control our children.

---

[25] K. Gire, *Windows of the Soul* (Grand Rapids, MI: Zondervan, 1996), 36.

Unfortunately, the effects of using guilt and shame can live for a lifetime in our children's souls. Yet love and respect are gifts parents can give their children. These build trust, confidence, safety, and security. Children need all of these things to live productive and spiritually healthy lives. "Young children need to sense that they are lovable and competent from the important people in their lives not only because of the message it imprints on their sensitive psyches, but also because these people are the only concrete representations of God and Jesus they know."[26]

Jesus said, "Greater love has no one than this, that he lay down his life for his friends" (John 15:13 NIV). Certainly every parent would say that they love their children. They know that their children are gifts from God. Most would offer their very lives for their children, without hesitation, if the moment called for it.

Jesus said that the greatest of all the commandments is "Love the Lord your God with all your heart and with all your soul and with all your mind and with all your strength. The second is this: 'Love your neighbor as yourself.' There is no commandment greater than these" (Mark 12:30–31 NIV). Then, John tells us, "We love because he first loved us" (1 John 4:19 NIV). So for today's children to be successful lovers of God and others, they must experience what love is for themselves. True love. Genuine love. The kind of love designed by God Himself.

The Greek word for this is *agapē*—a love that is unconditional, self-sacrificing, and active. This kind of love is divine. As we offer God's kind of love to our children, we must be diligent to love the way He loves. We have the responsibility to train them how to live by using *this kind* of love.

In Romans 2:4 we recognize the unique nature of God's love and its impact: "Or do you show contempt for the riches of his kindness, tolerance and patience, not realizing that *God's kindness leads you toward repentance?*" (NIV, author's emphasis). There are times when we must give grace to our children purely because they do not deserve it. We must show kindness and love when they are certain they will receive our wrath. We must do this because it reflects the absolute paradox of loving the way God loves instead of loving the way the world loves.

John Westerhoff cautions us, "Of course, it is easier to impose than reflect, easier to instruct than share, easier to act than to interact. It is important, however, to remember that to be with a child in Christian ways means self-control more than child-control. To be Christian is to ask: What can I bring to another? Not: What do I want that person to know or be? It means being willing to learn from another, even a child."[27]

---

[26] I. Beckwith, *Postmodern Children's Ministry: Ministry to Children in the 21st Century* (Grand Rapids, MI: Zondervan, 2004), 48.
[27] J. Westerhoff, *Will Our Children Have Faith?* (Toronto: Morehouse, 2000), 17.

This environment of love and respect demands more of parents than they have available in their own strength. Therefore, it compels every parent to rely on God's Spirit. Only He can make us love our children in a way that affirms His image in them. Only God can help us pass on His kind of love, to show respect in the way I discipline, speak, and listen to their lives. As we let Him do these things through us, we have the opportunity to understand in greater ways the love God has for each of us and the grace He extends to us simply because we are His.

9. The Environment of Knowing. The environment of knowing God stands in sharp contrast to what the world says is true. The world says there is no God, and if there is, He is irrelevant. The world says there is no Creator and no absolute truth. God's Word says, "Yes, there is, and you can know Him—you can actually know God the Father through His Son Jesus in the power of His Spirit." There is absolute truth, and it trumps all experiences and all counterfeits.

Parents today are raising their children in a postmodern world that denies this truth. As parents seek to create an environment that upholds and displays God's truth, they offer their children a foundation that is based on knowing God, believing His Word, and having a relationship with Him through Christ. These are the essentials for our faith, and they all begin with knowing God. Michael Anthony states, "We know God as we build a relationship with Him. He has beckoned us to come, and we have accepted His invitation. Along the way we interact, dialogue, and commune. Some days are filled with excitement and discovery while others are quiet and contemplative. Our relationship is anything but predictive, but as we 'do life together' we feel alive and encouraged by His presence."[28]

Throughout the history recorded in the Bible, God confirmed this reliability by orchestrating events in order that people would *know* that He alone is God. The phrase "so that you might know that I [alone] am God" is recorded more than a hundred times in His Word. In addition, the apostle Paul said, "How beautiful are the feet of those who bring good news!" (Rom 10:15 NIV). Parents are meant to be messengers of good news to their children. God has ordained parents to share it—and for children to *know* God personally through that truth. Although the church can aid parents in this task, the church simply does not have enough time or influence with each child to do this effectively alone.

My husband and I had the privilege of being the ones who brought this good news to our children and prayed with them to receive Christ. Those are moments we will never forget—our children's tender prayers asking Jesus to forgive their sin and inviting Him to begin a relationship

---

[28] M. J. Anthony, ed., *Perspectives on Children's Spiritual Formation: Four Views* (Nashville, TN: B&H, 2007), 33.

with them. There is no greater joy than to give the good news to another, especially our children, whom we love so dearly. Paul prays this for the church in Ephesus:

> I keep asking that the God of our Lord Jesus Christ, the glorious Father, may give you the Spirit of wisdom and revelation, so that you may know him better. I pray also that the eyes of your heart may be enlightened in order that you may know the hope to which he has called you, the riches of his glorious inheritance in the saints. (Eph 1:17–18 NIV)

Knowing God includes knowing the hope to which He has called us. What a great prayer for parents to pray for their children. This knowledge answers the epic questions: "Who is God? How has He appointed me to live my life? What is my calling? What is my purpose here on earth?" The hope of our calling, through the power of Christ, is the reason we live and breathe. As my children have grown older, I can see that these are the fundamental questions they wrestle with. It is imperative that parents equip their children to know whom to go to for the answers to these questions.

It is easy to get swept away with the tide of knowing *about* God. We can memorize a host of Bible verses and facts and still not truly know God. This was true of the religious people of Jesus' day, and it can be true today if we are not cautious. Knowing God must always be the center of all we do; otherwise our children will know that it is not authentic and real.

In our world people think truth is relative to perception, opinion, and experience. In Rom 1:25, Paul speaks about the depravity we have in our society as a result of *exchanging the truth of God for a lie.* When children have a vacuum of truth in their lives, they will accept a lie because that feels more real to them than anything else. Spiritual parents must choose to inspire their children by constantly reminding them that there is capital-T Truth and then living lives in authenticity and congruency to it.

Jesus says He alone is the truth, and no man comes to the Father except through Him (John 14:6). Furthermore, the truth He offers will set us free (John 8:32). Today's children are inspired when they begin to see the correlation between the capital-T Truth and freedom. Unfortunately, the church has often packaged this kind of truth around a framework of mindless obedience that is equated with a long list of do's and don'ts. The end result is a lifestyle of bondage that rivals the Scribes and the Pharisees.

When children see that truth actually leads to freedom, they begin to taste what Jesus said when He said, "I have come that they may have life, and have it more abundantly" (John 10:10). What young person does not want the full life with true freedom? These are words they will run to instead of away from, if they *know* the God who said them.

10. The Environment of Modeling. In regard to the environment of modeling, Polly Berrien Berends once said, "The best things your children will learn about God will be from watching you try to find out for yourself. Jesus said, 'Seek and you will find.' They will not always do what you tell them to do, but they will be (good and bad) as they see you being. If your children see you seeking, they will seek—and the finding part is up to God."[29]

Perhaps the best way to understand modeling in the context of children is in the way Paul said, "Be imitators of God, therefore, as dearly loved *children*" (Eph 5:1 NIV, author's emphasis). He knew the nature of children to imitate and desired that to be our posture before our Heavenly Father. Imitating God is always a good thing. He is perfect. We cannot fail when we choose to behave the way Christ modeled for us.

Of course parents are not perfect. They are not perfect models—and their actions are not always going to be congruent with their beliefs. But what makes ill behavior congruent in the environment of modeling is when parents simply acknowledge that fact. Parents become models whether they are modeling the correct way God would want them to do something or acknowledging that their behavior fell short.

Modeling is the environment that creates a marriage with the other environments. It is a perfect union because modeling demonstrates the "how" to the "what" that each environment reveals. In the other environments parents are challenged to learn about who God is and encouraged to live their lives in His power. Perry Downs notes that the influence parents have on their children is "due in part to the fact that children cannot see the invisible God, but they can see their parents who they may understand to live in God's presence."[30]

Modeling answers the questions: "How do I practically put into practice what I have learned? How do I live in relationship with God and others? How do I obey God's Word? How do I abide in Christ? How do I let His Spirit guide me?" Parents become living, breathing examples of the answers to these questions. They put flesh on faith.

The two concepts of *abiding in Christ* and *allowing His Spirit to guide our lives* are processes of spiritual growth. In any relationship, as we grow to know and understand the person we love, we grow in our understanding of how to best respond. The Christian life is all about responding to God. From the moment we choose to surrender our lives to God and accept the gift of salvation offered through Jesus, we begin the journey of relational transformation.

---

[29] P. B. Berends, *Gently Lead* (New York: Harper Collins, 1991), 8.

[30] P. G. Downs, *Teaching for Spiritual Growth: An Introduction to Christian Education* (Grand Rapids: Zondervan, 1994), 147.

Parents have an ever-narrowing window of opportunity to maximize their influence in their children's lives. The fields of psychology and sociology tell us that parents are the primary influencers in our children's lives from birth until 12 years old.[31] They must be shrewd to use this window of influence and capitalize on it in childhood.

Conclusion

This is the vision for spiritual parents: Each parent perseveres in loving Christ in his or her heart and by faithful action in trusting in Him for what only He can give and then modeling *this* to his or her children. Spiritual parents persevere, and they do not give up. They do not abdicate to somebody else. They do not make excuses for the way they were parented or the resources they did not have. They walk by faith, and they thank God, the one who entrusted their children to them in the first place. They fight the good fight *every day,* knowing that they cannot model something that they do not already possess.

As spiritual parents pray and ask God to empower them to parent in a way that strengthens their faith and that of their child, perhaps they would pray a prayer like this:

> Dear Heavenly Father,
>
> Thank You for entrusting these children to me. Thank You for giving me the privilege of pointing them to You, even though at times I feel so undeserving of this role. Help me to be a spiritual parent—with eyes to see what matters most to You.
>
> I pray that You will show me how to create these environments in my home and in my life in ways that will reflect the truth of who You are to them. I want them to know You accurately and fully.
>
> May our home be a place where truth and love prevail above all else, and may Your plans for my children, and myself, be fulfilled as we submit ourselves to Your desires. Please reveal Your desires to me, and craft my heart so that I will listen and obey. I trust Your Spirit to guide me and give me the wisdom and power to do the things that You desire.
>
> I am Yours. Our home is Yours. These children are Yours. Be glorified!
>
> Amen.

[31] G. Barna, *Transforming Children into Spiritual Champions* (Ventura: Regal Books, 2003), 12.

11 Children's Ministry in the Context of the Family for Spiritual Formation

Michelle D. Anthony
Kit Rae
ROCKHARBOR Church

Wesley's war cry in eighteenth-century England was, "Make Christians, my dear, make Christians!" Wesley uttered these words to Mary Bishop, who operated a school for girls in the English towns of Bath and Keynsham.[1] Wesley was deeply convinced that Christians weren't simply born but made. Wesley viewed this process of making Christians as one that will be most informed by devoted and diligent teaching. In light of this, his ministry gave special attention to the importance of preaching, worship, the sacraments, and Christian disciplines. He believed that people of all ages needed to be taught God's truth and how to live the Christian life. Because of this belief Wesley highly valued the spiritual formation of children and emphasized their training in the home and the church.

The mere mention of the word *children* invokes many feelings and emotions. To one it is a magical word of youth and freedom. To another it conveys the idea of an annoying, loud nuisance. In our society we idolize the *idea* of childhood with romantic notions of carefree days at the baseball diamond or tender moments with a teddy bear and tea sandwiches. We spend enormous amounts of money entertaining, feeding, and clothing children, but we rarely spend adequate time investing in their spiritual formation.

In almost every aspect of human life we isolate ourselves from them. We have created day cares, baby sitting, and nurseries to ensure that our time with them will be limited to the bare necessities. The effects of such a system is that our generations are isolated from one another. Children

---

[1] T. Jackson, *The Works of the Reverend John Wesley* (London: Wesleyan Conference Press, 1872), 388.

today know fewer and fewer adults and have fewer opportunities to relate with and learn from them than did their parents or grandparents.[2]

The net result is that we have neglected the social, emotional, and spiritual development of our children. Clark notes, "The sweep of history seems to trace a moving pattern in child training as follows: (1) all training is in the matrix of the home and is informal; (2) child training is shared by parents and relatives and is still informal in nature; (3) training is organized by the tribe or subculture group to transmit an increasingly complex body of treasured values and is carried on in both formal and informal ways; (4) child training is delegated to education specialists without regard to their values, and procedures are almost entirely formal, both unrelated to the teacher's values and related only with difficulty to the real world."[3] In other words, spiritual development and formation has moved from the informal safe environment of the family unit to the formal instruction almost void of familial attachment.

Although the understanding, views, and definitions of family structure may be diverse, controversial, and conflicting, the Bible speaks directly and indirectly about family structure. A biblical theology of the role of the family is foundational for understanding and applying God's truths. The Bible teaches that one man and one woman were joined together and that God then blessed them with children; both the Old and New Testaments reveal a God that is concerned about families, marriage, and children. The Bible presents a God who loves and cares for marriages, families, and children and speaks of the importance of them (1 Cor 7; Ps 139; Deut 6; Gen 2; Eph 5; Mal 2; Mark 10; Ps 78). Throughout His Word, God provides His idea of the family structure and the role of family for the spiritual formation of the next generation.

The role of the family is to provide spiritual nurturing and training, to evangelize, disciple, and raise godly children. However, we exist in a fallen world, and family life is often broken. The role of the church is to support and assist the parents and family in this process, in providing spiritual development when it is absent in the home. The church is to be a place of commitment to marriages, families, and children in the context of community.

Robert N. Bellah in his epilogue writes, "Churches are at present infirmaries for sick families, and they must continue to be so under present conditions. But if the illness is to be cured, they must bring the family back into the common life through activities and celebrations that join rather than isolate. . . . Thus, if we really want to re-appropriate the 'traditional' family, it will not be the idealized Victorian house with

---

[2] M. Anthony, "Children's Ministry and Christian Education," in *Evangelical Dictionary of Christian Education* (Grand Rapids, MI: Baker Books, 2001), 121.

[3] R. Clark, L. Johnson, A. Sloat, *Christian Education: Foundations for the Future* (Chicago: Moody Press, 1991), 128.

Mom and Dad by the fireside but rather the much older idea of the family embedded in community.[4]

Bellah's argument that the family model of ministry is in actuality a "much older idea" that is embedded in our church tradition is worthy of investigation. With children's ministry adopting the new family ministry model, practitioners and parents alike are being awakened to the fact that it is not *new* at all. A look at biblical history, human development, and church history all point to the family as the place, in the earliest of years, where faith can be nourished and formed.

God's Perspective: Children's Spiritual Formation

The Bible begins with the story of a family. After Adam and Eve were created, they were instructed to be fruitful and multiply (Gen 1:28). It was always God's intention that children would be part of His world. Because this is true, what does God say about how we should minister to children, teach them, and help them grow in faith-learning experiences? A look at the differences between Old and New Testament models will help us gain perspective on biblical principles that can be applied in our ministries today.

Old Testament Teachings

The most striking principle, gleaned from Old Testament teachings for children, is that the spiritual educational process for the child is done completely within, not separate from, the members of the community. Children are assumed as part of, rather than separated from, the body of believers.[5]

Also compelling is the primary source of religious education, which is exclusively the responsibility of the parent. It was God's intention that the home would be the classroom for the most important of all life's lessons, and the commands, which He gave, would be passed on through this means. In Deut 6:6–7, God says, "These commandments that I give you today are to be upon your hearts. Impress them on your children. Talk about them when you sit at home and when you walk along the road, when you lie down and when you get up" (NIV). This was to be a natural part of the Old Testament family life, which was also strengthened by their calendar year of festivals and memorials.

Each festival in Israel's year recapitulated significant events in their salvation history. For a child these must have held the wonder similar to what our children experience at Christmas today, with all the anticipation

---

[4] R. N. Bellah, "Epilogue: It Takes a Society to Raise a Family," in *Family Transformed: Religion, Values, and Society in American Life*, ed. S. M. Tipton, J. Witte Jr. (Washington, DC: Georgetown University Press, 2003), 296.

[5] L. Richards, *The Ministry Handbook for Children's Ministry* (Grand Rapids, MI: Baker Books, 1983), 83.

and excitement. As the family prepared the meal or sacrificed the lamb, the child was ever present and participating in the reliving of her nation's past that has shaped its faith. These were times of teachable moments and days of Sabbath rest and play. In Exod 12:25–27 God instructs, "When you enter the land that the LORD will give you as He promised, observe this ceremony. And when your children ask you, 'What does this ceremony mean to you?' then tell them, 'It is the Passover sacrifice to the Lord, who passed over the houses of the Israelites in Egypt and spared our homes when he struck down the Egyptians'" (NIV). It was always God's plan that the family home would be the greenhouse for the growth of faith formation.[6]

New Testament Teachings

Although little is mentioned in the New Testament Scriptures in regard to teaching and training children spiritually, we know that they are to obey their parents (Eph 6:1); that fathers are to bring them up in the "nurture and admonition of the Lord" (Eph 6:4); that bishops, deacons, and elders are to be faithful and successful in the rearing of their own children (Titus 1:6); and that fathers are to be careful not to deal too harshly with their children (Col 3:21). With this short list, we can see the brevity of New Testament instruction regarding child-rearing. However, there is no evidence to believe that the responsibility of religious education was outside the home or had changed since God outlined His original Old Testament plan.[7]

Because home groups were the primary meeting place for early church gatherings, the children were, most likely, in close proximity to the teaching of God's Word. Whether they formally participated in the spiritual practices, or scurried in and out among their parents, they were a vital part of faith community, gleaning from the modeling and instruction of their family members.[8] In addition to the biblical teachings, as Christians we believe that God created our minds, bodies, and souls and the developmental process by which we come into maturity. A look into childhood development also informs ministry to children's spiritual formation in the context of the family.

Developmental Issues in Children's Spiritual Formation

Childhood faith formation begins at an early age. In fact, some theorists suggest that faith development begins before a child is even born. Research shows that brain development begins in the womb within the

---

[6] Ibid., 129.

[7] M. Anthony, "Children's Ministry" in *Foundations of Ministry: Christian Education in the 21st Century*, ed. M. J. Anthony (Grand Rapids, MI: Baker Books, 2001), 206.

[8] C. Stonehouse, *Joining Children on the Spiritual Journey* (Grand Rapids, MI: Baker Books, 1998), 23.

second week after conception and that a sense of security is necessary for this to take place. Likewise, this same security is a foundational concept for faith development and could be argued that faith formation and brain development go hand in hand in the hidden environment and protection of the womb.[9] Psalm 139:15–16 states:

> My frame was not hidden from You, when I was made in secret, and skillfully wrought in the depths of the earth; Your eyes have seen my unformed substance; and in Your book were all written the days that were ordained for me, when as yet there was not one of them. (NASB)

Regardless of when true faith formation begins, God is intimately involved in the process and desires for each person to grow up in faith to reach his or her highest potential on earth through the power of His Spirit. Karen Yust argues that church ministries and parents often try to keep their children merely entertained until they are "old enough" to participate in true spiritual development practices. She explains, "[C]hildren are real people, capable of real faith, who deserve better than what they usually get in religious education, both in church and at home."[10] Yust does not recommend treating children as miniature adults, capable of adult responses to their experiences of God, although she does insist that children are born with a capacity for wonder, joy, and love and can, within the limits set by their psychological development, respond to the presence of God in their lives.[11]

As we begin to take a closer look at the developmental issues related to a child's spiritual formation and the impact the family and the church can have in a child's life, we first must start by understanding the psychological effects of the fall in Genesis 3. In Gen 3:7 we see sin enter humanity for the first time and Adam and Eve experience the feeling of shame. This is the deep awareness that "something is wrong with me and I don't want others to see me in my bad condition." Pathologically, shame leads us to "cover" ourselves—using anything in life to keep ourselves and others from seeing us for who we truly are. The feelings of shame were quickly followed by a deep sense of guilt as seen in Gen 3:8–10—the feeling of judgment, being found out, or abandoned.[12] Our pathological response to guilt is simply to hide—to hide our true selves, personality, and identity, only allowing what is acceptable to be seen by others.[13]

---

[9] S. K. Morganthaler, N. A. Lass, "Two Miracles Together: The Brain and Faith Development," in *Lutheran Education* 136 (2): 87–93.

[10] K. M. Yust, "Real Kids, Real Faith: Practices for Nurturing Children's Spiritual Lives," in *The Christian Century* 121 (14): 33.

[11] Ibid., 34–35.

[12] J. Coe, "Effects of Original Sin" (class lecture in *Developmental Spirituality* at Talbot School of Theology, La Mirada, CA, January 29, 2007).

[13] K. Horney, *Neurosis and Human Growth* (New York: Norton, 1950), 203.

The reality of sin and our pathological responses to cover and hide are at work in children from the earliest of ages. A great example of this can be seen in the story of a young boy who went out to play basketball on the first day of school. As he stood there, the older boys picked teams, and he was made fun of and not chosen for either of the schoolyard teams. When the next day came and the teacher dismissed the children to go out to recess, this little boy stayed behind and asked the teacher if he could stay in and help clean the chalkboard erasers. The teacher thought nothing of it and gladly welcomed the boy to stay in and help, showering him with compliments and appreciation for desiring to help. This pattern went on for months until teacher/parent conferences came around. It was then the teacher went on and on to the parents about how their little boy is such a servant and willing to sacrifice in order to help and serve others. That evening the parents took the little boy out to his favorite restaurant and praised him for his acts of service and selflessness, all the while unknowingly solidifying the deep belief that there was something wrong with him and the only way for him to receive love, and deal with the sense of shame and guilt he had experienced during recess, was to be a good kid and serve others.

Through the work of the Holy Spirit, the family can be used in a significant way to counter the effects of sin in a child's life. This can be seen primarily in the area of attachment and the relational dynamics that are developed between the child and parent. The greater the attachment and ability of the parent to be present with their child in their good *and bad* times, the less likely the child will feel the need to cover and hide from themselves and others.

Relational dynamics developed between a parent and child during the earliest years of life will be the same relational dynamics the child will establish between themselves and God. Will the child have the ability to bring their good and bad before God in such a way that they can be fully known, or will they only be able to bring the acceptable parts of who they are because their relationship with their parents and significant others has perpetuated the effects of sin? In addition to this parental approach of reflecting a correct theology in a child's mind, three areas of developmentalism also affect spiritual formation: behaviorism, humanism, and cognitivism.

Behaviorism

The behavioristic approach to learning and development is based on the premise that learning occurs primarily through the reinforcement of desired responses. At the core of this theory is the word *reward*, and although the reward may be extrinsic early in the process, the goal is to internalize the reinforcement so that the new behavior is an intrinsic reward in and of itself. Behavioral scientist B. F. Skinner successfully used reinforcement to teach pigeons to bowl. Simply, if the pigeon moved the ball toward the pins, he was given a piece of grain; if he did not, he did not receive anything. The techniques used in the model of behaviorism include prompting, cuing, modeling, role play, skill drills, and positive reinforcements.[14]

The behavioristic model is used frequently in the formation of children's spirituality. Children's ministries offer reward systems to children for memorizing verses, bringing their Bible to church, and even paying attention in class. Sometimes these rewards are simply a pleasant or positive response from the teacher, whereas other times the reward can be a ribbon, pin, or even a trophy. In general, the church and Christian parents often seek to modify a child's spiritual behavior through positive reinforcement; verbal and nonverbal cues; and modeling worshipful acts such as prayer, giving, and corporate singing.

Humanism

In contrast to behaviorism, the humanistic approach is founded on the theory that learning occurs primarily through reflection on personal experience. The role of the teacher is not to put anything into the mind of the learner but to extract lessons from the learner's own insight and experiences and to look for ways to engage the affective domain of the student. The knowledge is somehow already there, so the teacher focuses not on rewards and behavior but on asking the right questions. These questions stimulate the learner to make new and deeper connections.[15] They explore ways to connect the content to the attitudes, emotions, and values of the learner.[16] Humanistic instructional methodologies have been popular in North American classrooms since the 1970s. Humanistic teachers go beyond the mere transmission of content and look for ways to connect the material in a more holistic way (e.g., mind, body, and heart).[17]

Although this is a difficult model to use in early childhood, aspects of this theory are used in their spiritual development within the context of children's ministry. For example, when a teacher tells a vivid Bible story and allows the students to use their creativity to fill in the gaps of how the animals on the ark might have smelled or what it would feel like to be in the belly of a whale, the teacher encourages them to draw on these stories to gain a deeper understanding of the story and its meaning to their lives.

Cognitivism

The cognitivism approach is based on the more academic aspects of learning and development. The basic principle in this domain is that learning occurs primarily through the exposure to logically presented

---

[14] T. Kramlinger, T. Huberty, "Behaviorism versus Humanism," in *Training and Development Journal* 44 (12): 41.
[15] Ibid., 41.
[16] W. Yount, *Created to Learn* (Nashville, TN: B&H, 2010), 234.
[17] M. Anthony, "Humanism in Christian Education," in *Christian Education Journal* 12:1 (1988): 79–88.

information. "Cognitive learning theory emphasizes the thinking of students, rather than their behavior or attitudes."[18] A good analogy of this concept is to picture two pails, in which the full pail of the wise teacher pours its contents into the empty pail of the learner. The emphasis here is on "telling" another what he or she should know.[19] But it doesn't stop there; from this point in the lesson the learner processes the new information and uses their thinking and reasoning capacities to reflect on the new material.

Children's ministry in spiritual development often uses this model, with the structure of a well-informed teacher standing with the Bible open guiding the students in a journey of discovery. If the students listen carefully and engage their thought processes, there is a greater likelihood they will learn and, as a result of the methods used, remember and transfer this new material to real-life application. Learning and transformation take place where information is presented and the learner spends time reflecting on ways to apply the gleaned insights. This approach values self-selected discovery learning, problem-solving activities, and small-group discussion.[20]

Implications of Learning Approaches

Although each approach has its strengths and weaknesses, any of them used in isolation can be detrimental to the spiritual formation process in a child's life. God created each individual with different learning styles and personalities. Each person brings great diversity to the learning process, and children are no exception. Christian educators and parents need to make room for a blending of these approaches to make sure that correct information is being taught and processed (cognitivism) and clear and unmistakable objectives are given on how children are to live their lives according to God's plan and Word (behaviorism), while allowing them to experience the creative outflow of their uniqueness and the wonder of God through diverse learning environments that engage the mind, will, and heart of the learner (humanism). In this balance the spiritual formation process has a more balanced approach and better reflects the ineffable nature of God.

Because the home offers the best environment for children to be introduced to each of these developmental processes, and the individuality of each child can be ascertained, parents must be brought into the spiritual formation process from the earliest stage. The Church can also evaluate their methodologies in light of God's Word and developmental

---

[18] Yount, *Created to Learn*, 191.
[19] Ibid., 42.
[20] R. Biehler, J. Snowman, *Psychology Applied to Teaching* (Bellmawr, NJ: Houghton Mifflin, 2008), 341.

theories and take a look back historically on the teachings and leaders who shaped Christian education for the child and the family.

Historical Perspective: Children's Spiritual Formation

In Christian educational history, there were centuries where no provision was made for children to gain education of any sort, in literacy or the Christian faith formation process. It was not until the Reformation that tremendous focus on basic literacy and Bible study began. Martin Luther was dedicated to this education process for children and touted the family as the place where true spiritual formation began and was nurtured. Luther called parents to participate actively in their children's faith formation and to be the primary nurturers of this process. He saw the church as a supportive entity in this endeavor but identified parents as the ones who would make a lasting legacy of faith in their children's hearts. Then Comenius in the late sixteenth century committed himself to make broad Christian education available for all children.[21]

In 1703 another voice would begin its addition to the strong family formational values that Luther and Comenius had begun. John Wesley was born in England. His father, a graduate of Oxford and a Church of England rector, was also at this time the father to John's 14 other siblings. His mother Susanna Wesley was known for being educated, prayerful, and a woman who saw her role as a mother by vocation. Samuel Wesley was a scattered man that was short and temperamental, a poor provider, and absent for much of John's early years.[22] Susanna Wesley made the education of her children her top priority. Under no circumstances would Susanna permit her children to have any lessons until they were five years old, but starting on their fifth birthday their formal education would begin. On their first day of class they were to finish the day by knowing the entire alphabet. They would soon after begin reading the Bible as their main text.

In addition to this they were to learn Latin and Greek and were tutored in classical studies that were traditional in England at the time.[23] Susanna would also set aside time for each child each week so she could check in with them on their studies, spiritual growth, and progress. Susanna, in a letter she wrote to her husband, stated:

> I am a woman, but I am also the mistress of a large family. And though the superior charge of the souls contained in

[21] M. Anthony, "Children's Ministry and Christian Education" in *Evangelical Dictionary of Christian Education* (Grand Rapids, MI: Baker Books, 2001), 159–60.
[22] B. Barber, "Wesley Intro" (Class lecture in *History and Theory of Christian Soul Care and Direction* at Talbot School of Theology, La Mirada, CA, October 30, 2008).
[23] H. Ingvar, *John Wesley* (New York: Abingdon, 1961), 14–15.

> it lies upon you, yet in your long absence I cannot but look upon every soul you leave under my charge as a talent committed to me under a trust. I am not a man nor a minister, yet as a mother and a mistress I felt I ought to do more than I had yet done. I resolved to begin with my own children; in which I observe, the following method: I take such a proportion of time as I can spare every night to discourse with each child apart. On Monday I talk with Molly, on Tuesday with Hetty, Wednesday with Nancy, Thursday with Jacky, Friday with Patty, Saturday with Charles.

Through his mother's instruction and education John became acquainted with daily prayer, a reliance on the Lord, and a giving of one's self to the service of others. At the beginning of John's education at the age of five, his house caught on fire, and John was trapped in the attic of the house where his bed was located. When John became aware he was not able to escape, he leaned out the window and thereby was rescued by his father. From this point until his death he believed that he was set apart and saved for a special task. John later referred to himself as "a brand plucked from the fire," referring to a passage in Zech 3:2.[24]

In John's adult years he wrote his mother, requesting her to write an account of the child-rearing methods she used with her ten kids who survived to adulthood.[25] From his mother's influence on him as a theologian and an educated theorist, John quickly learned the power of a good Christ-centered education in the home and the impact it could have on society. As John Wesley developed his approach to the education and spiritual formation of children we can be sure to attribute much of it to his mother, Savannah Wesley.

Wesley believed in the capability of even young children to experience conversion and mentioned many of them in his writings and journal. Wesley believed that sanctification was a gift from God that was received by the hearts and minds of those who were receptive through the teaching ministry of the family and the church. He viewed education as a means of grace or an instrument that the Holy Spirit could use to work in the life of the believer. Because of these theological underpinnings and the previously mentioned influences, Wesley structured and carried out his ministry.[26]

As Wesley entered into this process, he knew that first and foremost this training needed to start in the home. He viewed the home as a little

---

[24] K. W. Ross, R. Stacy, "John Wesley and Savannah" (Savannah Images Project), http://www.sip.armstrong.edu/Methodism/wesley.html, accessed December 4, 2008.

[25] R. W. Ward, R. P. Heitzenrater, *The Works of John Wesley,* vol. 18 (Nashville, TN: Abingdon, 1998), 286–91.

[26] G. C. Felton, "John Wesley and the Teaching Ministry: Ramifications for Education in the Church Today," in *Religious Education Association of the United States and Canada* (Winter 1997): 1.

church in which children and young people were to learn the Bible and moral values of being a Christian. To aid parents in this endeavor, Wesley encouraged and promoted the use of the catechetical method. Parents were to teach their children using the catechism. Although some parents said they did not have enough time to teach their children, Wesley and other preachers would remind parents of long winter evenings and how they should be using their time on Sundays after the church service.[27]

In 1746 John began a four-volume set of *Lessons for Children,* which was essentially an abridged version of the Old Testament. With these materials in place, Wesley also published three sermons that dealt with the role of the family and its importance in the continuation of authentic Christianity. He wrote *On Family Religion* based on Josh 24:15; *On Education of Children,* using Prov 22:6; and *Obedience to Parents,* based on Col 3:20.[28] In all of these, Wesley emphasized that the home influenced and had a profound impact on the child even *before* the church did and that parents are the first religious teachers of their children. Wesley then concluded that the foundations for spiritual development in the life of a child must be built and nurtured in the context of family life.[29] With the family life serving as the foundation in a child's spiritual formation, Wesley knew that the role of the church was to help these children and their families to mature and continue their education in the Christian community.[30]

These early writings for children in the area of Christian education were the antecedent of the Sunday school movement. The first school for religious instruction was likely established in 1769, in High Wycombe, by Hannah Ball. Through many letters and visits Wesley encouraged Ball in the establishment of her school.[31]

When America was first established, in part as a revolt against the spiritual oppressions of Europe, the early schools taught and embraced the teachings of the Bible. The Bible was one of the primary textbooks and its truths were upheld in society. As the school system became more secularized, the need for outside Christian education became more critical. Parochial schools served to promote some religious training, but ironically, it was not until England's Robert Raikes established Sunday school in 1780 in Gloucester that a revival of Christian education would infiltrate the American system.[32]

---

[27] T. Jackson, *The Works of the Reverend John Wesley* (London: Wesleyan Conference Press, 1872), 293.

[28] A. C. Outler, *The Works of John Wesley,* vol. 3 (Nashville, TN: Abingdon, 1986), 347–60.

[29] Felton, "John Wesley and the Teaching Ministry," 3.

[30] J. E. Kirby, R. E. Richey, K. E. Rowe, *The Methodists* (Westport, CT: Greenwood, 1996), 169.

[31] Felton, "John Wesley and the Teaching Ministry," 4.

[32] R. Choun, *Children's Ministry Manual for Pastors and Teachers* (Grand Rapids, MI: Baker, 2000), 17.

As need for Sunday school materials became apparent, Wesley went to the task of writing these materials. A guiding principle for him was that children should truly comprehend, not simply learn by rote memory. Wesley stated, "I must entreat you to take good heed how you teach these deep things of God. Beware of that common, but accursed, way of making children parrots, instead of Christians. Labour that, as far as possible, they may understand every single sentence which they read." Wesley's concern was that this information simply did not become something the children could recite back to their parents or teachers but something that God was using to transform their hearts.[33]

As Sunday schools continued to grow Wesley continued to resource the family by writing a publication called *Prayers for Children* containing a variety of prayers for mornings, evenings, and prayers for relationships and friends. Many of these prayers contained strong echoes of the *Book of Common Prayer* with which these children's parents would be familiar. In addition, each prayer he wrote in this publication ended with the Lord's Prayer for the child to recite.[34]

Wesley went to great lengths to care for the souls of children. He believed these practices needed to be grounded in the home and be supported by the church for continued maturity. To this end he spent much time and effort establishing Sunday schools and writing children's curriculum, children's prayer books, and (with the help of his brother) hymns for children. Wesley wrote in a letter to a friend regarding ministry to children within the context of the family, "It seems, these will be one of the great means of reviving religion throughout the nation."[35]

Children's Spiritual Formation in a New Millennium

A quick glance over the past couple of centuries that the church has been in existence shows us that there are distinct eras of pronounced attention to specific ministries. For instance, beginning in the final decades of the nineteenth century, foreign missions exploded in interest and growth in England and then in America. The most passionate speakers and pastors were preaching about the lost in countries of which most had never even heard. Likewise, in the late 1960s and early 1970s, tremendous focus began to be placed on the youth of society. Like never before, children and youth were facing unprecedented issues of sex, violence, war, divorce, and drug dependence. The church responded with both church ministries and para-church ministries for youth/children such as Child Evangelism Fellowship, Pioneer Clubs, Youth for Christ, and Young

33 Felton, "John Wesley and the Teaching Ministry," 4.
34 Ibid., 5.
35 Ibid., 6.

Life, while the position of youth pastor and children's pastor became an essential element in most churches.[36]

At the same time technology was growing, a heightened value on children and their well-being began to emerge, the family was continuing to decline, and the megachurch was moving into the spotlight. In light of these new developments, a church called Willow Creek in South Barrington, Illinois, was coming onto the scene with their "Seeker Sensitive" movement. As many churches began to emulate their programming philosophy, this led to a new way of ministering to children.

Led by a woman named Sue Miller, who had a new vision for reaching today's child for Christ and coined the phrase, "Making your children's ministry the best hour of every kid's week!" Her goal was to have "Sunday school" be the time that children looked forward to most out of their entire week. She was tired of boring Bible lessons, large classrooms that looked like school rooms, teachers that had no business teaching kids, and kids not being known. She wanted to create a new environment that was specifically designed for kids, a place where a child would be known week after week by the same small-group leader, a place that brought God's Word to life in a way that could be applied to life, a place where the teachers were serving out of their giftedness instead of serving out of guilt, and a place that would be fun. She wanted to create the best hour of a child's week.

As this new vision for ministering to today's child began to shape churches all over the country, it found its power in six values. The following values were to shape the way ministry happened to children. The values are: (1) *child targeted,* meaning that everything from the building to the songs and lessons being taught were designed with the child in mind from a developmental perspective; (2) *safe environment,* which would allow every kid to feel comfortable and secure; (3) *relevant Bible teaching,* ensuring that each lesson was designed so that a child could remember the content and then live it out Monday morning on the playground at school, focusing on Christian behavior and attitudes; (4) *creative teaching,* through drama and skits, video, lights, sound effects, or whatever is needed to convey the appropriate lesson in a creative way; (5) *small groups,* allowing for the shepherding of children to happen in a small group of eight to ten kids with one leader; and (6) *fun,* where Miller says, "The reason for this value is quite simple—kids won't come back willingly if it's not fun and they certainly won't invite their friends. An absence of fun will result in an absence of kids."

These six values have literally shaped the face of ministry today for children in the church. Across the country, and even on an international

---

[36] M. Anthony, "Children's Ministry," in *Foundations of Ministry: Christian Education in the 21st Century,* ed. M. J. Anthony (Grand Rapids, MI: Baker, 2000), 207.

level, people who minster to children are looking at how to incorporate these values into their ministries.

With this paradigm in mind, we can now compare and contrast this view to the ministry that Wesley offered to children. Both ministries share a value to have resources that are age appropriate to ensure that kids can understand what is being taught. In this area today's church can stand on the many shoulders that were between Wesley and Miller in order to engage kids in a better manner. With the media and visuals that are at our disposal, the church can allow God's Word to come to life in ways that it has never been able to in the past.

In light of knowing each one of the children and shepherding each heart, a small-group leader is a great addition to the child's spiritual formation. This small-group environment allows the child to feel accepted, part of the group, and known and have the ability to ask questions, hear about life experience, see God working in other kids lives, be held accountable, and even learn how to pray and hear God's voice. Because this was a value for the adults Wesley ministered to, often, to his dismay, children were taught in large-group settings outside their home.

However, one aspect that is not mentioned in the modern values previously listed is that of the family. For Luther, Wesley, and those found in the biblical accounts, the family created the foundation for all Christian education and spiritual formation. Our spiritual forefathers actively developed resources and encouraged parents to be the primary spiritual nurturers in their child's life. They saw the church as a support in the early years of a child and primary in the later adult years. This stands in stark contrast to the contemporary children's ministry model. Its desire for a child's time at church to be the best hour of one's week undermines this belief. Seldom is there mention about creating resources to strengthen parent primacy, even involvement. This role in many ways enables the "drop off" mentality parents face in life in regard to their children. This view seems to unintentionally abdicate the role of the parent to the church.

Last, in the model of modernity, children's ministry can quickly become about fun, creativity, and entertainment as an *end* rather than a *means.* Although this is never stated, these values can quickly take priority over introducing children into a relationship with God, learning to hear His voice, and learning to respond to it in desired obedience through the power of God's Spirit. In light of this caution, it is possible that these values, when used appropriately, can aid in the pursuit of a deeper and more intimate relationship with God.

Today children are at the greatest risk ever, and the need for Christian educators to understand spiritual formation both theologically and developmentally is great. Although the church and its educators play a significant role in the spiritual endeavors of its children, an alarming number of parents have forgotten, ignored, or are ignorant of what their responsibilities are in the child-rearing process. Parents have strayed far from the biblical ideal for family life, and this gap between what is and what should be makes clear the need for a comprehensive yet empowering family ministry within the church.[37]

Spiritual Formation Issues in Ministry Application

This generation of children is in the spotlight more than ever. Their rights, their care, their nourishment, their minds, and their education are at the center of conversation and controversy. Both their well-being and their exploitation are seen at every level of societal structure. In addition, the battle for their souls is being waged not simply in the classrooms and political arenas, but also on what some refer to as a "mind-altering drug"—the Internet.[38] Our culture proposes that we care for our children by granting them certain rights. Traditionally, these have been fundamental protections and opportunities relating to health, safety, nutrition, and education, but recently these rights have extended into issues of autonomy and the right of choice in almost every aspect of life. In this societal shift comes a right to choose religious practices also.

The conflict Christian families face today in raising their children with values of faith in Christ lies within the fact that Christian values are no longer the values of society's norm. A postmodern way of thought and practice calls for educators to design opportunities for children and families to develop spiritually in a hostile environment. Although culture and society are in constant change, there are issues of spiritual formation that remain constant. These theological, cognitive, historical, and faith development issues allow the educator to find stability in a time of uncertainty. The stabilizers serve to remind us of how God works within individuals, redemptively, throughout the centuries in a diversity of cultural barriers.

The goal for all who care about the church's children is that we each become spiritually strong ourselves, living the practice that we preach. We must understand the delicate workings of all developmental aspects in order to make the most of every age in every situation. We must pay special attention to the first six years in the life of a child and champion the parents who are in closest proximity to the child during this stage.[39] Ultimately, God as the Creator of the human mind, soul, and spirit transcends the issues that might appear to stand in the way of spiritual growth and formation. Psychology can help to remind us that there is a mastermind behind the complexities of life and the human mind and spirit. Remembering this truth allows us to persevere and remain faithful in our endeavors. Children are

---

[37] R. Choun, *Children's Ministry: ABC's for Volunteers* (Grand Rapids, MI: Baker, 1998), 74.

[38] R. Maas, "Christ as the Logos of Childhood: Reflections on the Meaning and Mission of the Child," *Theology Today* 56, no. 4 (2000): 464.

[39] G. Barna, *Transforming Children into Spiritual Champions* (Ventura, CA: Regal, 2003), 22.

a precious gift from God and bear the indelible stamp of the image of God and thus bring incredible significance to the mission of family ministry.

Children's and youth ministries today need to run to the aid of parents if they want to care for the souls of today's generation. Many parents have not seen parenting modeled in a way they would want to emulate. Parents have deep desires to raise their kids in healthy ways but are looking for resources and models to help them on their journey. In this arena the church needs to reevaluate the way we are ministering to children and invite parents back into the process. As the church does this, it will need to inspire parents to their God-given role, equip them with tools and resources that will aid in the effort, and support them in the process. As this takes place we will be able to recover the lost ground that Wesley so rightly instituted. We as the church need to set up and establish parents as the primary faith builders in their children's lives and anticipate the church to play a supportive role in this process.

The church must assume the role as a training ground for parents to be the soul doctors for their children, giving parents tools to be with their children and learn how to sit with them in their misdeeds and sin in order to bring spiritual healing to that which we have all inherited. To help them understand how God wanted them to view their children's souls and to love them and learn how to have spiritual conversations with them are primary facets of spiritual parenting. Parents must learn how to really be present with their children and to create space for contemplation and reflection in their homes.[40]

The church potentially creates a great danger for children by taking this role away from their parents. As the church assumes this role, it will eventually hurt the child's faith development and ultimately lead children to a compartmentalized faith—one that is practiced on Sundays for 60 minutes. In contrast, Deuteronomy 6 offers a good reminder toward an overarching ministry to children. In this passage we see that the parents are called to love God first, to make this primary, and then they are called to teach this to their children. We need a generation of parents that can model the role of the Holy Spirit to their children and model what an authentic faith looks like in everyday situations. This will ultimately build the foundation for spiritual formation to children.

In addition, the spiritual formation of children within the context of children's ministry will need to develop recourses that are not merely focused on knowing information or morality but rather on true spiritual transformation. Too often ministry to children can be considered a success if they can recite long lists of biblical facts or they outwardly look and act a certain way. The sad reality of this is that research tells us that

---

[40] H. C. Allen, *Nurturing Children's Spirituality: Christian Perspectives and Best Practices* (Eugene, OR: Cascade Books, 2008), 242.

up to 80 percent of our youth are walking away from the faith after high school.[41] This is a tragic indictment, and unless a closer investigation is made into the resources that are being used to care for the souls of this new generation, the same rate of attrition will occur.

Wesley was quick to remind his preachers and teachers that we do not want kids simply to learn rote information but to learn the information in a way that affects the soul. The same is true today. If the church adopts the informational route or the moral formation route, it will still produce a generation void of a genuine relationship with God.

If this generation of ministry to children fails to make relationship with God the priority, or excludes the importance of this within the context of the home, we may unknowingly opt to replace that worthy endeavor with that of a programmatic approach toward a model that offers mere information *about* God. If we choose to invest actively in a generation that can know God, hear His voice, and be in submission to Him through a relationship to Him, then we will have far fewer young people walk away from their faith upon the emergence of adulthood.

The new paradigm of children's ministry will need to adopt a holistic view of the child in the context of the family and provide resources that will open up the child's heart to be receptive to the work of the Holy Spirit. In addition, ministry to children will need programming that creates space for God encounters, time for kids to wonder, dream, and respond to what God might be calling them toward. We need to create space for kids to simply be in the presence of God. If young people are able to taste authentic relationship with God and others, their fun- and entertainment-driven culture will not be as appealing.

The decline of the family has led to the church's running to the aid of the children in an effort to rescue them, but in doing so, it is leaving parents behind in the process. It is time to bring the parents back into the process and reestablish them as the foundational element in the spiritual formation of their children.

The church is positioned in this millennium to have a profound impact on the lives of children and their families by serving as a greenhouse in the nurturing and preserving of spiritual formation from the earliest of years. Likewise, the church must call on parents to be awakened to their God-given roles as the spiritual nurturers of their children's faith. If we do this effectively, we can raise a new generation of children who may have an impact on this world that has yet to be seen. We cannot be negligent in the endeavors of our spiritual formation if we are to pass our faith down to the following generations.[42]

---

[41] Ibid., 37.
[42] M. J. Dawn, "'Until Christ Is Formed in You': Nurturing the Spirituality of Children," *Theology Today* 56, no. 1 (1999): 73–85.

2 Youth Ministry from a Family Perspective

David Keehn
Talbot School of Theology

A Tale of Two Teens

I first met Chris during his sophomore year of high school. A friend in our ministry introduced him to us, and it wasn't long before his fun-loving and charming personality quickly won him many new friends in our youth group. Chris began regularly attending our midweek gathering and soon the Sunday morning Bible study. As I listened to Chris share his story of divorced parents, I also sensed a hunger to know God's truth. He was eager to study the Bible, and I connected him to Brad, one of my most experienced youth mentors. They quickly developed a strong bond, and I was proud to see Brad spend additional hours with Chris outside the hours at church.

Chris became a strong peer leader in our ministry during his junior year, providing a powerful influence on the underclassmen. He was the "poster child" of what a youth ministry could do in the life of a teenager. However, during Chris's senior year he began to be routinely absent from church programs. Rumors began to circulate that Chris was binge drinking alcohol regularly and was having sex with various girls at school. Brad was distraught as his efforts to pursue Chris and bring him back to church went ignored at first and then later were rejected.

As I looked back at what went wrong, I realized I had ignored Chris's stories about splitting time between living with his codependent mom and his alcoholic, womanizing dad. The handful of hours each week that Chris spent with our church and his mentor, Brad, paled in comparison to the spiritual vacuum he returned home to each night. Even worse, the toxic messages he was receiving from his dad were marginalizing what he was learning at church. In the end Chris walked away from a church family that loved him and gave him more attention than most students received.

Becky was the middle child of a strong Christian family at my church. Her older sister was the model of perfection—she was beautiful, smart, caring, and fully devoted to Jesus. Becky was determined to be the problem child. During her middle-school years, Becky began ditching school. Her parents reached out to me as her youth pastor to try to talk some sense into her before it got any worse. She did not want to talk. Becky's freshman year began a cycle of drugs, drinking alcohol, and dating guys that had only one desire for her. I would sit with her heartbroken parents and suggest various youth programs to involve her in. They thanked me for my concern, but Becky never got connected.

Once in a while I would see Becky for a few weeks when the latest life crisis was too overwhelming, but as soon as it was over, she was gone again. I decided to give my attention to students who were more responsive to growing in their faith. However, during Becky's post-high school years she began to attend our college Bible study. Then Becky volunteered to help with the nursery. Soon people were telling me stories of Becky's radical transformation. Becky grew in devotion to God: She married a strong Christian man; is the mother to two beautiful children who love God; and even joined the staff of a church-plant in our area, giving spiritual leadership to this new fellowship. I wish I could take some credit for the miraculous change, but I cannot. What caused such repentance and restoration in Becky? Her parents never gave up on her. Her dad faithfully invested time and love in her, even while she angrily pushed him away.

The difference in the lives of these two teenagers can be found in the approach taken by their parents and the home environment fostered for their kids. It was not a result of our youth ministry's programs. God's original design, as already discussed throughout this book, has been to work through parents and the family. Right from the beginning God wanted children to be raised in a spiritual community. We saw this first in His teaching of the law and then later in the worship found at the tabernacle. It culminated in a community of believers in the local church where Christian parents worked together to raise godly children to become young adults. It is unfortunate that pastors have forgotten these lessons from our biblical heritage. As a result, misguided programs have substituted resources for spiritual formation.

Journey to Discovery

Looking back over 22 years of youth ministry, I can see that I have not always valued parents and their involvement in my ministry as much as I should have. At first I simply tolerated parents, allowing a select few to join my volunteer team. I saw parents as confused, misinformed, and sad examples of spiritual maturity for their children. In time God broke me of my spiritual pride. One of the defining moments along this journey can be traced back to when I became a parent myself. It was at that point I discovered my own ignorance.

I repented of my arrogance and the harm I had perpetuated in that first decade of youth ministry. God graciously allowed me to see my ministry to youth through a new lens, and it has made all the difference. During this past decade of youth ministry, I have come to realize that parents are my highly invested partners in it. I am obviously not the first youth pastor to come to this conclusion. A recent groundbreaking national study of youth and religion concludes, "We believe that the evidence clearly shows that the single most important social influence on the religious and spiritual lives of adolescents is their parents."[1] Another study of more than 1,300 college students concerning active church involvement found "the religious life of the family during the teenage years has an impact on continued church attendance during the young adult years."[2] These studies have provided new motivation wholeheartedly to invest time and resources through strategic programming to help parents become the primary spiritual influences of youth.

Ancient Roots of Youth Ministry

Adolescence is a relatively new phenomenon. G. Stanley Hall was probably the first to use the term when he wrote *Adolescence: Its Psychology and Its Relation to Physiology, Anthropology, Sociology, Sex, Crime, Religion and Education* in 1905.[3] However, it was the emerging education system of the 1800s that created an age group that presented unique needs and parental desires. In 1875 the government permitted the first public high school to "educate young people prior to college."[4] Prior to this era, the expectation of pubescent children was to take on adult responsibilities. Although a few churches had begun various types of Sunday school efforts to teach children the gospel, "the discovery of adolescence both from a legal perspective and from an educational point of view meant that youth work would have to change."[5]

Confusion about how to communicate with this age group has raged for many years. Mark Twain is said to have given an amusing piece of advice concerning adolescence when he declared his preferred method of interacting with teenagers. "When a boy turns 13 put him in a barrel and feed him through the knot hole. When he turns 16, plug up the hole."

---

[1] C. Smith, M. Denton, *Soul Searching: The Religious and Spiritual Lives of American Teenagers* (New York: Oxford University Press, 2005), 261.

[2] W. Black, "Youth Ministry That Lasts: The Faith Journey of Young Adults," *Journal of Youth Ministry* 4:2 (2006): 27.

[3] M. Senter III, *The Coming Revolution in Youth Ministry* (Wheaton, IL: Victor Books, 1992), 93.

[4] Ibid., 93.

[5] Ibid.

This reflects a communal frustration of what to do with adolescents who are struggling to transition from childhood to adulthood. Many parents wring their hands in worry as they contemplate the decisions made by their aging children. Godly parents search the Scriptures looking for insight on how to raise these young adults who are no longer mere children. The difficulty is that the Bible is silent about teenagers because adolescence was not a mind-set in that culture. However, this lack of specific instruction does not necessitate reverting back to Mark Twain's methods of "parenting" young adults.

From a developmental perspective, age 13 appears to begin the transitional years from childhood to adulthood. Although the onset of puberty seems to be coming earlier in recent years, 13 still seems to be the average for most teenagers, particularly boys. Many cultures have ceremonies celebrating this arrival into adulthood, although the exact age varies greatly from age seven in some Hindu cultures to as late as 20 in Japanese celebrations.

The Jewish bar and bat mitzvah celebrations have their roots in the Old Testament and have subsequently become cultural institutions unto themselves. However, these elaborate parties also have significant spiritual roots. Dating back to the time after the exile, Jewish leaders wanted to teach their children the Hebrew language so they could study the Torah. Not wanting to see their faith extinguished with age, the synagogue schools became the primary means for the instruction of reading, writing, and speaking the Hebraic language. "Young boys attended once they reached the age of manhood at thirteen."[6] This rite of passage entitled the boy to privileges and responsibilities of adult men, such as serving with other men in the synagogue and in the courts. The Hebrew roots of youth ministry can also be found in the educational roles of the priests. Only boys were allowed to participate in formal education, and older boys from the tribe of Levi were apprenticed by older priests.[7]

Providing a "language" for young people is a primary need in adolescent faith development. The Jews understood this, and we have much to learn from their practices. Although not specifically discussed in Scripture, some of these earlier approaches to communicating values and instilling faith in their children form the early roots of what has become known as the modern-day youth ministry movement. Today we have the same general objectives: equipping our students to live their faith daily and eventually be equipped to pass on their faith to the next generation.

In a further and more formalized approach to religious instruction of young people, the prophet Elijah establish "prophet schools"

---

[6] M. J. Anthony, *Exploring the History and Philosophy of Christian Education: Principals for the 21st Century* (Grand Rapid, MI: Kregel, 2003), 53.
[7] Ibid., 28.

that provided in-depth teaching about God's Word (2 Kgs 4:38). This advanced leadership training institute was present in ancient Israel for the purpose of raising the next generation of spiritual leaders through instruction and training in spiritual acts of service.

Looking back through the pages of the Old Testament reveals a particular pattern. It began with godly families that lived out their faith on a daily basis and was punctuated through participation at the various feats and national religious ceremonies. Then the boys in the community were gathered together for instruction in reading the Torah so as to instill a deep and abiding respect for God's Word. Eventually, for those boys who showed spiritual maturity and insight, prophet schools were created to instruct and provide training in service to God's kingdom. This general pattern formed a basis for what we might look back on from today's vantage point and call a *biblical pathway to facilitate the spiritual formation of youth.* This biblical model could be summarized in the following diagram:

Biblical Pathway of Youth Ministry

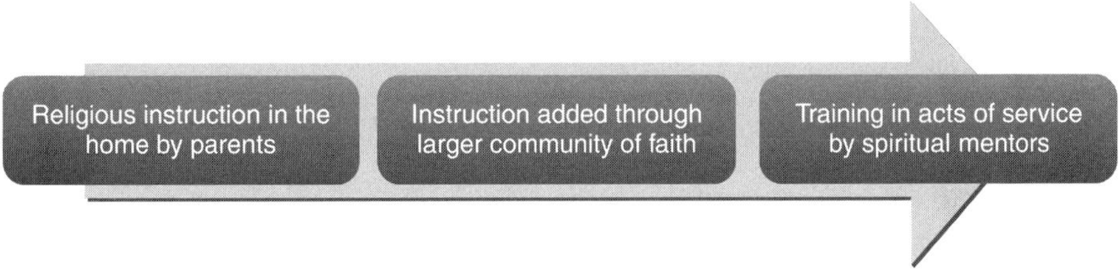

Old Testament Rationale for Youth Ministry

Although there are no explicit examples of youth ministry in the Old Testament, ample principles can be drawn from the Scriptures to help us understand the importance of ministry to all members of the family. To begin to grasp the rationale for youth ministry in the Old Testament, we first need to understand the various Hebrew terms used to describe the life stage we have come to know as adolescence. The NIV Bible translates the word *youth* 55 times and the term *young man* 41 times from a variety of words. The commonality of these words often obscures the true understanding of this age range. For example, the Hebrew word *na`ar*, can be translated *newborn* for the baby Moses (Exod 2:6), and it can also refer to a young adult about age 20 when it is used to described Joseph (Gen 41:12).[8]

[8] W. E. Vine, ed., *Vine's Expository Dictionary of Biblical Words* (Nashville, TN: Thomas Nelson, 1985), 299.

Another caveat to understanding the various terms is found in an examination of Eccl 11:9. Here we read, "Be happy, young man *(bachur),* while you are young *(yalduth)* and let your heart give you joy in the days of your youth *(bĕchuroth)*" (NIV). Here in this one short sentence we find three different Hebrew words that speak of this season of life. The Hebrew word *yalduth,* describes the time of youth, which differs from the Hebrew word *bĕchuroth,* which is used to describe a group of people (e.g., young men); this is one of the three verses utilizing this arrangement.[9] The latter word has its root in the Hebrew word *bachur,* which commonly (e.g., 89 times in 45 Old Testament verses) describes a young man of mature age but unmarried, as in Ruth 3:10, or of fighting age as in Isa 31:8.

The variety of these three terms used in the Old Testament adds to the difficulty often associated with making definitive declarations. However, we can also look to biblical narratives to bring more clarity regarding God's desire for youth to enter into a relationship with Him as early as possible and to serve Him throughout the days of their lives. In doing so, we see that it is His expectation for young people to be mentored by older spiritual leaders for the purpose of training for ongoing service and for passing on the baton of faith to future generations. Let me illustrate this through three axioms.

Old Testament Axiom 1: Seek God In Your Youth. God called Samuel when he was a young boy. The word *na`ar* is used to describe Samuel's age, leading many to assume Samuel was just a small child when God sought a relationship with him. Samuel's mother, Hannah, is reported to have brought Samuel to the temple when he was weaned (1 Sam 1:24), which would be approximately two or three years of age.[10] Just how old Samuel was at the time God first spoke to him we will never be able to pinpoint; Jewish historian Josephus says Samuel was 12 years old at the time.[11] This word, and its close companion *na`uwr* are translated as "youth" the majority of times because we often see them linked to young-adult experiences (e.g., marriage, Prov 5:18 and Mal 2:15, and child-bearing, Ps 127:4). This word is also used to define a time when a young man could be expected to join a battle for his family's honor or tribe's survival. We find this in 1 Sam 17:33, where it tells us Goliath was a champion for his tribe since his youth.[12] The point I am making is that Samuel

---

[9] Strong's Lexicon for Hebrew, http://www.blueletterbible.org/lang/lexicon/lexicon.cfm?Strongs=H5288&t=KJV and http://www.blueletterbible.org/lang/lexicon/lexicon.cfm?Strongs=H979&t=KJV, accessed December 17, 2009.

[10] J. A. Thompson. *Handbook of Life in Bible Times* (Downers Grove, IL: InterVarsity Press, 1986), 83.

[11] D. Guzik, *Study Guide for 1 Samuel 3* (2009), http://www.blueletterbible.org/commentaries/comm_view.cfm?AuthorID=2&contentID=7556&commInfo=31&topic=1%20Samuel.

[12] These characteristics seem to be the defining issue for discussion of what differentiated a childhood boy from a young man: able to be married, have a family, and fight for his family and people.

was a young boy when God called to him and initiated a relationship with Samuel.

Solomon supports this thesis in Eccl 11:9–12:1. He believes the ultimate goal of life is to worship, "remember," God while one is young and still able to determine the course of one's life, holding off the effects of age and unwise decisions. This truth is emphasized by the repetition of the Hebrew words that can be translated as "youth." Solomon has pursued many of the most "popular" pathways of life, seeking fulfillment of purpose, and has come up empty. Many of these pathways are exalted by youth today through song, movies, television, and even academia, as each young generation before this one has chased after them. It is for this reason Solomon addresses his conclusion to youthful readers. Many of us have become entangled in the affairs of the world, missing the peace and joy that God designed us to live by according to His truth. The purpose for all youth ministries is to teach, equip, and motivate young people to "remember" their Creator before life is "troubled." This axiom can be summarized many ways, but we can all agree the benefits of a young life fully devoted to the Lord, living out his or her full potential to make a godly kingdom impact, is worth all the sacrifice and efforts made by youth workers around the world.

Old Testament Axiom 2: God Calls Youth to Serve. Two individuals support this Old Testament axiom for youth ministry: Joseph and Daniel. We read in Gen 37:2 that Joseph was a young man of 17 when God interrupted his sleep with amazing dreams. The Hebrew word used here is *na`ar,* confirming our previous discussion regarding the range of this word focused around adolescence. After the betrayal of his family and being sold into slavery, Joseph maintained a dedicated spiritual life by refusing to have sex with the wife of his employer. He made this decision because he realized God had chosen him for a special purpose. He declared, "How then could I do such a wicked thing and sin against God?" (Gen 39:9 NIV). God called Joseph to serve Him in a special capacity as Egypt's chief resource administrator. The dedication that marked his youth would be an abiding character quality throughout the years of his service to God.

Daniel was one of many "young men" taken captive around 586 BC during one of the first campaigns by Nebuchadnezzar. The Hebrew word *yeled,* is used here in reference to the fact that these boys were "off-spring" of nobility.[13] Although this word is often used to describe a young son, it can also be used to identify a young man. Genesis 4:23 uses this word to describe a man worthy of death for injuring Lamech. It is absurd to think that such a

[13] Strong's Lexicon for Hebrew, http://www.blueletterbible.org/lang/lexicon/lexicon.cfm?Strongs=H5288&t=KJV and http://www.blueletterbible.org/lang/lexicon/lexicon.cfm?Strongs=H979&t=KJV, accessed December 17, 2009.

penalty would be given to a young child, let alone that even an older child could cause such injury. It can be reasoned that Daniel was between 13 and 17 years old when taken to Babylon to be trained in such academics as the "language and literature of the Babylonians" (Dan 1:4 NIV).

When confronted with the luxurious food and wine served at the king's table, Daniel and his friends take a radical stand to eat only vegetables and drink water. They believed God had an anointing on them for a specific purpose, which went beyond their personal comfort. Later, when Daniel's three friends faced death by fiery furnace, they stood by their conviction to serve the true God, Yahweh, and refused to worship the golden image. This intense commitment to the Lord in the midst of crisis speaks of their dedicated service to God dating back to their youth.

Old Testament Axiom 3: Mentor the Next Generation. When Moses interceded with the Lord in the tent of meeting outside the camp, Joshua would go with him. After Moses received the message to pass onto the people, he would leave, "but his young aide Joshua son of Nun did not leave the tent" (Exod 33:11 NIV). This unique benefit of being Moses' young protégé was part of God's plan to rise up Joshua one day to be the next leader of Israel.

Joshua's mentoring curriculum included watching Moses' leadership style change from single ruler to developing layers of leadership (Exodus 18), listening in on intimate conversations between Moses and Yahweh (Exodus 33), and taking on challenging assignments given by Moses (Exodus 17) (e.g., Joshua led the battle against the Amalekites while Moses prayed).

Joshua's strong leadership was developed through the many years of mentoring by Moses. The fruit of this mentoring resulted in the nation of Israel following in the laws of God after the death of Moses. "Israel served the Lord throughout the lifetime of Joshua and the elders who outlived him and who had experienced everything the Lord had done for Israel" (Josh 24:31, NIV). However, somewhere along the line between subsequent generations, parents failed to instruct their children and mentor the young men within their communities. The result was a spiritual apostasy and an eventual removal of God's blessing. We later read, "After that whole generation had been gathered to their fathers, another generation grew up, who knew neither the Lord nor what he had done for Israel" (Judg 2:10 NIV). This highlights the third Old Testament rationale for youth ministry: God desires for each generation to be mentored because the adage is true that the church is just one generation away from extinction.

New Testament Axioms for Youth Ministry

Just as there are important ministry axioms to be found in the Old Testament that relate to developing a sound theology of youth ministry, the New Testament is also replete with examples that can guide and shape our rationale for youth ministry. We will highlight a couple here for that purpose.

New Testament Axiom 1: Model a Balanced Life. Perhaps the greatest picture we have of the outcomes of a healthy and effective youth ministry is the one given to us in the Gospel of Luke when describing Jesus as a young teenager. Luke 2:42 states that when Jesus was 12 years old He went with His parents to the temple in Jerusalem. During this season of life, He encountered the challenges all teenagers face: obedience to parents, developing a self-identity, puberty, and relationships with others and with God.

Think of what it must have been like for the well-educated teachers of the law to be conversing with a 12-year-old boy about the details of theology. His questions must have shown an unusual degree of critical thinking, reasoning ability, and logic. Evidently, these religious leaders were asking Him questions too because we read in verse 47 that those who were gathered around Him were amazed at his understanding *and his answers.*

We read in Luke 2:52 that Jesus kept increasing in wisdom (cognitive development) and in stature (physical development) and in favor with God (spiritual development) and man (social development). Indeed, for a 12-year-old young man, he was a remarkable individual. These holistic growth objectives give all youth workers targets for which to aim their ministries.

Jesus was not disobedient when He separated from them to spend time in the temple, but rather at 12 years old He was naturally developing His self-identity as the Messiah. As youth workers we must help teenagers process and become who God created them to be, establishing a healthy interdependence with their family and community. Jesus returned home with His parents "and was obedient to them" (Luke 2:51 NIV). The family dynamics were surely not as simple as the Gospels briefly discuss; Jesus' natural-born siblings did not understand who He was and tried to keep Him from continually embarrassing the family (Mark 3). However, in spite of the obvious realities of life as both God and man, Jesus maintained this healthy balance in the midst of tensions both within His own family and from society around Him.

The teenage years are generally seen as being egocentric and certainly one of the greatest challenges for parents and youth workers alike. Jesus modeled what a life growing in healthy relationships around Him looked like. Jesus' stature with God was recognized at His baptism as the Heavenly Father's voice boomed His approval and love (Luke 3:22). Too often this is the only focus youth workers have—developing students' spiritual life—and, although it is important, it is not the only aspect of a student's development in which we must invest. God made us intellectual, physical, relational, and spiritual beings, so the effective youth ministry must incorporate elements of each in order to foster a healthy environment in which spiritual formation to occur.

New Testament Axiom 2: Replicate Yourself. One of the greatest compliments I ever received was from a student who rose to speak at a thank-you celebration when I left my first church. I had been involved in youth ministry at this church for 14 years, the last ten as the youth pastor. I had begun to recognize the benefits of developing the "new pathway" of youth ministry and invested many hours in the lives of a few young men. All five of these men are currently serving in full-time ministry today, most as youth pastors. This particular student, James, is one of those five I poured myself into during the last few years at that church. As many people stood to say nice things to my family and me, this young man silenced the room when he simply said, "You are my Paul and I am your Timothy!" And with that he sat down. The emotion I had been trying to control burst forth at that moment and I realized I was finished. I had completed the task God had called me to at that church.

Paul began his religious training early in life, yet it was on a road leading to his next conquest that he truly met God. We read in the book of Acts that Barnabas spent a year replicating himself in the life of Paul while serving the church in Antioch (Acts 11). In the same way Paul later replicated his life in the lives of other church leaders: John, Mark, Silas, and finally Timothy, whom he called his spiritual son (1 Tim 1:2).

We do not know Timothy's exact age, but we can assume he was a young adult. Paul revisited Lystra on his second missionary trip, approximately five years after his first. It may be that Timothy's family became Christians during that first visit. If so, Timothy matured in his family under the spiritual guidance of his mother and grandmother because Paul notes the family's spiritual environment in his last epistle, "I have been reminded of your sincere faith, which first lived in your grandmother Lois and in your mother Eunice . . ." (2 Tim 1:5 NIV).

Timothy joined Paul during his second missionary trip and was trained for ministry service at the hand of the great apostle himself. After sufficient training he commissioned Timothy to serve the church in Ephesus and to correct false teachings that had infiltrated the church. In essence, he entrusted Timothy with the care of a church he himself had once established. The Pastoral Epistles, two of which were written to Timothy, have become the cornerstone upon which church leadership continues to be built upon today. Paul had chosen "in effect, that Timothy become his heir in ministry and his representative to the church in Ephesus."[14] Paul could finish strong knowing that the ministries he birthed would continue under the leadership of Timothy and others (i.e., Titus).

---

[14] C. Arnold, ed., *Zondervan Illustrated Bible Background Commentary: Vol. 3, Romans to Philemon* (Grand Rapids, MI: Zondervan, 2002), 449.

This final New Testament axiom for youth ministry states simply: replicate yourself. Jesus modeled this leadership practice when he selected his 12 disciples. "Jesus went up on a mountainside and called to him those he wanted . . . that they might be with him and that he might send them out to preach and to have authority to drive out demons" (Mark 3:13–15 NIV). Both Jesus and Paul selected younger believers to invest in with the purpose of expanding God's kingdom through them. Timothy is an example of what God can do in the life of a young adult who plants deep spiritual roots in the family home (mother and grandmother), is encouraged and strengthened through the local church (in Lystra), and is trained to serve in ministry by an intentional leader.

Youth Ministry Viewed in the Context of Family Ministry

Some of you may be thinking this does not sound too different from how youth ministry has traditionally been done: larger community of faith instructing teenagers, or even the latest emphasis of connecting them to mentors. *The difference is seen in its context.* Let me give you an example of what I mean.

NASA learned this lesson in a tragic way back in 1986. Like so many Americans that fateful morning, I sat in horror watching the Space Shuttle Challenger explode just 73 seconds into its mission. The cause of the destruction was later determined to be a fault in the O-ring design at the base of the right rocket booster. Adding to the greater tragedy was discovering NASA knew about the faulty O-ring design nearly ten years earlier but failed to act sufficiently to change its design.

This sad story illustrates the importance of perspective. Obviously, some engineers did not consider the O-ring to be a critical part given the hundreds of thousands of parts that comprise the Space Shuttle. What some might have considered an insignificant piece turned out to be the critical component because they lost their perspective. They failed to understand that every part must function properly or the entire system fails. No one part works in isolation of the others.

The same can be said when looking at the various age-level related ministries in the local church. The system (using this metaphor) is the family. The parts that support the system are the various ministries that are sponsored by the church (e.g., children, youth, singles, choir, missions, etc.). When any one part starts functioning in isolation from the greater whole, a system failure is bound to occur.

Because of the nature of this important principle, the rest of this chapter will focus on how youth ministry leaders can develop a *biblical pathway* mind-set, which works in harmony within the greater context of family ministry. In doing so, they will be establishing a firm foundation for building healthy families in the church and contributing to the first phase of this pathway.

Pathway Mind-Set 1: Approach the Youth Through the Parents. Most youth workers have a natural "radar" for teenagers. We cannot help but see students, whether it is around the church or out in the community. We engage them with ease, focusing our attention on them almost exclusively. To begin this *biblical pathway* of youth ministry we must first broaden our perspective and see the teenager in the greater context of their family. Otherwise we are prone to see them in isolation, as if somehow operating outside the greater system of their family. This involves some intentionality on our part.

Having this family systems mind-set will affect all the subsequent decisions on which our youth ministry is built. The mind-set is seen in how we walk through the church campus, saying hello and connecting with parents of our students. Having this mind-set may force some youth ministry leaders out of their comfort zone, where years of functioning in isolation from the other age-level ministries of the church has created a kind of insulation and barrier. But if this barrier is not broken down and new healthy patterns established the *biblical pathway* discussed earlier in the chapter will never be established. A few practical ways I live out this new first mind-set include:

- When meeting new students, their parents are usually there also. After welcoming the new student and connecting them to other peers, I spend time with the parents, telling them about our youth ministry's focus and programs. An important element of this initial meeting is to ask them questions about their spiritual journey as a family. In essence, I want to understand their student in the greater context of their family system. I want to partner with the parents in the spiritual formation of their teenager and not appear like our youth ministry operates in isolation from them.

- As the youth program is getting started, I position myself outside, in the "drop off zone," to meet and greet the students. My volunteer team handles the youth interactions inside our room, while I remain outside to focus on being available to parents. Although some parents do not stop long enough to talk with me, some take a few moments to provide me with valuable insights about what is happening at home or perhaps, more specifically, in the life of their child. This greater context can make all the difference when trying to reach them where they are.

- I expect our volunteer youth leaders to connect with each of their students every other week by phone. I prefer they call the house phone rather than the student's cell phone. Here is why: Calling the house phone allows the student leader to speak to the parent first because it is often the parent who answers the phone at home. We do not simply say, "Is Tom there?" We start out the conversation with "Hi, Mrs. Smith, this is John, your son's volunteer small-group leader at church. I'm calling to check in with Tom and see how he's doing this week. May I speak with him, please?" This approach alleviates any concern about who is calling their teenager and models our partnership with parents. For those parents who do not attend our church, it alleviates anxiety about what the adult on the other end of the phone is doing with their child.

Pathway Mind-Set 2: View Yourself as a Family Shepherd. The biblical metaphor of a shepherd, which describes the roles and responsibilities of a pastor, are striking. Leading sheep is far more difficult than it appears to the uninformed. The same can be said for leading youth. Black's study of an adolescent's spiritual journey found the family had a tremendous impact on whether or not a teenager "stuck" with their faith after adolescence. He states:

> The type of home in which teenagers grew up has an impact on church participation in young adulthood. Those whose parents were divorced, those who grew up with a single parent, and those who live with step siblings during their teenage years tend to drop out following high school graduation.[15]

This second mind-set of the *biblical pathway* of youth ministry requires a change in the way you look at your role as youth pastor. If you see yourself as the one who leads the young people at your church, then you have a perspective that is far too narrow. You are not just leading the youth—you also have some influence over the entire family system. As such, you should see your role as one who shepherds in partnership with others to facilitate the greater goal of spiritually healthy families.

If you feel inadequately trained to lead classes on parenting or marriage enhancement, partner with the community at large to meet this need in the church. No doubt professional counselors in the community (perhaps even in the church) can come alongside you and provide training toward this end. Providing resources for family going through crisis may seem like an extra burden for the youth worker, but if that is the

---

[15] Black, *Youth Ministry That Lasts*, 28.

case, view these classes as "job security" because helping families results in greater student retention. It will also bolster your role as a valuable pastoral resource rather than merely a "babysitter of youth."

Most seminaries offer courses in premarital or marital counseling. Maybe you took one in your degree program. If so, now is the time to dust off the notes and put the coursework into practice. You can start by offering enrichment seminars that get the parents together. You may find as you offer this resource that deeper issues will surface. Some of these issues may require expertise beyond what you trained for in school. That is time for you to refer the couple to someone with a higher level of professional qualifications. This is not a sign of weakness but of recognizing your abilities. More harm can be done by someone who ventures into areas beyond their training, so view the referral as your way of ensuring a successful outcome. There is much to be said about knowing and respecting your limitations. You did your part by bringing the issue(s) to the surface where they can be examined under the light of Scripture and healed through the skilled hands of a wise counselor.

Some specific examples where I have provided family counseling and made appropriate referrals include:

- I host a monthly parent class during one of the "parent of teen" Bible studies that meets at our church. This class serves two additional purposes besides providing training on parenting skills. It is a time for connecting new parents of the church to an existing network of parents for support and encouragement. Second, I pick training topics that are felt needs so I can appeal to parents from nonchurched families. Topics have included preparing your teen for college, teaching your teen to handle money, and communicating for a change. These are topics that even nonchurched parents care about and may be willing to attend a church for help in this area.

  I use parents to call and invite other parents for these events. For example, I will ask a seventh-grade parent to call the other seventh-grade parents because they have natural connections. I have seen nonchurched parents attend a parenting class looking for the parent who called them. It provided the link the nonchurch parent needed to begin attending our church.

- Develop a referral list of the professional, Christian counselors in your area. I take the time to interview these individuals to understand the area of their expertise so as I can make a more knowledgeable referral when the time arises.

- One of the most important training topics I've found concerns seasons of parenting. In this seminar I help parents remember that the goal of biblical parenting is to prepare the child for eventual life outside the home as a responsible young adult. Wes Black talks about this approach to parent training. He refers to it as parenting style. "Parenting style—guiding youth toward making wise choices in friendships, lifestyle, and priorities when they are older and away from the direct influence of the parents."[16] The key word here is "guiding." The youth worker must point out that as the child grows older, the parenting style needs to adjust from "controlling" (elementary years) to "coaching" (teenage years) to "consulting friend" (young adult years). As one student whose parent went through this course said, "It's really cool when your dad thinks of you as an adult and you have your dad's respect. Now I submit to him because I want to and not because I have to."[17]

Pathway Mind-Set 3: Empower Parents to Be the Spiritual Leaders of Their Home. Perhaps one of the reasons youth ministry has been allowed to operate in isolation from the family environment is that in many cases parents have allowed others to assume the responsibility for the spiritual formation of their teenagers. New parents are passionate about parenting their young children. However, as the child grows and new challenges are faced, some parents feel intimidated and unsure about how to handle the nest stage of their child's development. As a result, they may back off from their role as spiritual leader and default to the youth pastor to take control.

Brain Haynes proposes two possible reasons for this. First, parents feel it takes a "professional" to shape the spiritual formation of their children and they are unsure how to do "be the primary faith influencers."[18] These two issues may be closely related: "Just as parents take their children to soccer practice to be taught by a trained coach, they take their children to church to facilitate spiritual growth."[19] Just as parents partner with specialized sports coaches, they figure they should also partner with "spiritual coaches" for the faith development of their children. It sounds reasonable, but it is not biblically accurate. As we clearly stated in Chapter 10, there is no biblical substitute for the parents being the primary spiritual leaders of the family.

Although it may be understandable for parents to have some anxiety about spiritually leading their teenagers, your job as a shepherd of families with youth is to train them to do their job effectively. As we said earlier, it

---

[16] Ibid., 39.
[17] Ibid.
[18] Hayes, *Shift: What It Takes to Finally Reach Families Today* (Loveland: Group, 2009), 36.
[19] Ibid.

does not have to be profound and elaborate. Sometimes it is just as simple as making a meal and sitting down to eat it together. That environment can open up a healthy dialogue about the issues of concern in the teenager's life. Black found that "[t]hose who regularly ate meals with their families and talked about spiritual matters during the teenage years had different attendance patterns during the young adult years from those who did not."[20] A simple family meal can reap long-term benefits.

This is an aspect of youth ministry done in the greater context of family ministry. The youth worker should work hand in hand with the family ministry team to provide resources for parents to grow in their own spiritual development. The youth worker can provide simple questions to facilitate family discussions that will encourage dialogue between parents and teens. By giving our parents tools to initiate spiritual discussions with their teenagers, we will help empower them in their God-given role as the spiritual leaders of their home. A couple of additional examples include:

- Rather than simply sending out a news flyer, I prefer to develop a monthly newsletter. This expanded format allows me to include discussion ideas for family talks, news about upcoming youth events, resources for parents, and a host of creative ideas.

  If you find it hard to be creative in these kinds of ventures, I suggest you try the resources of various publishing companies such as Group, David C. Cook, or LifeWay. For example, Group provides an incredible resource called "The Parent Link" for $99 a year, giving the youth worker the template for a newsletter filled with topical articles on parenting and discussion starters for the family. They also include analysis of current music and movies so parents can be aware of what their teenagers are listening to and watching.
- I have found good success by providing a weekly e-mail, and now text blast, to parents after our youth program. This e-mail provides parents with the key thought of the night, the biblical passage that was discussed, and some follow-up questions they can ask to engage their teen in the following days. I do not recommend parents trying to get into the questions on the car ride home from youth group, but to simply allow the teenager to share their feelings of the night and any highlights they want to voluntarily discuss.

---

[20] Black, *Youth Ministry That Lasts*, 28.

- I encourage the parents in my ministry to have a weekly "date" meal with each of their teens to discuss life; this is a prime time for a spiritual discussion based on the subject matter the teenager was already discussing in our youth ministry.

Pathway Mind-Set 4: Help Parents Celebrate Their Child's Rite of Passage from Adolescence to Adulthood. There are key milestones in the life of a child. In the same way milestones in the lives of teenagers mark their transition from childhood into adulthood. These should be set apart and celebrated as appropriate. When the family chooses to mark these moments, it is our job as youth ministry leaders to come alongside the parents as they maximize their spiritual impact in the life of the family.

These rites of passage have three elements: preparation, challenge, and celebration. If a milestone is allowed to pass with little preparation or only a brief celebration, it will have lost its opportunity to be a significant spiritual formation experience for both the teenager and the family. The milestones are connected to key decisions that a teenager must make: baptism (following a personal decision of faith in Jesus Christ as Savior and Lord), purity commitment (following a decision to begin dating but prior to their first date), and blessing ceremony (following high school graduation as the teenager decides to pursue God's kingdom purposes).

Each rite of passage should begin with a time of preparation, which can be a class, reading a book and then discussing it with a parent, or meeting with a mentor. Our youth ministry developed a rite of passage for younger boys entering the transition of middle school to high school. We lead the boys, with their fathers, through monthly discussions on various topics of godly manhood. These topics are divided into three main arenas and are introduced through a day-long event of fun and challenge.

For example, to launch our first series of discussions about the courage it takes to live with godly convictions, we took the fathers and sons paintballing. This became a great bonding experience as fathers and sons battled beside one another. We have also used rock-climbing gyms and inner-city mission trips to unite fathers and sons in this year of transition. The key to its success was the preparation. Each of the young men had regular discussions with their fathers together with situations designed to challenge their strength and perseverance. The year concluded with each family hosting a celebration of their young man, bringing in other influential men who could speak blessing over that boy becoming a man.

This became a powerful tool for dads to invest as spiritual leaders in their sons. We did not forget about the many single moms in our church. In these situations, we provided an older adult male mentor from our church to become "dad" for this important milestone in the young man's life.

Conclusion

The local church must transition to operating as an intergenerational family of faith to reach this emerging generation.

> As culture has changed and there is a greater recognition of the scope of the church's responsibility to take seriously and ultimately assimilate the young into the local body of Christ, the need for a more sophisticated and integrated ecclesiology, for example, is slowly emerging.[21]

This will require new ideas of how the church ministries can work together to empower parents to be the spiritual leaders of their home. Parents need and want the youth ministry to provide relevant programs and resources for their teenagers, but this should not be taken as permission to hijack the spiritual formation of adolescents away from the family. Churches need to provide resources to parents who may be uninformed about their role or self-conscious in their ability to succeed. The ways of doing youth ministry isolated and removed from the other age-related programs of the church must end. Youth ministry must be fully integrated into the greater context of the family. It has been my goal in this chapter to articulate what may appear to many to be a new approach to conducting youth ministry in the local church. However, there is clear biblical evidence through the pages of both the Old and New Testaments that this new pathway to youth ministry has its roots in the expectations of God Himself. It is His desire that ministry leaders "prepare God's people for works of service, so that the body of Christ may be built up until we all reach unity in the faith and in the knowledge of the Son of God and become mature, attaining to the whole measure of the fullness of Christ" (Eph 4:12–13 NIV).

---

[21] C. Clark, "Youth Ministry as Practical Theology," *Journal of Youth Ministry* 7, no. 1 (2008): 11.

Name Index

Subject Index

Scripture Index